To all the Beatles fans who have kept the memories and the music alive. And to my family, whose love and encouragement made these books possible.

The word is love.

Backbeat Books
An Imprint of Hal Leonard Corporation
7777 West Bluemound Road
Milwaukee, WI 53213

Trade Book Division Editorial Offices
33 Plymouth St., Montclair, NJ 07042

Published in 2016 by Backbeat Books

Printed in China through Colorcraft Ltd., Hong Kong

Originally published by Chuck Gunderson/Gunderson Media, LLC

On this spread: The view from behind the stage at the Atlantic City Convention Hall, August 30, 1964.
Photograph by Mirrorpix

On the cover: The Beatles rock the house in Detroit on September 6, 1964.
Photograph by Tony Spina

Library of Congress Cataloging-in-Publication Data

Names: Gunderson, Chuck, author. | Naboshek, Mark, editor. | Eubanks, Bob writer of foreword.
Title: Some fun tonight! : the backstage story of how the Beatles rocked America : the historic tours of 1964-1966 / by Chuck Gunderson ; edited by Mark Naboshek ; foreword by Bob Eubanks.
Description: Milwaukee, WI : Backbeat Books, 2016. Contents: Volume 1 : 1964 --
Identifiers: LCCN 2016021644 | ISBN 9781495065675 (pbk.)
Subjects: LCSH: Beatles. | Beatles--Travel--United States. | Concert tours--United States. | Rock concerts--United States--History--Chronology. | Rock music--United States--1961-1970--History and criticism.
Classification: LCC ML421.B4 G86 2016 | DDC 782.42166092/2--dc23
LC record available at https://lccn.loc.gov/2016021644

ISBN 978-1-4950-6567-5

www.somefuntonight.com
www.backbeatbooks.com

SOME FUN TONIGHT!

*The Backstage Story of How the Beatles Rocked
America: The Historic Tours of 1964–1966*

Volume 1: 1964

Chuck Gunderson

Edited by Mark Naboshek

FOREWORD BY BOB EUBANKS

Backbeat Books

An Imprint of Hal Leonard Corporation

1964

Foreword

WHEN I FIRST READ EXCERPTS FROM *SOME FUN TONIGHT*, I was totally blown away. I read things about my years with the Beatles that I didn't know existed or simply forgot. This is the most complete, factual material you will ever read about a band that changed the music in America forever.

The Beatles took America by storm. Everyone wanted to be involved. The media would make up stories just to get recognition as part of the Beatles' world. It was a crazy but wonderful time.

They not only changed the world of music, but also changed the live concert world into what it is today. With exception of Elvis, no other act toured the United States playing multiple cities in a short period of time. The Beatles paved the way for the British Invasion of musical talent, such as the Rolling Stones, Eric Clapton, the Dave Clark Five, and the Who, just to name a few. I was lucky enough to be involved with all of these acts, but nobody had the effect on music lovers that the Beatles did.

In 1964, I was working at the number one rock 'n' roll station in Los Angeles, KRLA. I wasn't a very good disc jockey, and I knew I'd better do something to make myself more important. So when the Beatles did the Ed Sullivan variety show and announced they were going to tour America, I went to work. I had never produced a concert in my life, but those who had, turned them down, because nobody—not even Frank Sinatra— was getting $25,000 per night. So my business partner, Mickey Brown, and I borrowed $25,000 on a house that we owned, and we presented the Beatles at the Hollywood Bowl on August 23, 1964. That night changed my life. Little did I know the impact they would have on America and the world.

To know that I was a small part of that musical phenomenon still amazes me. It was fascinating to watch people from all walks of life gravitate to those four lads from Liverpool. The rich, the famous, and the youth of America were taken in by their incredible talents and their glib personalities. Nobody had ever attracted such a large and loyal following in such a short period of time.

The innocence I saw in 1964 was replaced by a reserved attitude in 1965. Their popularity had increased and their musical performance was better, although still only thirty minutes in duration. But their wide-eyed innocence, the air of being amazed by all that was around them, was gone. And by 1966 they were a totally different group of guys: harder to please, a change in personalities, and, I believe, tired of their world. I paid them $100,000 for a thirty-minute show at Dodger Stadium. I figured out that after they paid their manager, agency, opening acts, security, chartered airplane, and hotel rooms, they probably made about $4,000 apiece that night. So they were tired of touring, tired of each other, and ready to move on. They had accomplished everything possible in the world of live music.

Like all of us, they were human. They all had strengths and weaknesses. Their personal lives soon got in the way of their professional lives, as you will read in these books. Like so many talented performers, their business talents didn't match their creative talents. They were so cohesive as performers and yet four different personalities, all with different goals in life.

I was privileged to be one of the only three promoters to produce a Beatles concert during each of the three years they toured. That is one of my proudest achievements in my business life.

My partner, Teri Brown, called me one day and suggested we put together a fiftieth-anniversary celebration of the Beatles' first North American tour, to be held in Los Angeles in August 2014. We were going to recreate the excitement that Beatlemania brought to all of Southern California. But after much thought, we realized nothing would ever come close to the magic these four young geniuses blessed us with.

I sent Paul an email when we first started working on the idea, asking if he would be interested in participating. He responded immediately. I will share with you part of his response, after he explained that he would be on holiday during that period of time. Here is what he told me to tell his fans if we went forward with the celebration:

> *Hey Beatles fans, I hope you will have a completely fab evening celebrating our first visit to Los Angeles. It was a fantastic time for us, and I still have many wonderful memories of the things we got up to. It was great to play the Hollywood Bowl, even though our music was completely drowned out by the screams of our lovely fans. Many thanks to Bob Eubanks and Teri Brown for organizing this special event; we have many fond memories in common, and we all look back on that phenomenal period with great warmth and joy. Have a great evening—sing a lot, laugh a lot, and love a lot!*

George was quiet; Ringo, distant; John, glib and intense; and Paul, friendly and interested in all around him. There are no words to explain my pride in being involved with the most talented, magical group in musical history.

I produced the concerts of country star Merle Haggard for ten years. So when I saw Paul McCartney and Merle Haggard being honored at Lincoln Center in 2010 by the president of the United States, I got a big lump in my throat. To think that I had a small part of their careers is my proudest achievement in the entertainment world. Yes, even more than *The Newlywed Game.*

Enjoy this fabulous book, because I believe it will go down as the Bible of Beatles concert history.

—**Bob Eubanks**
Los Angeles
September, 2013

Author's Note

SOME YEARS BACK, BEATLES HISTORIAN MARK LEWISOHN wrote *The Beatles Live!*, the first book that chronicled the group's live touring career, from their first stage appearance as the Quarrymen in 1957 to the final bow at Candlestick Park in August 1966—a truly fabulous book, but limited in detail and high-quality images. My goal for these two books was to give the reader an all-inclusive "backstage" story of how the Beatles rocked America during their historic tours from 1964 to 1966.

As I began to research the subject, I found that no cohesive history of the North American tours existed, just bits and pieces scattered in newspaper clippings, college archives, the web, books, and the memories of those who were there. Lewisohn's painstaking research for his book inspired me to dig and search further than anyone had ever attempted.

My goal was to produce a factual account of every tour stop during those amazing three summers in the mid-1960s, from the moment the Beatles landed until the time they left. I also wanted to record the goings-on that occurred before the band ever set foot in each town, such as local promoters dueling for the rights to promote them, "boss" radio stations squaring off to sponsor the shows, and fans lining up for tickets that would be snapped up in a matter of hours. And I wanted to give a special nod to the fourteen supporting acts that shared the bill with the biggest band on the planet.

Of course the books had to be filled with high-quality images of the Beatles onstage and backstage, press conferences, hotels, limousines, airports, and the fans who followed them. Many of the images in these pages have seldom been seen, having been unearthed from long-forgotten files and dusty archives.

Lastly, rare images of the colorful concert memorabilia that promoters produced to bring the masses to the arenas and stadiums across North America had to be featured. And each volume had to include an update, at the end, of the current status of every concert venue and hotel visited by the Fab Four.

To achieve this vision, lots of interviews had to be conducted, thousands of emails sent, hours upon hours of research and fact-checking done in newspaper morgues, and tremendous expense incurred to license high-quality photographic images—let alone compiling the actual history!

In writing the book, I found it interesting that the Beatles stood on North American soil for only a brief moment in their careers—a grand total of just ninety days. By the time they first visited America, in February 1964, the band had logged over 1,400 concerts, and those live shows defined a large part of their history. They didn't spend long hours in a sterile recording studio in their early years, trying to get their sound just right; they perfected their craft on cramped, rough-and-tumble, sweat-soaked stages in their native Britain and Hamburg that led them all the way to sold-out stadium shows around the globe.

My hope is that you find the story of the North American tours as interesting as I did. So fasten your seat belt and enjoy this comprehensive history. When all is said and done, it's a tribute to the fans—the first generation and beyond. Look carefully at the faces of the fans in these books; they may be your friends, parents, grandparents—or even you!—but together, they made Beatlemania happen.

And if you happen to find something cool related to these fascinating concert tours, like a picture you took or your ticket, send me an email—I never tire of finding new things and learning more about these tours.

—*Chuck Gunderson*
September 2013
www.somefuntonight.com

1964

August, 19—September, 20

©KAI SHUMAN

"In the more than fifteen years that I have been in this business, I do not know of any attraction that has come close to this sort of money in so short a tour."
—Norman Weiss, vice president of General Artists Corporation

IT WAS RECORD-SHATTERING, PRECEDENT-SETTING, groundbreaking, earth-shaking, and moneymaking. The Beatles' 1964 tour of North America would turn the entertainment business on its ear and forever change the landscape of the concert touring industry. In February 1964, after finally achieving a number one hit in America, the Fab Four came to the country with high hopes, performing on the wildly popular *Ed Sullivan Show* in both New York City and Miami and playing concerts at Carnegie Hall and the Washington Coliseum. In just fifteen short days, the Beatles conquered America. (Over the years, the Beatles' February 1964 visit has been incorrectly referred to as their first American tour. The fact is, it was nothing more than their American debut visit. Their first full-fledged North American tour didn't begin until August of that year.)

A month later, in March, teenagers filled the nation's theaters to see a closed-circuit rebroadcast of the group's February 11 concert in Washington, D.C., but that alone wasn't enough to cure Beatlemania. Allen Tinkley, who later partnered with Lou Robin to promote the group in San Diego, said, "Fans had already seen the Beatles on three televised appearances on *The Ed Sullivan Show*. What they wanted was to see them live." Unbeknownst to fans, the efforts to bring the

March 31st, 1964

General Artists Corporation
640 Fifth Avenue
New York, New York

ATTENTION: Mr. Norman Weiss

Gentlemen:

This letter will serve to authorize you to act as our exclusive agents for
a personal appearance tour of the act known as THE BEATLES, in the United
States and Canada, such tour to commence on or about August 18, 1964 and
continue through September 20, 1964.

All terms of any engagement contracts to be negotiated by you on our behalf
for THE BEATLES shall be subject to our approval and signature.

In consideration of your services, it is agreed that we shall pay you, and
you shall have the right to receive and retain, a sum equal to 5% of the
gross proceeds payable to us with respect to said engagements.

Very truly yours,

NEMS ENTERPRISES, LTD.

BY: _____
BRIAN EPSTEIN

AGREED TO:

GENERAL ARTISTS CORPORATION

BY: _____
NORMAN WEISS

MIRRORPIX

The contract (above) between Brian Epstein and General Artists Corporation to present the Beatles in America. Epstein (above right) was the Beatles manager from 1962 to 1967. Epstein's notes on an envelope (lower right) with tour dates.

Beatles back to North America had already begun.

In January 1964, Norman Weiss, vice president of General Artists Corporation (GAC), one of New York's finest talent agencies, was in Paris with one of his clients, a singer-songwriter named Trini Lopez. Lopez shared the bill with the Beatles for a marathon twenty-day/twenty-night run of shows at the city's Olympia Theatre. It was at the Olympia that Norm Weiss met Beatles manager Brian Epstein for the first time. The two would later agree to work together to bring the Beatles back to North America for a series of concerts.

Weiss, without a formal contract but with a gentleman's agreement from Epstein, immediately began to draw up the Beatles' first North American tour—one that would make music-entertainment history. On the heels of the successful Ed Sullivan performances, Weiss instructed his talent agents (which included such future legends as Frank Barsalona, Irv Dinkin, and Bob Astor) to contact promoters in their area of influence to offer the services of the Beatles. Not surprisingly, promoters from all over the United States and Canada were hungry for the opportunity to present the group. By the end of March, Weiss was prepared to present Epstein with an ambitious tentative tour schedule. But first, he needed the Beatles' manager to formally commit to GAC's services.

COMPLETE U.S.A. TRIP OF THE BEATLEBOYS

Put your finger anywhere on the map, showing the top major arenas and concert halls in the U.S.A. and Canada ... and you would find the Beatles performing there with an evening of entertainment during August and September. The sensational Beatleboys are making their second visit across the ocean a long and grueling month-long tour of the North American Continent.

As tickets went on sale across the country, there were unprecedented sell-outs. Showmen were astounded at the way tickets were bought up ... causing stampedes at the box offices everywhere.

The Hollywood Bowl was completely sold out in two hours after tickets were placed on sale there ... with the top price for a seat selling for $7.50. In Detroit, tickets sold out so fast that a second show was scheduled earlier in the day ... which was completely sold out to those forming a long line hoping to get to the window in time to get a seat. A third show, planned for the Detroit date, was nixed by the Beatleboys ... so many Detroit Beatle-fans will be heartbroken.

The Beatleboys asked for a guarantee of $25,000 or 60% of the gate receipts ... whichever is higher ... and they received it. Among the contract agreement is their request that a minimum of 100 uniformed policemen or guards be on hand to protect them from the public.

The complete schedule, is listed here.

AUGUST 19	COW PALACE, SAN FRANCISCO, CALIFORNIA
AUGUST 20	CONVENTION HALL, LAS VEGAS, NEVADA
AUGUST 21	MUNICIPAL STADIUM, SEATTLE, WASHINGTON
AUGUST 22	EMPIRE STADIUM, VANCOUVER, B.C., CANADA
AUGUST 23	HOLLYWOOD BOWL, LOS ANGELES, CALIFORNIA
AUGUST 24	OPEN
AUGUST 25	OPEN
AUGUST 26	RED ROCKS STADIUM, DENVER, COLORADO
AUGUST 27	THE GARDENS, CINCINNATI, OHIO
AUGUST 28 & 29	FOREST HILLS STADIUM, FOREST HILLS, N.Y.
AUGUST 30	CONVENTION HALL, ATLANTIC CITY, N. J.
AUGUST 31	OPEN
SEPTEMBER 1	OPEN
SEPTEMBER 2	CONVENTION HALL, PHILADELPHIA, PA.
SEPTEMBER 3	INDIANA STATE FAIR COLISEUM, INDIANAPOLIS, IND.
SEPTEMBER 4	AUDITORIUM, MILWAUKEE, WISCONSIN
SEPTEMBER 5	INTERNATIONAL AMPHITHEATRE, CHICAGO, ILL. OLYMPIC STADIUM, DETROIT, MICHIGAN
SEPTEMBER 7	MAPLE LEAF GARDENS, TORONTO, ONT., CAN.
SEPTEMBER 8	THE FORUM, MONTREAL, QUEBEC, CANADA
SEPTEMBER 9	OPEN
SEPTEMBER 10	OPEN
SEPTEMBER 11	'GATOR BOWL, JACKSONVILLE, FLORIDA
SEPTEMBER 12	BOSTON GARDENS, BOSTON, MASSACHUSETTS
SEPTEMBER 13	CIVIC CENTER, BALTIMORE, MARYLAND
SEPTEMBER 14	CIVIC ARENA, PITTSBURGH, PA.
SEPTEMBER 15	PUBLIC AUDITORIUM, CLEVELAND, OHIO
SEPTEMBER 16	CITY PARK STADIUM, NEW ORLEANS, LA.
SEPTEMBER 17	OPEN
SEPTEMBER 18	MEMORIAL COLISEUM, DALLAS, TEXAS
SEPTEMBER 19	COLT STADIUM, HOUSTON, TEXAS
SEPTEMBER 20	CHARITY SHOW, NEW YORK CITY

Other cities who tried to get on the Beatleschedule included St. Louis, Washington D.C., Allentown-Bethlehem, Louisville, Kansas City, Minneapolis, Memphis, and Des Moines ... to mention a few.

82

On March 31, 1964, a letter of agreement was signed between GAC and NEMS Enterprises for GAC to act as "exclusive agents for a personal appearance tour of the act known as THE BEATLES, in the United States and Canada, such tour to commence on or about August 18, 1964 and continue through September 20, 1964." Weiss and GAC demanded 10 percent of the gross proceeds of the tour,

AMERICAN FLYERS AIRLINE CORP.　　　*CHARTER SERVICE*

PRESS
The Beatle's Show

NEMS press officer Derek Taylor with his wife, Joan, (top left) relax at the rented L.A. mansion. Taylor was instrumental in managing the American press. All four Beatles signed this American Flyers brochure (above left). A press pass for one of the concerts (above right).

but Epstein resisted and the two men finally settled on 5 percent. The next day, on April 1, Weiss sent Epstein a cover letter with a tentative tour schedule. Weiss stated in his letter, "As per the attached, which covers 24 to 28 playing dates, we have guarantees of $630,000 to $700,000, depending on which deals you take.... The potential of the Beatles' share on a sell-out basis is between $1,000,000 and $1,400,000."

With the tentative schedule in hand, the Beatles' able manager began to pore over dates, cities, and venues, while projecting the potential gross. Epstein considered such diverse cities as Honolulu, Nashville, and Albuquerque as well as historic venues such as Fenway Park in Boston and the Los Angeles Coliseum. He was careful to not overexpose his "boys" and rejected offers for a show at the 50,000-seat Tiger Stadium in Detroit, an 80,000-seat show at the L.A. Coliseum in conjunction with Disneyland, and nine shows over a three-day period at New York's Freedomland. The ever-conservative Epstein was more comfortable booking smaller places such as the Hollywood Bowl in L.A., Denver's Red Rocks Amphitheater, and the Tennis Stadium at Forest Hills in New York. In fact, the largest venue played on the 1964 tour was Jacksonville's cavernous 60,000-seat Gator Bowl; the average venue was approximately 17,000 seats. Epstein even considered booking New York's Shea Stadium on September 13, a full year before the band's record-shattering performance there on August 15, 1965. Once he had listed his

GAC representative, Roy Gerber, with the individual Beatles during the Los Angeles stop. Gerber was the inspiration for the Oscar Madison character in Neil Simon's play, "The Odd Couple." North American Tour program (below) that was sold at every concert.

venue preferences, he sent them to Weiss, who began to formalize the final tour schedule.

On May 9, 1964, while Epstein was staying at the Americana Hotel in New York, Weiss delivered the formalized "Beatles Tour." In the cover letter, he explained, "As you can see, because of the changes in the venues, that you wanted made, THE BEATLES' potential share is just shy of $1,000,000 to be earned within twenty-three working days." The average guarantee for each city would be around $25,000. GAC concluded that the supporting show would cost approximately $30,000, and air, bus, and limousines would run in the neighborhood of $35,000 to $40,000. Ultimately, GAC and Epstein contracted with American Flyers Airline to transport the Beatles and their entourage from city to city at a cost of $37,950.50. GAC also stated that it would "arrange for all hotel accommodations with adequate police protection."

The tour was now set, with the exception of one add-on concert that would take place on

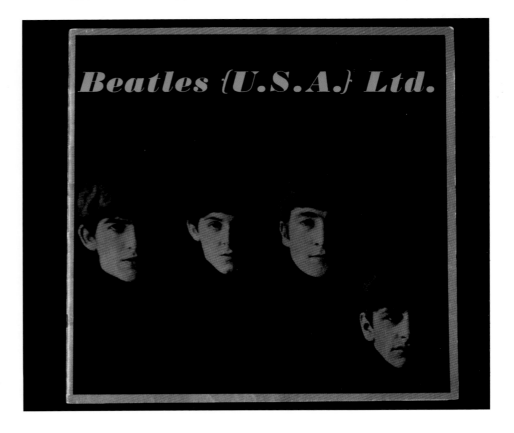

Beatles (U.S.A.) Ltd.

September 17 in Kansas City. The guaranteed appearance fee offered by an eccentric promoter would make entertainment history. By the time the tour ended, the Beatles would play a staggering thirty-two shows in twenty-six venues in twenty-four cities in just thirty-three days. The group would log 22,621 miles by air and road and spend sixty-three hours making the trip to America, traveling the United States and Canada and returning home to London. It would be a road trip of massive proportions that would change the concert industry forever. It's estimated the Beatles earned nearly $1.2 million before expenses.

Tony Barrow, press officer for the 1965 and 1966 tours, quickly learned how Epstein would determine the fees promoters would be charged to book the group. According to Barrow, "Epstein told me he tried to find out the biggest fee previously paid to any top star to perform ... then he'd ask for double that amount." Epstein instructed Weiss to do just that. GAC agents began informing their contacts that, to secure the Beatles' services, they would need to ante up $20,000, $30,000, $40,000 plus 60 percent, or, in some cases, 70 percent of the gross gate receipts. Only one promoter opted for a simple flat fee of $50,000 and perhaps got the best deal on the tour. The guarantees left some promoters scurrying for loans, while other big-time promoters simply refused to pay such exorbitant fees to unproven talent. Superstars of the day such as Frank Sinatra, Bob Hope, and Judy Garland were commanding appearance fees of $10,000 to $15,000. Norm Weiss concluded that the Beatles could have charged three times those amounts and still sold out venues nationwide. Epstein inserted maximum ticket prices in each contract, however, and demanded that they remain affordable. During the 1964 tour, the average ticket price was $4.50, the highest $8.50, and the lowest $1.95 (not counting the $1.50 seats at the Paramount Theatre charity show).

Fans were excited to have the Beatles back in America after their brief visit in February. This display ad featured the Beatles records that were in release at the time of the tour.

With the cities and venues chosen, AM "Boss Radio" stations lined up toe-to-toe, going to war with each other over the official sponsorship of the Beatles' concerts. Some even resorted to fabrications to snag the show so they could have their deejays on stage to announce the group. Wildly popular on-air personalities such as Pat O'Day, Bruce Bradley, and "Jungle" Jay Nelson received the honors to do just that, in turn propelling their stations' ratings through the roof.

Just before the band left for the United States, the Massachusetts Mutual Life Insurance Agency insured each Beatle for $500,000.

Upon the group's arrival in San Francisco on the eve of the tour, a telegram arrived at Beatles headquarters at the San Francisco Hilton from none other than Colonel Tom Parker, Elvis Presley's manager. The message read in part, "On behalf of Elvis and myself, welcome to the USA. Our sincere good wishes for a successful tour and a wonderful trip to all your engagements." Of course, the group encountered total chaos in every city they played. They endured bomb threats, blackmail plots, teenagers who infiltrated their hotels dressed as maids, and even a prediction from a famous astrologer that they would all die in a plane crash.

Elaborate plans were drawn up to transport the Fab Four to hotels and venues. These included the use of ambulances, police cars, and, in one case, an empty fish truck. Hucksters as well as managers from fine hotels gathered up bed linens, pillowcases, and even the carpet the Beatles walked on to be cut up and sold off to fans who were eager to get their hands on anything the Beatles touched. Fans clamored and fought over cigarette butts left in ashtrays and grass the Beatles walked on, and some even resorted to removing doorknobs from the band's hotel rooms.

Perhaps no musical act before or since will ever rival the Beatles on their incredible groundbreaking tour of 1964. John Lennon, Paul McCartney, George Harrison, and Ringo Starr not only would leave an indelible impression on their fans in the United States and Canada, but would leave the continent with fans hungering for more in 1965.

Ringo shows his hand—the boys passed time playing cards in hotel rooms, airplanes and backstage.

THE MAY FAIR HOTEL
BERKELEY SQUARE . LONDON . W.1
CABLE ADDRESS · MAYFAIRTEL · LONDON
TELEPHONE MAYFAIR 7777

APRIL 1ST, 1964
NW/IK

BRIAN EPSTEIN, ESQ.
SUTHERLAND HOUSE
5/6 ARGYLL STREET
LONDON W.1.

DEAR BRIAN,

HERE IS THE PROPOSED US TOUR ON THE BEATLES. AS PER THE ATTACHED, WHICH COVERS 24 TO 28 PLAYING DAYS, WE HAVE GUARANTEES OF $ 630.000 TO $ 700.000, DEPENDING ON WHICH DEALS YOU TAKE, WHERE WE HAVE A CHOICE OF OFFERS.

THE POTENTIAL OF THE BEATLES' SHARE ON A SELL-OUT BASIS IS BETWEEN $ 1.000.000 AND $ 1.400.000, AGAIN DEPENDING ON WHICH OF THE DEALS YOU DECIDE TO TAKE.

IN THE MORE THAN 15 YEARS THAT I HAVE BEEN IN THIS BUSINESS, I DO NOT KNOW OF ANY ATTRACTION THAT HAS COME CLOSE TO THIS SORT OF MONEY IN SO SHORT A TOUR.

TO GIVE YOU A TRUE PERSPECTIVE, I AM ESTIMATING THAT THE COSTS WILL BE APPROXIMATELY

$ 30 - 40.000 FOR THE BALANCE OF THE SHOW
$ 25 - 30.000 FOR TRANSPORTATION FOR THE ENTIRE TOUR, AS PER THE ATTACHED PROPOSAL FROM UNITED AIRLINES FOR A CHARTER PLANE FOR THE ENTIRE TOUR
$ 5000 TO $ 7500 FOR PRESS MATERIAL, WHICH WILL IN-CLUDE THE PRESS KIT, AD AND PICTURE MATS, POSTERS, THREE SHEETS, ART WORK, GLOSSY PICTURES, COMMISSION TO GAC, WHATEVER THAT AMOUNT WILL COME TO.

ALSO YOU SHOULD FIGURE A COST OF ABOUT $ 2 -3000 PER WEEK

THE MAY FAIR HOTEL
BERKELEY SQUARE . LONDON . W.1
CABLE ADDRESS · MAYFAIRTEL · LONDON
TELEPHONE MAYFAIR 7777

CONT....

FOR HOTEL EXPENSES. BEAR IN MIND THAT THE HOTELS OUT OF TOWN ARE NOT AS EXPENSIVE AS THE PLAZA AND IN MANY CASES WE WILL BE ABLE TO GET SPECIAL RATES AND IN SOME CASES EVEN COMPLIMENTARY ACCOMMODATION.

I HOPE THIS GIVES YOU SUFFICIENT INFORMATION AND THAT YOU WILL BE ABLE TO COME TO A DECISION QUICKLY, BECAUSE MANY OF THE STADIUMS AND AUDITORIUMS THAT WE ARE CURRENTLY HOLDING FOR THESE SPECIFIC DATES, CAN ONLY BE HELD FOR A VERY SHORT TIME.

ALSO BEAR IN MIND THAT YOU WILL BE SELLING A SOUVENIR BOOK ON THIS TOUR, WHICH WILL BRING IN SOME VERY SUBSTANTIAL ADDITIONAL INCOME.

VERY TRULY YOURS,

NORMAN WEISS

GENERAL ARTISTS CORPORATION
NEW YORK

Norman Weiss of GAC sent Brian Epstein this letter (above) with the proposed tour schedule (right and following pages) for the 1964 summer tour. Weiss suggested some interesting venues and partnerships.

PROPOSED U.S. TOUR FOR THE BEATLES

DATE	CITY & LOCATION	SEATING CAPACITY	TICKET PRICES	APPROX. GROSS POTENTIAL	OFFER	BEATLES SHARE SOLD OUT
AUG.18-TUE	SAN DIEGO (BALBOA STADIUM (OUTDOORS)	34,000 ✗ out	2.50 - 3.50	$ 104,000	$ 20,000/60%	62,000
AUG.19-WED	SAN FRANCISCO COW PALACE	17,000	3.50 - 5.50	$ 73,000	$ 20,000/60%	43,800
AUG.20-THUR	LAS VEGAS CONVENTION HALL (MUST DO 2 SHOWS)	7,500	2.00 - 5.00	47,000	25,000/60%	28,000
AUG.21-FRI	SEATTLE, WASH. MUNICIPAL STADIUM	16,000	2.50 - 3.50	49,000	20,000/60%	29,000
AUG.22-SAT	VANCOUVER, CANADA EMPIRE STADIUM (OUTDOORS)	35,000	2.00 - 4.00	100,00	25,000/60%	60,000
AUG.23-SUN CHOICES	LOS ANGELES HOLLYWOOD BOWL (OUTDOORS)	17,000	3.00 - 6.00	65,000	25,000 PLUS 60% OVER 50,000	34,000
	LA COLISEUM (OUTDOORS)	80,000				
	1. SHOW IN CONJUNCTION WITH DISNEYLAND				50,000 FLAT	50,000

PROPOSED U.S. TOUR FOR THE BEATLES - CONT....

DATE	CITY & LOCATION	SEATING CAPACITY	TICKET PRICES	APPROX. GROSS POTENTIAL	OFFER	BEATLES SHARE SOLD OUT
	2. SHOW IN CONJUNCTION WITH DICK CLARK; A 4 HOUR MUSICAL EXTRA-VAGANZA		1.50	120,000	25,000/55%	66,000
	3. FELD & CO. (WITH RAIN DATE) (ON AUG. 24)		2.00 - 4.00	240,000	25,000/60%	144,000
AUG.24-MON	OFF					
AUG.25-TUE	OFF					
AUG.26-WED	DENVER, COLO 1. STADIUM (OUTDOORS)	22,000	3.50	77,000	20,000/60%	46,000
	2. REDROCKS STADIUM (OUTDOORS)	9,500	5.00 - 6.00	57,000	20,000/60%	34,000
AUG.27-THUR	CINCINNATI, OHIO 1. CINNC. GARDENS	12,000	3.00 - 5.00	45,000	20,000/60%	27,000
	2. CROSSLEY FIELD (OUTDOORS) (W.S.A&L. RADIO)	45,000	1.50 - 2.50	75,000	25,000/60%	45,000
	EVANSVILLE, IND.	12,000	3.00 - 5.00	45,000	20,000/60%	27,000

PROPOSED U.S. TOUR FOR THE BEATLES - CONT......

DATE	CITY & LOCATION	SEATING CAPACITY	TICKET PRICES	APPROX. GROSS POTENTIAL	OFFER	BEATLES SHARE SOLD OUT
	ALLENTOWN, PA STADIUM (OUTDOORS) CITY OF ALLENTOWN & WAEB RADIO	30,000	250 - 3.50	90,000	30,000 FLAT	30,000
AUG.28-FRI AUG.29-SAT OR	N.Y. FORREST HILLS STADIUM (OUTDOORS)	14,000 PER NIGHT	4.00 - 6.50	120,000 —2 nites	40,000 PLUS 60% OVER 80,000	64,000
	INDIANA STATEFAIR INDIANAPOLIS	108,000		108,000	40,000/50%	64,800
AUG.30-SUN	ATLANTIC CITY STELL PIER (3 SHOWS)		1.25	70-80,000	25,000/50%	35-40,000
AUG.31-MON	OFF OR RAIN DATE FOR FORREST HILLS					
SEPT.1-TUE	NEW HAVEN BOWDEN STADIUM (OUTDOORS)	19,000	3.00-5.00	75,000	20,000/60%	45,000
SEPT.2-WED	PHILADELPHIA CONVENTION HALL	13,000	3.00-4.50	45,000	20,000/60%	27,000
SEPT.3-THUR	BOSTON, FENWAY PARK (OUTDOORS)	30,000	2.50 - 3.50	74,000	25,000/60%	44,000

Epstein's working copy of GAC's proposed tour schedule included possible partnerships with Disneyland, Dick Clark and playing outdoor stadiums like Boston's Fenway Park.

The tour schedule continued—venues such as the 50,000 seat Tiger stadium and three shows daily over a three-day period at New York City's Freedomland, the East Coast's equivalent of Disneyland.

PROPOSED U.S. TOUR FOR THE BEATLES - CONT....

DATE	CITY & LOCATION	SEATING CAPACITY	TICKET PRICES	APPROX. GROSS POTENTIAL	OFFER	BEATLES SH SOLD OUT
SEPT.4-FRI	MILWAUKEE AUDITORIUM	11,300 ✓	1.75 - 4.75	42,000	20,000/60%	25,000
SEPT.5-SAT	CHICAGO INTERNATIONAL AMPH.	13,500 ✓	2.50 - 5.50	50,000	20,000/60%	30,000
SEPT.6-SUN	DETROIT					
	1. COBO HALL	11,000 ✓ *2 show agreable*	3.50 - 5.50	50,000	20,000/60%	30,000
	2. TIGER STADIUM (OUTDOORS)	50,000	2.00 - 3.00	120,000	20,000/60%	72,000
	3. OLYMPIC	14,000	3.00 - 5.00	50,000	20,000/60% 1 SHOW	30,000
					30,000/60% 2 SHOWS	60,000
	4. FAIRGROUNDS (OUTDOOR)	20,000	2.00 - 4.00	65,000	25,000/60%	39,000
SEPT.7-MON	TORONTO, CANADA					
	1. MAPLE LEAF GARDENS	15,000 ✓	3.00 - 5.00	50,000	20,000/60%	30,000
	2. CNE EXPOSITION GROUNDS	40,000	3.00 - 5.00	120,000	25,000/60%	72,000
SEPT.5-6-7	OR NYC FREEDOMLAND 3 SHOWS DAILY	*200,000 20,000 - 3 days*	1.00 - 2.00	250,000	60,000 PLUS 60% OVER 90,000	156,000

(CANNOT PLAY FORREST HILLS IF WE PLAY THIS)

PROPOSED U.S. TOUR FOR THE BEATLES - CONT....

DATE	CITY & LOCATION	SEATING CAPACITY	TICKET PRICES	APPROX. GROSS POTENTIAL	OFFER	BEATL SOLD
SEPT.8-TUE	OFF					
SEPT.9-WED	MONTREAL, CANADA					
	1. FORUM	15,000 ✓	3.00 - 5.00	50,000	20,000/60%	30,00
	2. EMPIRE STADIUM (OUTDOORS)	25,000	2.00 - 4.00	75,000	25,000/60%	45,00
SEPT.10-THUR	PITTSBURGH FORBES FIELD (OUTDOORS)	*Civic Centre* 34,000 *available possible*	2.50 - 4.50	95,000	20,000/60%	57,00
SEPT.11-FRI	JACKSONVILLE, FLA GATOR BOWL (OUTDOORS) RADIO STATION WVOK	*40,000* ✓			50,000 FLAT	50,00
SEPT.12-SAT	MONTGOMERI, ALA. CRAMPTON BOWL (OUTDOORS) RADIO STATION	26,000 ✓	3.00 - 6.00	70,000	25,000/60%	42,00
SEPT.13, SUN	BALTIMORE					
	1. CIVIC CENTER (2 SHOWS)	13,000 *per show* ✓	2.00 - 3.75	80,000	25,000/60%	48,00
	2. CIVIC CENTER (1 SHOW) (RADIO STATION WITH)		3.00 - 5.00	40,000	25,000/60%	24,00

PROPOSED U.S. TOUR FOR THE BEATLES - CONT.....

DATE OR NXEXSHE	CITY & LOCATION	SEATING CAPACITY	TICKET PRICES	APPROX. GROSS POTENTIAL	OFFER	BEATLES SH IF SOLD OU
	NYC SHEA STADIUM (X SHOW)	60,000	2.00 -4.00	180,000	50,000/50%	90,000
SEPT. 14-MON	OFF					
SEPT. 15-TUE	OFF					
SEPT. 16, WED	TO FILL	) HAVE OFFERS:	NORFOLK, VA MEMPHIS			
SEPT. 17, THUR	TO FILL	) DALLAS	WASHINGTON NASHVILLE			
SEPT. 18, FRI	TO FILL	) NEW ORLEANS) MIAMI	CHARLOTTE ATLANTA LOUISVILLE			
SEPT. 19, SAT	HOUSTON COLT STADIUM (OUTDOORS) RADIO STATION KNOZ	30,000	2.00 - 4.00	100,000	25,000/60%	60,000
SEPT. 20-SUN	TO FILL					

HAVE OFFERS FROM OTTOWA, BUFFALO, CONVENTION HALL - ATLANTIC CITY, HONOLULU, ALBERQUEQUE, TROY, GRAND RAPIDS.

Shea Stadium, with its 60,000 seats, was presented to Epstein in the spring of 1964 as a venue to consider (left). The manager favored smaller venues. (Below) Weiss' letter to Epstein with the finalized schedule attached. The Beatles would make just shy of a million dollars in twenty-three working days—even more with Kansas City added.

May 9th, 1964

Mr. Brian Epstein
NEMS Enterprises Ltd.
%The Americana Hotel
811 Seventh Avenue
New York, New York

Dear Brian:

The attached is the completed list of THE BEATLES' tour.

As you can see, because of the changes in the venues, that you wanted made, THE BEATLES' potential share is just shy of $1,000,000 to be earned within twenty-three working days.

Just so that no misunderstanding can arise on the details, I would like to spell out the following:

The supporting show (which I am estimating will run around $30,000 for the tour. Naturally, if we can buy it for less, we certainly will.)

Air, Bus and Limousine transportation for the entire company. (This will run between $35,000 and $40,000. We are now in the process of getting the costs and feasibility of doing at least portions of the tour, by regular commercial flights, in order to cut these costs down as much as possible.)

We shall arrange for all hotel accommodations with adequate police protection. THE BEATLES will pay for their own hotel accommodations, wherever we cannot get the accommodations gratis. (We already do have gratis accommodations in a number of cities and we hope to get more.)

GAC will pay for and provide a company manager. However, you have agreed to pay his hotel and transportation expenses.

Page Two
Mr. B. Epstein

The agreements attached hereto shall be the general form agreement used.

Please bear in mind that we must get the contracts for the individual dates signed as quickly as possible. Please let me know as soon as you are ready to sign these yourself, or have them signed by whomever you authorize.

Also, bear in mind that you will be getting additional income directly from the sale of the Souvenir Programs, and indirectly from the sale of a great deal of the various BEATLES merchandise that will be on sale at these venues.

I would appreciate your signature below as an acknowledgement of receipt and confirmation of the foregoing.

Kindest Personal Regards.

Sincerely,
GENERAL ARTISTS CORPORATION by

NORMAN WEISS

NW:mm

ACCEPTED AND AGREED TO :

NEMS ENTERPRISES, INC.

BRIAN EPSTEIN _____

The final tour schedule (right). Additional shows were added in Indianapolis and Montreal. Note that Boston was handwritten in late and Kansas City on September 17 had not yet materialized.

DATE:	LOCATION:	DEAL:	APPROXIMATE POTENTIAL:	BEATLES' SHARE (Approx.)
August 19	COW PALACE, San Francisco California	$25,000 agst. 60%	$82,000	$49,000
August 20	CONVENTION HALL, Las Vegas, Nevada (TWO SHOWS)!	$25,000 agst. 60%	$47,000	$28,000
August 21	MUNICIPAL STADIUM, Seattle, Washington	$20,000 agst. 60%	$60,000	$36,000
August 22	EMPIRE STADIUM, Vancouver B. C.	$25,000 agst. 60%	$70,000	$42,000 (Canadian Funds)
August 23	HOLLYWOOD BOWL, Los Angeles, California	$25,000 plus 60% over $50,000	$80,000	$40,000
August 24	O F F			
August 25	O F F			
August 26	RED ROCKS STADIUM, Denver, Colorado	$20,000 agst. 60%	$40,000	$24,000
August 27	THE GARDENS, Cincinnati, Ohio	$25,000 agst. 60%	$45,000	$27,000
August 28	FOREST HILLS STADIUM, F.H. New York	$40,000 plus 60% over $80,000	$130,000	$70,000
August 30	CONVENTION HALL, Atlantic City, New Jersey	$25,000 agst. 60%	$63,000	$38,000
August 31	O F F			
September 1	O F F			
September 2	CONVENTION HALL, Philadelphia Pennsylvania	$20,000 agst. 60%	$45,000	$27,000
September 3	INDIANAPOLIS STATE FAIR COLISEUM INDIANAPOLIS, INDIANA	$25,000 agst. 60%	$50,000	$30,000

DATE:	LOCATION:	DEAL:	APPROXIMATE POTENTIAL:	BEATLES' SHARE (Approx.)
September 4	AUDITORIUM, Milwaukee Wisconsin	$20,000 agst. 60%	$43,000	$26,000
September 5	INTERNATIONAL AMPHITHEATRE Chicago, Illinois	$20,000 agst. 60%	$45,000	$27,000
September 6	OLYMPIC STADIUM, Detroit Michigan (TWO SHOWS)	$30,000 agst. 60%	$94,000	$57,000
September 7	MAPLE LEAF GARDENS, Toronto Canada (TWO SHOWS)	FIRST SHOW: $20,000 agst. 60% SECOND SHOW: $25,000 agst. 70%	$130,000	$85,000 (Canadian Funds)
September 8	THE FORUM, Montreal, Canada	$40,000 agst. 60%	$100,000	$60,000 (Canadian Funds)
September 9	O F F			
September 10	O F F			
September 11	THE GAITER BOWL, Jacksonville, Florida	$50,000 FLAT		
September 12	*BOSTON GARDENS*	*25,000/60%*		
September 13	CIVIC CENTER, Baltimore, Maryland (TWO SHOWS)	$25,000 agst. 60%	$80,000	$48,000
September 14	CIVIC ARENA, Pittsburgh Pennsylvania	$20,000 agst. 60%	$50,000	$30,000
September 15	PUBLIC AUDITORIUM, Cleveland Ohio	$30,000 agst. 70%	$50,000	$35,000
September 16	CITY PARK STADIUM, New Orleans Louisiana	$20,000 agst. 60%	$80,000	$48,000
September 17	O F F			
September 18	MEMORIAL COLISEUM, Dallas Texas	$22,500 agst. 60%	$40,000	$24,000

INITIAL HERE [   ]

DATE:	LOCATION:	DEAL:	APPROXIMATE POTENTIAL:	BEATLES' SHARE (Approx.)
September 19	O F F			
September 20	CHARITY SHOW, NEW YORK CITY			

INITIAL HERE [   ]

Each of the Beatles was insured for $500,000. This policy below was for John. (Lower page) The official "tour rider" that accompanied each performance contract is shown below. This rider was for the Vancouver show.

LAW OFFICES
WALTER HOFER
221 WEST 57TH STREET
NEW YORK, NEW YORK 10019
—
JUDSON 2-5030
—
THOMAS R. LEVY

CABLE
HOFERESQ NEWYORK

July 16, 1964

Mr. Brian Epstein
New Enterprises, Limited
Sutherland House
5-6 Argyll Street
London W. 1. England

Dear Mr. Epstein:

At the request of Mr. Hofer, we are enclosing herewith, ledger statements from the Massachusetts Mutual Life Insurance Company, concerning John Lennon, Ringo Starr, Paul McCartney and George Harrison; concerning their proposed insurance.

Kindest personal regards.

Very truly yours,

Bob Casper

Robert L. Casper

/ps
Encs.

AGENCY 065 HBN

LEDGER STATEMENT
DIVIDENDS LEFT TO ACCUMULATE AT INTEREST

Epstein

PROPOSED INSURED John Lennon   AGE 24   AMOUNT OF INSURANCE $ 500,000.00
PLAN EXECUTIVE SERIES CONVERTIBLE LIFE   DATE JUNE 25, 1964   ANNUAL PREMIUM $ 8,228.00

YEAR	TOTAL DEATH BENEFIT END YEAR	ANNUAL PREMIUM DEPOSIT	YEARS INCREASE IN TOTAL CASH VALUE	COST OF INSURANCE FOR YEAR	TOTAL PREMIUM DEPOSITS	TOTAL CASH VALUE END YEAR	TOTAL COST OF INSURANCE	TOTAL PAID-UP INSURANCE
1	500,350.00	8,228.00	1,735.00	6,493.00	8,228.00	1,735.00	6,493.00	5,045.00
2	500,990.00	8,228.00	8,155.00	73.00	16,456.00	9,890.00	6,566.00	28,160.00
3	501,930.00	8,228.00	8,595.00	367.00CR	24,684.00	18,485.00	6,199.00	51,535.00
4	503,185.00	8,228.00	7,045.00	1,183.00	32,912.00	25,530.00	7,382.00	69,680.00
5	504,790.00	8,228.00	7,535.00	693.00	41,140.00	33,065.00	8,075.00	88,350.00
6	506,750.00	8,228.00	8,025.00	203.00	49,368.00	41,090.00	8,278.00	107,485.00
7	509,095.00	8,228.00	8,550.00	322.00CR	57,596.00	49,640.00	7,956.00	127,115.00
8	511,830.00	8,228.00	9,080.00	852.00CR	65,824.00	58,720.00	7,104.00	147,190.00
9	514,975.00	8,228.00	9,640.00	1,412.00CR	74,052.00	68,360.00	5,692.00	167,735.00
10	518,540.00	8,228.00	10,205.00	1,977.00CR	82,280.00	78,565.00	3,715.00	188,695.00
11	522,380.00	8,228.00	10,620.00	2,392.00CR	90,508.00	89,185.00	1,323.00	209,670.00
12	526,505.00	8,228.00	11,050.00	2,822.00CR	98,736.00	100,235.00	1,499.00CR	230,670.00
13	530,995.00	8,228.00	11,490.00	3,262.00CR	106,964.00	111,725.00	4,761.00CR	251,690.00
14	535,690.00	8,228.00	11,940.00	3,712.00CR	115,192.00	123,665.00	8,473.00CR	272,725.00
15	540,785.00	8,228.00	12,395.00	4,167.00CR	123,420.00	136,060.00	12,640.00CR	293,790.00
16	546,250.00	8,228.00	12,870.00	4,642.00CR	131,648.00	148,930.00	17,282.00CR	314,905.00
17	552,100.00	8,228.00	13,355.00	5,127.00CR	139,876.00	162,285.00	22,409.00CR	336,065.00
18	558,335.00	8,228.00	13,830.00	5,602.00CR	148,104.00	176,115.00	28,011.00CR	357,255.00
19	564,980.00	8,228.00	14,335.00	6,107.00CR	156,332.00	190,450.00	34,118.00CR	378,495.00
20	572,045.00	8,228.00	14,845.00	6,617.00CR	164,560.00	205,295.00	40,735.00CR	399,805.00
æ55	680,275.00	8,228.00	20,890.00	12,662.00CR	255,068.00	403,105.00	148,037.00CR	637,490.00
æ60	753,530.00	8,228.00	24,290.00	16,062.00CR	296,208.00	517,630.00	221,422.00CR	753,390.00
æ65	846,515.00	8,228.00	28,160.00	19,932.00CR	337,348.00	650,445.00	313,097.00CR	879,100.00

ANNUAL PREMIUM 8,228.00   20 YEAR AVERAGE ANNUAL INCREASE IN TOTAL CASH VALUE 10,264.75

THIS ILLUSTRATION INCLUDES DIVIDENDS WHICH ARE BASED ON THE CURRENT SCHEDULE AND ARE NOT GUARANTEED. THE FIRST YEAR DIVIDEND IS CONTINGENT ON PAYMENT OF THE ENTIRE SECOND YEAR PREMIUM. UNDER PRESENT TAX LAWS, THE DEATH BENEFIT IS EXEMPT FROM FEDERAL INCOME TAX.

MASSACHUSETTS MUTUAL LIFE INSURANCE COMPANY

RIDER "A" TO CONTRACT DATED **June 9, 1964** BETWEEN NEMS ENTERPRISES LIMITED (HEREINAFTER REFERRED TO AS "PRODUCER") AND **A. P. Morrow, Pacific National Exhibition** (HEREINAFTER REFERRED TO AS "PURCHASER").

1. The PURCHASER agrees, at his sole expense, to supply police protection to the BEATLES of not less than one hundred uniformed officers, for the engagement covered herein, and said policemen will be present at least one hour prior to performance and thirty minutes following completion of performance.

   If, in PRODUCER's opinion, additional police protection is required, PURCHASER agrees to hire such additional police at PURCHASER's sole expense.

2. PURCHASER will furnish at his sole expense the following:

   a. A hi-fidelity sound system with adequate number of speakers, four floor-stand Hi-Fi mikes with detachable heads and forty feet of cord for each microphone. If sound system and microphones do not meet with PRODUCER's satisfaction, PRODUCER has the right to change or augment the system in order to meet PRODUCER's sound requirements. Any costs in relation to such changes shall be borne solely by the PURCHASER.

   b. Not less than two Super Trouper follow spotlights with normal complement of gelatins and necessary operators.

   c. A first-class sound engineer who will be present for technical rehearsals, is required by PRODUCER and this same engineer will work the entire performance.

3. PURCHASER will submit to PRODUCER for PRODUCER's approval, a list of people PURCHASER wishes to include on his complimentary ticket list; in no case will the number of complimentary tickets exceed one hundred.

4. No interviews of the BEATLES or any other artists to appear on the show will be scheduled by the PURCHASER without the express written consent of the PRODUCER.

5. The PURCHASER will arrange for one general Press Conference the day of the engagement. The exact time of that Press Conference to be approved by the PRODUCER.

6. Artists will not be required to perform before a segregated audience.

- 2 -

7. PURCHASER will comply with exact billing requirements as furnished to PURCHASER by PRODUCER not later than 90 days prior to engagement.

8. PURCHASER will make available, at his sole expense, the place of performance, fully staffed for necessary music and technical rehearsals on the day of engagement. PURCHASER to be notified of exact rehearsal time by PRODUCER, not later than 30 days prior to date of engagement.

9. PURCHASER warrants that no seating of audience will be permitted behind stage.

10. In event of outdoor appearance, PURCHASER warrants that stage will be covered.

11. Attached contract together with this rider must be signed by PURCHASER and returned to GENERAL ARTISTS CORPORATION accompanied by deposit as outlined in contract no later than May 1, June 15 1964.

12. PURCHASER will be required to furnish the Master of Ceremony for this engagement

ACCEPTED AND AGREED TO:

PURCHASER
PACIFIC NATIONAL EXHIBITION
General Manager
Assistant General Manager

PRODUCER
NEMS ENTERPRISES LTD
SUTHERLAND HOUSE
5/6 ARGYLL STREET
LONDON W.1.

Musician's Union
27. JUL 1964

Support Acts
1964 Tour

PHOTOGRAPH BY BOB BONIS ©NOT FADE AWAY GALLERY

The Bill Black Combo

The Bill Black Combo on stage in Kansas City, Missouri, on September 17, 1964. Sadly, because of illness, Black could not go on the tour.

THE BILL BLACK COMBO WAS THE FIRST SUPPORTING ACT to appear onstage during the 1964 North American tour. The band was the workhorse of the summer bill, not only performing their own set but also backing the Righteous Brothers, the Exciters, Jackie DeShannon, and Clarence "Frogman" Henry, who replaced the Righteous Brothers when they left the tour after the Atlantic City appearance. Bill Black, the namesake of the band, had been famous for a decade as the stand-up bass player for Elvis Presley. Black never made it on the Beatles tour, however; he had been seriously ill for some time and was unable to travel. In 1963, at his request, the band had hired a replacement for him on bass and continued without him. Despite his absence, the combo provided the all-important backbeat to the other supporting acts on the Beatles tour.

Along with Elvis Presley, William Patton "Bill" Black Jr. led the way in popularizing rockabilly music. Born in 1926, Black was the oldest of nine children, and his father inspired him to learn to play music. After a brief stint in the U.S. Army, Black met and married his wife. The pair moved to Memphis, Tennessee, where he went to work at the local Firestone plant.

In 1952 he teamed up with guitarist Scotty Moore and other musicians to play in Doug Poindexter's band, the Starlight Wranglers. Black's "slap-style" bass fiddle playing enthralled audiences and, in 1954, he and Moore formed a trio with a local Memphis kid named Elvis Presley. Sam Phillips of Sun Records

The group being introduced on stage at Maple Leaf Gardens, September 7, 1964. An album of hits the band recorded is shown below.

fame had asked Black and Moore if they would back up the then-unknown Presley and record some songs. After Elvis sang an upbeat version of Arthur Crudup's "That's All Right (Mama)," Black was heard to say, "Damn. Get that on the radio and they'll run us out of town!"

With a few cuts under their belt, Black and Moore left the Starlight Wranglers for good to become Elvis's backing musicians, earning 25 percent on their recordings with the future "King of Rock 'n' Roll." First recording as "Elvis Presley, Scotty and Bill," the trio soon adopted the name "Elvis Presley and the Blue Moon Boys." After adding drummer D. J. Fontana, the now-quartet toured and recorded extensively. Presley's manager, Colonel Tom Parker, became concerned that Black's comedy routines and aggressive bass playing were detracting from Elvis's stage presence. Gordon Stoker of the Jordanaires, who provided backing vocals on recordings, told Black, "Hey man, you've got to cut this out. You're not the star. Elvis is the star."

In the fall of 1957, Black and Moore left the trio because of poor wages, although Black continued to record with Elvis into 1958. The following year, Black formed the Bill Black Combo. The original lineup included Joe Lewis Hall on piano, Reggie Young on guitar, Martin Willis on sax, and Jerry Arnold on the drums. The combo had a string of hits and were voted *Billboard* magazine's number-one instrumental group of 1961. The group also appeared in the 1961 movie *The Teenage Millionaire* and on *The Ed Sullivan Show*.

In 1963, due to poor health, Black replaced himself on bass with Bob Tucker; in 1964, when the Beatles requested "the best honky-tonk band in America" for their tour, Black was unable to go. Doctors discovered a brain tumor, and despite two operations and lengthy hospital stays, he died on October 21, 1965, during his third operation. There's no doubt that he'd been regularly updated on his combo's travels with the Beatles on the whirlwind 1964 tour.

Even though Black never personally experienced the Beatles phenomenon, there's still a connection between him and one of the Beatles. In the mid-1970s, Linda McCartney purchased Black's original stand-up double bass as a present for Paul. According to Paul, "We knew this guy in Nashville who knew Bill Black's family. At that point, Bill had died and the bass was sitting in his barn. They didn't know what to do with it. So Linda got hold of it. When it arrived, I was astonished. It was all intact, right down to the white trim around the sides, except that the letters spelling 'Bill' had fallen off." Referring to "Heartbreak Hotel" (which prominently features Black using the bass), Paul added: "When I hear it, I always get this image in my head ... Elvis driving his Lincoln down the interstate on a clear night in Tennessee. The stars are twinkling. The air is balmy. They're on their way to a show, Bill Black and Scotty Moore in the back, with Bill's double bass strapped to the car roof. And now that bass belongs to me. It's my link to 'Heartbreak Hotel.'"

Paul used Black's bass in the video *The World Tonight,* on his version of "Heartbreak Hotel," and on the recording of "Real Love" by the three surviving Beatles in 1995.

Black was inducted into the Rock and Roll Hall of Fame in 2009.

Because of various lineup changes, the only original Bill Black Combo member from 1959 playing on the Beatles tour was guitarist Reggie Young. The rest of the group included Bob Tucker on bass, Bubba Vernon on piano and vocals, Ed Logan on saxophone, Bill English on tambourine, and Sammy Creason on drums.

PHOTOGRAPH BY BOB BONIS ©NOT FADE AWAY GALLERY

The Exciters

The Exciters perform in Kansas City. The Bill Black Combo backed up this quartet on stage.

IN LATE 1962, THE POWERHOUSE DUO OF JERRY LEIBER AND MIKE STOLLER produced a hit titled "Tell Him." In January 1963, the song peaked at number four on the *Billboard* Hot 100. The group that recorded "Tell Him," the Exciters, was originally an all-girl ensemble from the Jamaica neighborhood in Queens, New York. After adding a male member, the group landed on the Beatles' 1964 North American summer tour.

The original members of the group (initially called the Masterettes) were lead singer Brenda Reid, Sylvia Williams, Carolyn "Carol" Johnson, and Lillian Walker. By 1961 Williams had been replaced by Penny Carter, and by 1962 Carter was replaced by record producer and bass singer Herb Rooney (who married Reid in 1964).

In early 1963, well before the Beatles had an international hit with "She Loves You," the Exciters sang "yeah, yeah, yeah" in their recording of the Ellie Greenwich–Tony Powers composition "He's Got the Power." That same year, the Exciters were the first to record the song "Do Wah Diddy Diddy" (which became a massive hit for Manfred Mann the following year, but shouldn't be confused with the Bo Diddley–Willie Dixon classic "Diddy Wah Diddy," which the Remains covered on the Beatles' 1966 summer tour). The Exciters' hits also included "Get Him" and "Blowing Up My Mind."

Legend has it that Dusty Springfield changed her direction in music after listening to "Tell Him." Springfield was en route to Nashville to record a country album when a layover gave her some free time to explore the streets of New York City. She was walking past the Colony Record Store when she heard the Exciters' hit blasting out onto the sidewalk. Inspired by the feel of the tune, Springfield gravitated from folk-country toward a more pop-soul musical style.

Touring with the Beatles was a major boost for the Exciters' music and stage presence, but that success also came with challenges. For the first half of the tour, the Exciters were the only black artists on the bill, and they became the targets of racial slurs on many of the stops. While they were performing in Denver, some members of the audience screamed, "Niggers go home!," reducing Lillian Walker to tears and forcing her to run offstage. Herb Rooney comforted her and encouraged her to go back out and knock the audience dead. The Exciters did exactly that, and at the end of their set, the crowd yelled for an encore and gave them a standing ovation. The Beatles were sympathetic to the trials endured by the black musicians who accompanied them on tour. When they were informed that the George Washington Hotel in Jacksonville was segregated, manager Brian Epstein cancelled all reservations. Rather than stay overnight, the entire entourage flew on to Boston after the Gator Bowl show.

The Exciters' set most likely consisted of "Tell Him," "He's Got the Power," "Get Him," and the show-stopping "Do Wah Diddy Diddy."

Although the group experienced several lineup changes through the years beginning in the late 1960s, the members continued to tour in America and abroad. Herb Rooney and Brenda Reid had a son, Cory Rooney, a successful songwriter and record producer who has worked with such artists as Mariah Carey, Mary J. Blige, Jennifer Lopez, and Jessica Simpson. As of this writing, two members of the group have passed away—Herb Rooney in the early 1990s and Carol Johnson in 2007.

BILLBOARD SAYS ...TWO IN A ROW WITH THIS EXCITING DISK
Pick CASHBOX SAYS ...ITS A FANTASTIC DRIVER..SURE FIRE!

THE EXCITERS
"HE'S GOT THE POWER"

UNITED ARTISTS RECORDS · 729 SEVENTH AVENUE · NEW YORK 19, NEW YORK

With a string of hits like, "He's Got The Power," and "Tell Him," the Exciters were the perfect choice to get the crowd ready for the Beatles.

PHOTOGRAPH BY BOB BONIS ©NOT FADE AWAY GALLERY

The Righteous Brothers

The Righteous Brothers on stage at the Hollywood Bowl. Their music was popular on the West Coast with songs like "Little Latin Lupe Lou." A Righteous Brothers' album cover is shown (right).

THE RIGHTEOUS BROTHERS' MASSIVE HIT, "You've Lost That Lovin' Feelin,'" was not released until after the Beatles tour, in December 1964, and it did not reach the top spot on the *Billboard* Hot 100 until February 6, 1965. Written by the trio of Bill Mann, Phil Spector, and Cynthia Weil, it is thirty-fifth on *Rolling Stone's* list of the 500 greatest songs of all time. Had the song been released prior to the tour, the Righteous Brothers—Bill Medley and Bobby Hatfield—would have ridden a wave of success by association and achieved a whole new fan base. Instead, the singing duo enjoyed just six shows in the western states, where their music was better known, then had to labor through four more shows on the eastern swing of the tour before quitting.

Tired of competing with chants of "We want the Beatles! We want the Beatles!," Medley and Hatfield approached manager Brian Epstein during the stop at Forest Hills, New York, and asked to leave the tour. Epstein and General Artists Corporation (who booked the group) granted their request and released them from their contract. Their final show on the tour was in Atlantic City, New Jersey, on August 30, 1964, and from that point on, they were replaced on the bill by Clarence "Frogman" Henry. The Righteous Brothers were the only group to leave a Beatles North American tour before it ended. Their later recording successes, however, cemented their place in the history of popular music. The duo was elected to the Rock and Roll Hall of Fame in 2003.

Pioneers of "blue-eyed soul," Bill Medley and Bobby Hatfield began their careers in the music business as part of a five-member singing group called the Paramours. During a gig in Los Angeles, a U.S.

The soulful duo of Bill Medley and Bobby Hatfield decided to call the tour quits after the New York City shows at Forest Hills. They had grown tired of fans chanting, "We want the Beatles," during their stage act.

Marine stood up after a song and shouted, "That was righteous, brothers!"—a description that obviously stuck with Medley and Hatfield when they embarked as a duo. As partners, Medley sang the soulful bass parts while Hatfield sang the higher-register tenor parts. In addition to "You've Lost That Lovin' Feeling," the singers struck gold in the mid-'60s with such hits as "Unchained Melody," "(You're My) Soul and Inspiration," "Ebb Tide," and "Just Once in My Life."

On the Beatles tour, the Righteous Brothers usually followed the Bill Black Combo (who remained onstage to back them as well as the Exciters, Clarence Henry, and Jackie DeShannon). The duo's set most certainly included their 1963 hits "Little Latin Lupe Lou" and "My Babe." It has been reported that the 1964 summer tour was not the first brush the singing duo had with the Beatles. Some sources cite the pair as one of the supporting acts for the boys' American debut concert at the Washington Coliseum on February 11, 1964.

In *The Beatles Anthology*, George somewhat incorrectly recalled the Righteous Brothers' departure from the tour. He correctly remembered the duo's displeasure when the Beatles' helicopter noisily buzzed the Forest Hills Tennis Stadium during their performance. But he said the group was singing "You've Lost That Lovin' Feelin,'" which in fact was not released until December 1964. George noted that "all the people were up in the stands, pointing up to the sky, screaming and shouting, paying not a blind bit of notice to the Righteous Brothers, which pissed them off a little." He then humorously added, "In fact, they got so pissed off that they decided to leave the tour. Righteous indignation." Hatfield recalled his time on tour with the Fab Four this way: "We were fine in L.A. and San Francisco, but once we got east of Denver, nobody knew us." Epstein was sad to see the duo leave the tour and even offered to manage them, only to be turned down.

Leaving the tour proved to be a blessing for the Righteous Brothers, as they began appearing on popular teen shows such as *Shindig* and *Hullabaloo* and were instantly propelled to international stardom. They split up in 1968 and, after a six-year separation from each other, reunited in 1974, scoring a come-back hit with "Rock and Roll Heaven." While the two continued to record and tour together, Medley also had solo success. In 1987, he scored what would be his last number-one hit—and a 1988 Grammy Award—by teaming with Jennifer Warnes for the song "(I've Had) The Time of My Life," which was featured in the finale of the movie *Dirty Dancing.* The song also won an Academy Award for Best Original Song in 1987 and a Golden Globe Award for Best Original Song in 1988.

A resurgence in the duo's popularity took place in 1990, when "Unchained Melody" was featured in a now-iconic scene in the enormously popular film *Ghost.* They continued to tour the country until November 5, 2003, when Hatfield was found dead in his hotel room in Kalamazoo, Michigan, only a half hour before the Righteous Brothers' scheduled appearance at Western Michigan University. Medley still tours and, as of this writing, performs on a regular basis.

PHOTOGRAPH BY BOB BONIS ©NOT FADE AWAY GALLERY

Jackie DeShannon

JACKIE DESHANNON, NÉE SHARON LEE MYERS, began her musical career at the age of six, singing country tunes on local radio in her native Kentucky. By 1964, she found herself joining the Beatles on their whirlwind North American tour. Her spot on the program was immediately before the Beatles, so by the time she'd whipped the crowd into a frenzy with her good looks, gyrating dance moves, and up-tempo tunes, everyone was ready for the headliners.

DeShannon was born into farm life, but when that became too difficult she and her family moved to Illinois, where her songwriting ability impressed industry executives. By the time she reached her teens, she had recorded under the names Sherry Lee, Jackie Dee, and Jackie Shannon. In 1957 she appeared at the Uptown Theater in Philadelphia, and two weeks later she scored a spot on Alan Freed's "Big Rock 'n' Roll Show" at the Paramount Theatre in New York City. (She would return to the Paramount on September 20, 1964, to open for the Beatles at the charity performance that concluded their first North American tour.)

In 1960, after using a number of stage names, she settled on Jackie DeShannon (taken from an Irish ancestor), signed with Liberty Records, and recorded "Lonely Girl," but it would be two more years

before she had her first *Billboard* Top 100 song—"Faded Love," which barely slipped in at number ninety-seven in February 1963. Later that same year, she fared a little better on the American charts with the self-penned "When You Walk in the Room" and the Sonny Bono–Jack Nitzsche song "Needles and Pins." In Canada, the latter became a number-one hit, making it a surefire crowd-pleaser for the Beatles shows in Vancouver, Montreal, and Toronto.

Many critics agree that DeShannon's greatest attribute was her versatility. The singer-songwriter ventured into several musical genres including pop, rockabilly, country, and gospel. She also forged relationships, both musically and socially, with such artists as Jimmy Page, Ricky Nelson, the Everly Brothers, Marianne Faithfull, and the Byrds (who featured her composition "Don't Doubt Yourself, Babe" on their debut album). The low-voiced, soulful singer dated Elvis Presley and even starred in a pair of movies—*Surf Party* with Bobby Vinton and *C'mon, Let's Live a Little* with Bobby Vee.

Arguably, one of her biggest career breaks came in 1964 when General Artists Corporation convinced Brian Epstein to place her on tour with the Beatles. Musically, she hit her peak the following spring with her powerful version of the Burt Bacharach–Hal David-penned "What the World Needs Now Is Love," which became her signature song. In 1969, "Put a Little Love in Your Heart," which she cowrote, hit number four on the Hot 100 chart.

Although she didn't produce any more Top Ten singles of her own, DeShannon's compositions have been covered by other artists who had hits with them. She and songwriter Donna Weiss cowrote "Queen of the Rodeo" and "Bette Davis Eyes," the latter of which became a worldwide number-one hit for Kim Carnes in 1981, earning DeShannon and Weiss the 1982 Grammy Award for Song of the Year. In 2010, DeShannon was inducted into the Songwriters Hall of Fame.

DeShannon captivates the crowd at Red Rocks Amphitheater, in Morrison, Colorado. She was the last act to perform before the Fab Four hit the stage. Some of DeShannon's hits are shown on an album cover (below left).

Clarence "Frogman" Henry

Clarence "Frogman" Henry on stage in Kansas City. Henry replaced the Righteous Brothers beginning with the show in Philadelphia and performed through the end of the tour.

IN 1956, AFTER AN EXHAUSTING LATE-NIGHT CONCERT at the Joy Lounge in New Orleans, Clarence Henry penned a song that would land him a spot on the lineup of the Beatles tour eight years later. The song, "Ain't Got No Home," was an instant success, and the tune's signature "croaking" sounds and a deejay's praise soon earned him the nickname "Frogman."

Henry wasn't one of the four original supporting acts chosen for the '64 summer tour. When the Righteous Brothers bowed out, however, GAC had to scramble to find a replacement. The duo had been a great supporting act for the Beatles—all the way back to the group's first American concert, at the Washington Coliseum on February 11, according to some sources. Met with an audience chanting "We want the Beatles!" night after night, however, the two singers—Bobby Hatfield and Bill Medley—decided they wanted out of their contract with GAC once the tour headed east of Denver.

At the show in Forest Hills, New York, Beatles manager Brian Epstein and GAC asked the duo to remain with the tour until the Atlantic City, New Jersey, show on August 30. During the short break between the Atlantic City and Philadelphia stops, Bob Astor of GAC secured Henry for the remaining dates. The choice was natural and the transition was smooth because Astor, who had booked a few of the Beatles' tour dates, including Henry's native New Orleans, was Henry's manager. The Frogman filled the slot left vacant by Hatfield and Medley from the Philadelphia show, on September 2, until the end of the scheduled tour in Dallas.

Born in 1937 in the Algiers community of New Orleans, Henry idolized one of the artists who had been a major influence on the Beatles—Fats Domino. The Beatles and Domino would ultimately meet just before showtime in New Orleans on September 16, at a gathering arranged by none other than Bob Astor.

"Ain't Got No Home" was based on Henry's personal experience with a belligerent club owner who didn't want his musicians to leave early. Upon hearing that he had to stay and play longer, an exasperated Henry banged the keys on his piano and wailed, "Ooo oo oo oo oo oo oo oo oo," the song's signature tagline. Henry recorded the song for Chess Records, and deejay Poppa Stoppa would tell his listeners that he was playing a song by "the Frogman." From then on, Henry adopted "Frogman" as his stage name. The "ooo ooo" refrain has often been mimicked, most notably in Rod Stewart's hit "Some Guys Have All the Luck." Besides "Ain't Got No Home," the singer also had success with "(I Don't Know Why) But I Do" and "You Always Hurt the One You Love," both released in 1961.

During the Beatles tour, Henry's set list usually consisted of "Josephine," "But I Do," "You Always Hurt the One You Love," "I'm Going Home," and the crowd-pleaser "Ain't Got No Home."

Today, Henry is still a mainstay on Bourbon Street in New Orleans, and in 2007 he was inducted into the Louisiana Music Hall of Fame.

Henry's hit, "Ain't Got No Home," (left) was a crowd pleaser. He was most likely placed on the bill by his manager, Bob Astor who also worked for GAC.

THE ARRIVAL

**August 18, 1964
San Francisco International Airport
6:24 p.m.**

ON AUGUST 16, 1964, THE BEATLES PERFORMED THEIR LAST SHOW in the United Kingdom before departing for their second visit to North America in just six months. The show was at Blackpool's famed opera house, the last of six scheduled seaside gigs there. On the bill with the Fab Four were the Kinks and a "new R&B group" called the High Numbers. With a simple name change to The Who, this four-piece group would later conquer the world as well. The Beatles had recently returned from a frenetic first world tour, playing the Netherlands, Hong Kong, Australia, and New Zealand, as Beatlemania erupted around the globe. The concert at Blackpool was preceded by shows in such cities as Bournemouth and Scarborough, in small theaters that held a few thousand fans—a number that paled in comparison to the onslaught the Beatles would soon face in America.

The Beatles' highly anticipated 1964 North American tour would begin in San Francisco at the Cow Palace. They boarded their plane in London on August 18 at noon, waving good-bye to scores of fans who turned up to wish their boys luck. Their long Pan Am flight to the West Coast would require two brief layovers, one in Winnipeg, Canada, and one in Los Angeles. At 2:05 p.m., the Beatles' plane touched down in Winnipeg. The stop had not been anticipated, but because the information was leaked just prior to arrival, several hundred fans scrambled to the airport to be the first to welcome the Beatles on not only North American but Canadian soil.

The Beatles greet fans and the press at Los Angeles' International Airport during a brief layover after their flight from London. They would meet the press and then fly on to San Francisco where another press conference awaited them.

MIRRORPIX

Local area media personnel were also jockeying for the rights to be the first to interview the group on the eve of their tour. Local personality Bob Burns of Winnipeg's Channel 7 would win the honor. Burns recalls that the Beatles had absolutely no intention of even coming out of the airplane until their manager, Brian Epstein, convinced them it would be a public relations disaster if they didn't do so. Epstein wasn't about to disappoint all who had come out to see the group, especially right before the start of the tour. Decades later, Burns still relishes being the first to interview the Beatles on the eve of their soon-to-be-record-shattering tour.

Paul and Ringo sign autographs (above) while John strains to hear questions from the press (left). One journalist asks, "The burning question is, when are you going to get a haircut?" To which Ringo cheekily replied, "I had one last night, believe it or not."

Just as they were set to take off after refueling, one brave young man made a dash for the plane, almost reaching the cabin door before being subdued by local police officials. The incident warranted a front-page story the next day in the *Winnipeg Free Press*.

The stopover in Los Angeles was much more organized. A makeshift press area was crammed with reporters, microphones, and cameras. As the Beatles made their way into the room for a press conference, George dryly read, "Welcome to Los Angeles International Airport" from the sign directly ahead. Seated at a six-foot table with a Pan Am logo mounted in front, the group began to field the kind of questions that would be asked repeatedly at each stop: "What are you going to do with all the money you are making?" "Are you going to get a haircut?" Of course, the reporters would always get a dose of "Beatle payback." One journalist asked Paul, "How do you feel about all the enthusiasm that the teenagers display?," to which Paul replied, "We love it, it's flattering y'know. I mean wouldn't you feel the same if they displayed it for you!"

Dave Hull, a deejay from radio station KRLA, was able to interview the boys before they boarded the plane. Hull was asked by television station KTLA to get the interview, as they thought he had the best chance. This in turn angered the KTLA news department, who reminded management that they were professional journalists while branding Hull a "cockamamie Pasadena disk jockey!"

The plane carrying the Beatles touched down in San Francisco at 6:24 p.m., to the delight of thousands of screaming teenagers there to catch a glimpse of the phenomenon that was rocking the entertainment industry. In fact, the day before the Beatles' arrival, fans had already set up camp in an area they dubbed Beatlesville. A minuscule twenty-five-square-foot wooden platform had been erected three-quarters of a mile northwest of the main terminal, surrounded by a five-foot cyclone fence. The purpose was

The Beatles step off the plane in San Francisco (previous page). Police officials (top) had the daunting task to quell the approximately 5,000 fans gathered to greet the group. The Fab Four (above) survey the "Beatlesville" crowd.

to provide an area where energetic local deejays could welcome the Beatles to the city.

With only 180 San Mateo deputies available to quell the commotion, various Beatles clubs from the area took it upon themselves to police the area and keep Beatlesville orderly. The San Francisco fan club boldly dubbed themselves Beatles Bobbies, dressing in white shirts and red jackets sporting "BB" armbands. As the Beatles' arrival drew closer and the anticipation grew, the crowd at Beatlesville surged from several hundred to what the *San Francisco Chronicle* estimated was "between 5,000 and 10,000" nervous teenagers on the lookout for any plane in the sky.

The Beatles, having already conquered America during their February visit, were accustomed to the mob atmosphere. Gary Park, who worked for KCRA-TV and was on hand for the event, described the band to viewers: "In case you haven't heard, the Beatles are four young male singers from Great Britain ... all four of them rather ordinary except for the hair."

Upon arrival, the band was immediately driven to Beatlesville to greet fans and pose for photographers. Ringo was the first to ascend the platform, with the others following closely

An aerial view of "Beatlesville" (above) shows the crowd forming hours before the Beatles' plane landed. The small stage set up for the Beatles to pose for photos would be overturned by fans moments after the group left. Exhausted fans (right) are treated by police and medical personnel.

behind. A mob scene ensued as the unruly crowd pressed against the fence, some attempting to hurdle it. The Fabs, seeing a perilous situation unfolding before their eyes, hustled back into the limo and sped away, moments before the fence collapsed in the frenzy. According to Park, the event lasted a mere forty-two seconds.

In his report, Park quoted a police official at the event who screamed, "My God, let's get 'em outta here before somebody gets killed!" Girls sobbed uncontrollably, having waited hours to see their idols. Some were carried away unconscious, while others begged for a pinch of dirt from inside an enclosure strewn with undelivered love letters.

Also causing alarm in the Beatles' camp was the decision by San Francisco city officials to hold a ticker-tape parade down the city's main streets—before Beatles management raised a serious objection. George commenting in *The Beatles Anthology*, noted that President Kennedy had been shot in a public motorcade only nine months earlier and added, "I don't like littering the streets." The idea was quickly scrapped, not only for the San Francisco visit but for other cities as well; some mayors presented keys to the Beatles as a gesture of welcome instead.

AP IMAGES

Protesters (above) show their displeasure with the Beatles' arrival in San Francisco. Two fans (left) walk through the debris left in the aftermath of "Beatlesville". Brian Epstein would never attempt an event like this again.

SAN FRANCISCO

**August 19, 1964
Cow Palace
8 p.m.**

ANTICIPATION FOR THE BEATLES' RETURN TO AMERICA had been running high for months among fans and members of the press. But they were far from alone in their vigilance. In advance of the group's arrival, another interested party was watching and waiting: the Federal Bureau of Investigation. Having witnessed the chaotic scenes played out during the boys' first visit to America in February, and in other countries around the world in the months since, the FBI would be keeping close tabs on the group and the activities surrounding its upcoming appearances. As reported in FBI file number 157-6 and a memo dated August 19, 1964:

"The San Francisco and Los Angeles Divisions were on August 18, 1964 alerted to the fact that teenagers gathering for the appearances of 'The Beatles' in Los Angeles and San Francisco could be a perfect vehicle for riots if racial elements or organization, subversive or otherwise, would decide to capitalize on this vehicle. Los Angeles and San Francisco were instructed that in this connection they should very carefully determine whether any element or organization, either local or from the outside, might be present endeavoring to create a disturbance."

Of the group's arrival in San Francisco, the memo went on to say that *"although conduct was generally orderly, several persons were injured, and arrests of at least eight persons were made by the Sheriff's Office for disorderly person, disturbing the peace, and molesting. San Francisco has advised that no racial or subversive overtones were observed in the crowd."*

The memo concluded: *"We will continue to be alert for elements which may endeavor to capitalize on the emotional pitch of crowds of teenagers in conjunction with this appearance tour in view of the potential of such a situation."*

It was under the watchful eye of the local division of the Bureau that the Beatles landed in San Francisco early in the evening of Tuesday, August 18, and made their way to the San Francisco Hilton, located downtown in Union Square. The boys and their entourage occupied the entire fifteenth floor. Ivor Davis, who was assigned to ghostwrite George's tour diary for the *Daily Express*, was astounded at the scene laid out before him: "The hotel was under siege. Tens of thousands of people, most of them young girls and most of them with their teeth encased in metal braces, had completely surrounded the hotel and were screaming in the wildest example of mass hysteria I have seen before or since."

Members of the San Francisco Beatles fan club also made their presence known by pouring into the hotel lobby as early as 4 a.m. Hotel management then roped off an area for the club and provided

"The Palace For Cows." The Cow Palace was the site of the first concert to kick off the tour.

the boosters with tables and chairs on which members placed banners, photos, and literature about the group. Three club representatives went so far as to drag into the lobby a six-legged, 150-pound "Beatle Beetle" created from torn-up clothes. As the fan club dined on "Beatle Burgers" provided by the hotel, regular guests shook their heads in disbelief.

Later that night, John and Ringo, press officer Derek Taylor, and tour secretary Diana Vero managed to evade security and visit the Rickshaw, a club on nearby Ross Alley run by Mai Tai Sing.

While enjoying some rare moments out of the spotlight, they met television cowboy star Dale Robertson and renewed their friendship with Billy Preston, whom they'd first met in Hamburg, Germany, when he was Little Richard's keyboard player. Preston would once again cross paths with the Beatles in the late sixties when he was recruited by the band for the "Let It Be" sessions. And on January 30, 1969, he would appear with them on the roof of Apple's Savile Row headquarters for the group's last live nonpaying public performance.

The Beatles held a press conference the next day at the Hilton, shortly before the Cow Palace show. The usual questions were hurled at the group. One reporter commented to Ringo: "You didn't look too happy when you got off the airplane." The beleaguered drummer replied with a question: "If you'd been on it for fifteen hours, how would you look?" Another reporter asked: "What do you boys plan to do in San Francisco other than sleep?" John replied simply: "Sleep." And yet another asked why San Francisco had been chosen as the tour opener. "We don't plan the tours," John replied. "They're planned for us, you see ... with a hearty, healthy, hey! Jolly good." In fact, on the original tour plan drawn up in the early spring by General Artists Corporation's Norman Weiss and presented to Brian Epstein, the first stop was

The boys on stage (above). Cow Palace officials erected a wire fence to hold back fans. The press conference shortly before the Cow Palace show (left).

SAN FRANCISCO HILTON
SAN FRANCISCO, CALIF.

The group occupied the entire fifteenth floor at the Hilton (above), but were unable to use the luxurious rooftop pool area. A ticket envelope from the Cow Palace is shown (right).

COW PALACE

TICKETS

EXAMINE DAY AND DATE ON TICKETS

GENEVA AVE.
SAN FRANCISCO 24
JU 4-2480

@

to be San Diego on August 18. Due to contractual obligations back in the United Kingdom, however, the earliest date that could be honored was the August 19 San Francisco date.

John's words would ring true as businessman Charles O. Finley of Kansas City, Missouri, visited San Francisco during the Beatles' visit, making an offer for an unscheduled show that he felt Epstein couldn't refuse: a single performance in Kansas City for the previously unheard-of sum of $100,000 (some reports say $60,000—still triple the going offer for the band). Epstein refused, at least until Finley visited him again during the Beatles' stop in Los Angeles. In Epstein's presence, Finley tore up the $100,000 check, replacing it with another one in the amount of $150,000, a record at the time for the most money paid to any entertainer for a single performance. The Beatles trusted their able manager and agreed to the gig, sacrificing a valuable day of rest and a long-awaited visit to New Orleans to explore the jazz scene—although by the time they arrived in the Big Easy on September 16, it was clear the latter would have been impossible due to fan hysteria.

The chosen venue in San Francisco was the venerable Cow Palace, which at that time was considered a historic arena. The idea to build it was hatched in 1915 during the Panama-Pacific International Exposition, when city leaders noticed that the livestock exhibit was one of the more popular attractions. After numerous lobbying efforts in the 1930s, the California legislature appropriated $250,000 to purchase a suitable site on which to build an arena. With the Depression in full swing and the economy on the verge of ruin, however, a local newspaper ran a story asking, "Why, when people are starving, should money be spent on a 'palace for cows'?"—hence the name. The building was completed in 1941 and played host not only to cows but also to rodeos, circuses, and even troops as they went off to war. On a hot summer night in August, it would play host to the Beatles.

On August 19, 1964, the Beatles' long-anticipated summer tour of North America began as 17,130 hysterical fans packed the Cow Palace. Ushers at the venue wore Beatles wigs as they tore tickets for the fans.

The promoter for the show (as well as the Beatles' Cow Palace concert the following year) was Paul R. Catalana. A well-respected businessman and promoter in the San Jose area, Catalana began his career operating two drive-in movie theaters—the El Rancho and the Tropicaire Twin-Vue. In 1955, he had promoted the world heavyweight title fight between Rocky Marciano and Archie Moore using closed-circuit television, then in its infancy, at the San Jose Civic Auditorium. Aside from the Beatles,

Catalana also promoted the Rolling Stones, Herman's Hermits, and the Dave Clark Five at the San Jose venue.

He is best known, however, for conceiving, designing, and managing the Safari Room in downtown San Jose. This popular venue welcomed such artists as Wayne Newton, the Supremes, and the Everly Brothers. With the profits he made from the Beatles shows, Catalana even opened a French restaurant called Les Poupees and booked a relatively unknown group named the Syndicate of Sound, who would climb the charts in 1966 with their hit "Little Girl."

The booking for the San Francisco show was hotly contested between Catalana and Tom "Big Daddy" Donahue, who was then a popular disc jockey for radio station KYA. "Big Daddy" thought he had secured the rights for the show during a phone call with Brian Epstein *before* the band appeared on the Ed Sullivan shows. In fact, Donahue was so sure of Epstein's verbal commitment that he asked Cow Palace manager Ed Diran to clear the date for a concert at the building on August 19. Diran recalled that despite never having heard of the Beatles, he blocked the date on his calendar for the booking, writing in "Beettles." Still, with no contract signed, Donahue flew to London to meet with Epstein. Nothing ever materialized. "Big Daddy" did not end his dealings with Epstein there, as he was determined to do business with the Beatles manager. Later he would threaten Epstein with a lawsuit but then secure himself a place in history as the promoter of the

PRIVATE COLLECTION

The Beatles pose with Paul R. Catalana (above) the promoter for the 1964 and 1965 Cow Palace shows. A letter from the San Francisco Hilton (far left) documents that the bed sheets were used by the Beatles. A piece of one sheet is shown (left). The hotel used the gimmick to raise funds for Junior Achievement, a national high school club.

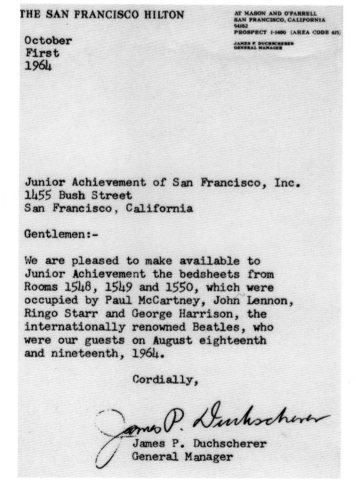

THE SAN FRANCISCO HILTON

AT MASON AND O'FARRELL
SAN FRANCISCO, CALIFORNIA
94102
PROSPECT 1-1400 (AREA CODE 415)

JAMES P. DUCHSCHERER
GENERAL MANAGER

October
First
1964

Junior Achievement of San Francisco, Inc.
1455 Bush Street
San Francisco, California

Gentlemen:-

We are pleased to make available to Junior Achievement the bedsheets from Rooms 1548, 1549 and 1550, which were occupied by Paul McCartney, John Lennon, Ringo Starr and George Harrison, the internationally renowned Beatles, who were our guests on August eighteenth and nineteenth, 1964.

Cordially,

James P. Duchscherer
General Manager

With the American flag proudly displayed in the background, the British imports rock the Cow Palace to the delight of 17,130 fans. The sold out show set American Beatlemania in motion once again. This was a night never to be forgotten— an historic venue, deafening screams from the fans, record tickets sales, and complete disorder in the crowd. During this 1964 tour, the Beatles would perform 32 concerts in 24 cities in just 34 days.

MIRRORPIX

Beatles' final concert performance, which took place at San Francisco's Candlestick Park on August 29, 1966. In the end, Donahue stated publicly that he "wished he had never heard of the Beatles."

Ed Diran was surprised when Catalana walked into his office to sign a contract for use of the Cow Palace for the August 19 show. Though Diran had never heard of Catalana, the promoter assured him that all was in order—that he had secured the show contract with Epstein. The contract between NEMS and Catalana was executed on April 17. Diran issued only one news release announcing the concert, in mid- to late April, which allowed all ticket orders to be quickly filled. Ticket prices were set at $6.50, $5.50, $4.50, and $3.50. Scalpers, it was reported, were commanding up to $50 per ticket.

Yet another press conference was held an hour before showtime in the Cow Palace cafeteria. The Beatles had to stand against a wall to field questions from the reporters who packed the room.

Meanwhile, the venue was brimming with excitement as the Bill Black Combo, the Exciters, the

Righteous Brothers, and Jackie DeShannon performed their hits to an impatient crowd that was already chanting for the Beatles. Backstage, the band was having a meet-and-greet with the celebrities in attendance. Shirley Temple's ten-year-old daughter Lori got to sit on Ringo's lap, and a telegram arrived from Elvis Presley and his manager, Colonel Tom Parker, wishing the band the best of success. As the show progressed, even DeShannon's hip-shaking music couldn't quell the commotion.

Backstage, Larry Kane, a journalist who was fortunate enough to travel with the Beatles on the entire 1964 tour, was with the group at the bottom of the stairs leading to the stage. He noticed that they were a bit nervous as they clutched their instruments and that George was biting his lip in the sultry atmosphere of the venue. As emcee Art Nelson of the Bay City's KEWB announced the group, the Beatles rushed up the stairs to the stage with John leading the way. Nelson's introduction of the band unleashed four minutes and forty-five seconds of relentless screaming. Ed Diran, who had witnessed many events at the historic arena, had never heard anything like it. He recalls that the noise level was "comparable to all the jet planes at San Francisco Airport taking off simultaneously."

The group plugged in, played a few warm-up notes, and then launched into a searing rendition of "Twist and Shout." One fan, Cyril Jordan, recounts, "The flash of the cameras didn't stop, the sound of screaming was a constant roar like the ocean, everyone was jumping over one another to get to the front … the whole city went nuts!"

The Beatles prepared about a dozen songs for their set list. After "Twist and Shout," the usual order was "You Can't Do That," "All My Loving," "She Loves You," "Things We Said Today," "Roll Over Beethoven," "Can't Buy Me Love," "If I Fell," "I Want to Hold Your Hand," "Boys," "A Hard Day's Night," and "Long Tall Sally." The song "Kansas City" was added at the Kansas City show and "Till There Was You" in Las Vegas.

Jelly beans peppered the stage during the concert, inspired by George's reported love for Jelly Babies—the soft English equivalent of the harder American candy—and despite Ringo's pre-show plea to the audience not to throw them.

The concert had to be stopped twice to restore order. Photos from the evening show kids seated behind the stage, separated from the band by only a wire fence, just a few feet from Ringo's drum riser.

MIRRORPIX

A San Francisco policeman stands at John's microphone in an attempt to restore order as Lennon backs off. KEWB's Art Nelson, who introduced the group, looks on. Note the jelly Beans that litter the stage.

By the time the show ended thirty-eight minutes later, with Paul belting out "Long Tall Sally," the Beatles had indeed made an impression. Fifteen-year-old Mary Murphy described the concert by saying simply, "It was traumatic."

For each show the Beatles played in North America, it was the promoter's responsibility to safely escort the group from the venue. While Elvis's promoters used the phrase "Elvis has left the building," the Beatles were much more creative in their escapes. Following the Cow Palace performance, the boys remained backstage, according to Diran, until he felt it was safe for them to board the limousines for the ride to the airport and their late-night flight to Las Vegas. The limos were besieged by fans, however, so an ambulance was called to dispatch the boys under cover to the airport. Ringo found the tour madness exciting: "I loved it. I loved the decoy cars and all the intricate ways of getting us to the gigs."

By the time all the jelly beans, ticket stubs, and spent tissues were swept up, the concert was deemed an incredible success. The momentum that other cities would soon experience had begun. The *San Francisco Examiner* quoted a deputy sheriff who said: "That's 16,000 kids who aren't out stealing hubcaps." A child psychologist who had attended the show with his wife and had witnessed many forms of mass hysteria commented: "This beats anything I've seen." Most newspaper accounts compared the noise at the concert to that of a jet engine, and one columnist made the preposterous claim that the shrieking had killed the venerable rats that made the Cow Palace their home.

The Beatles concert certainly caused a wave of excitement that would soon envelop the nation. Ed Diran was relieved it was over, but soon found himself besieged with calls from other arena managers asking for tips on surviving the onslaught they would soon face. The Palace had survived, but Diran recalls that it was a frightening, traumatic experience. Gross receipts totaled $91,670. The Beatles' share was their $25,000 guarantee plus 60 percent of the gross, for a very tidy profit. Paul Catalana did very little to promote the show, placing just a few newspaper ads. No posters or handbills were ever needed. Unused tickets from the concert in San Francisco are extremely hard to find, as are stubs. The ticket pictured belonged to a young girl whose parents forbade her to go. She placed the ticket in the family Bible, where she discovered it some forty years later.

The next stop on the tour was Las Vegas, where an incident involving John in a hotel room threatened to derail the entire tour—and possibly the Beatles themselves.

The Beatles belt out their hits (above) as a San Francisco police officer crouches at the ready. Jubilant fans look on from the seats behind the stage. Nervous arena managers from around the country sought advice from Cow Palace manager, Ed Diran, on how to survive the onslaught of Beatlemania. Paul and John (left) share a microphone, beautifully framed by their guitars.

LAS VEGAS

August 20, 1964
Convention Center
Two Shows, 4 p.m. and 9 p.m.

LAS VEGAS CONJURES UP IMAGES of a city that never sleeps—a 24/7 entertainment mecca where people the world over gather to try their luck in one of the many casinos, dine on everything from buffet to gourmet, and attend first-class shows and championship boxing matches. It's an expanding, fast-paced, multicultural oasis shining like a diamond in the barren desert that surrounds it. Today it is one of the nation's fastest-growing cities, with no end to development in sight.

In the early 1960s, however, Las Vegas was quite a different place, home to only a few casino properties and a scattering of permanent residents. It was into this somewhat sparse setting that the Beatles arrived in the early morning hours of August 20, 1964.

This second tour stop, with the group still fresh from the rousing performance in San Francisco a few hours earlier, would leave an impression on Las Vegas that remains today. Paul and Ringo have performed in the city over the years as solo artists, and John and George visited often. The Mirage Hotel and Casino honored their legacy in the summer of 2006 with the premiere of a dazzling Cirque du Soleil production titled *LOVE*.

Given the city's relatively small population at the time, one has to wonder why Beatles manager Brian Epstein booked Las Vegas as part of the group's 1964 tour. According to census figures, only 64,405 people lived there. The surrounding Clark County added 60,000 more, for a combined total of around 125,000. Vegas wasn't even in the top 100 most populous cities in the United States. It was by far the smallest visited by the Beatles on the tour, followed by Jacksonville, Florida, with a population of 460,000. The average population of the twenty-three American cities on the tour was 1.4 million.

So why did the Beatles play Las Vegas? The reason was simple. Brian and the boys wanted to see the city firsthand—its hotels, exotic casinos, and resort setting. Their entourage mistakenly assumed that they would be able to unwind by the pool in the warm desert sun and gamble undetected in the hotel casino. In reality, what they saw of Las Vegas was much like what they saw of every other American city: the airport, mobs of fans, a hotel room, a press room, a stage, and, once again, the airport. As always, the Beatles found themselves prisoners of their own success, unable to explore and enjoy Las Vegas and its trappings of excess.

After a raucous debut at the Cow Palace the night before, the Beatles' American Flyers Electra turboprop headed southeast for the short flight to Las Vegas. This had been an impromptu change, as the Beatles were scheduled to spend the night in San Francisco and then travel to Las Vegas the next

The iconic Sahara Hotel and Casino, where the Beatles were guests, closed its doors on the famous Las Vegas Strip in 2011. The group stayed on the twenty-third floor.

day. On board the flight, journalist Larry Kane, who traveled with the band for the entire tour, asked John what it felt like at the Cow Palace. John replied simply, "Not safe." The Beatles' hopes for increased security rested with the officials and promoters of the Las Vegas Convention Center. The venue was located just a short drive from their accommodations at the Sahara Hotel and Casino.

When the Sahara opened its doors on October 7, 1952, it was only the sixth resort on the Strip and the first Las Vegas casino to obtain financial backing from an actual bank. The hotel's futuristic convention center was added in 1959. Those wishing to see where the Beatles performed to two packed audiences are out of luck. The convention center was demolished in 1990 to make way for new, expanded convention facilities.

In 1961, the Sahara Hotel and Casino was sold to Del Webb, the construction magnate who had originally built the hotel. A lifelong baseball fan, Webb and two other partners purchased the New York Yankees for $2.8 million in 1945. He owned the team until it was sold to CBS during the 1964 season. He also built the Flamingo Hotel and Casino for reputed mobster Bugsy Siegel, owned a chain of roadside motels called Hiway House, and constructed the Mint Hotel and Casino. He is probably best known for developing the retirement community of Sun City, Arizona, one of the first of its kind. The Sahara later became the first Strip resort to go public and be traded on the New York Stock Exchange. At this writing, the Sahara sits vacant on the Strip, awaiting a transformation to its former glory.

Herb McDonald, a legendary Las Vegas figure who is credited with inventing the all-you-can-eat buffet, and Stan Irwin were the promoters for the Beatles' Las Vegas concerts. Irwin, who worked for McDonald, first arrived in the city in 1949 to do a comedy stint at Club Bingo, which had occupied the land where the Sahara now resides. His booking was for only eleven days, but he decided to stay and later became head of public relations and promotions for the newly built Sahara Hotel and Casino. Irwin stayed on for two decades, eventually rising to vice president of the Sahara Nevada Corporation.

"Gambling is evil," quipped John, but Paul looks enthralled with the action. Sahara management brought slot machines into the Beatles's suite for their enjoyment, something the now-powerful Nevada Gaming Board would never allow for today's celebrities and sports figures.

According to Irwin, the other resorts initially rejected the idea of bringing the Beatles to town. He recalls that it was Roy Gerber, an agent for General Artists Corporation (GAC), who initially worked his way down the Strip trying to find a buyer for the Beatles. The last casino Gerber visited was the Sahara. Irwin said that back then, the Hotel Association and the Publicity Directors Association worked together to bring what he called "traffic" to Las Vegas, usually from southern California. This partnership and the noncompetitive spirit of the association were directed at improving Las Vegas as a whole. In Irwin's words: "We all believed that that which was good for Vegas was good for the hotel, and what's good for the hotel or hotels is good for Vegas."

The resorts and the Publicity Directors Association were concerned about staging an event that largely attracted teenagers to a city that targeted and lured patrons over the age of twenty-one. Herb McDonald, who was in England at the time, received a call from Irwin at 4 a.m. begging him to go see the Beatles, to which McDonald replied, "Stan, I'm not an exterminator. Who are the Beatles?" Nonetheless, McDonald, together with James Bond actor Sean Connery, ventured out to see a performance and was smitten with the crowds and the screams. McDonald gave Irwin the go-ahead to book the group. Years later, Irwin would say: "I just knew it would be a hit to the Sahara, the Strip, and ultimately Las Vegas."

Irwin originally planned for the group to play two shows in the Sahara Hotel's Congo Room, which, if pushed to the limit, could seat 700 for each show (1,400 total). After witnessing the growing excitement over the band and conferring with GAC agent Stan Gerber, however, he switched venues and booked the 7,000-seat convention center. Irwin, with the prodding of GAC, then decided to promote

MIRRORPIX

the concert as a "Las Vegas" event and requested that the other hotels help by selling tickets and advertising it.

With the concert now scheduled for a larger venue, Irwin gambled further, keeping the same format he'd planned for the Congo Room. The Beatles would perform two shows—one at 4 p.m. and another at 9 p.m. He partnered with Irvin Feld (who promoted the 1964 Baltimore and Dallas concerts) and negotiated with GAC for a $25,000 appearance fee plus 60 percent of the gate for the two shows. This fee for both shows would prove to be one of the best deals any promoter would receive on the 1964 tour, with the exception of Feld's Baltimore and Dallas shows.

While planning the concert, Irwin devised a seating arrangement that would allow fans to sit behind the stage, adding 1,408 people per show and making the local fire marshal a nervous wreck. In 1990, when the original Las Vegas Convention Center was demolished, the Beatles' two performances on August 20 still held the record for attendance at a single event at that venue (16,816). Only a sold-out performance by Leonard Bernstein's New York Philharmonic Orchestra came close.

In the weeks following the announcement of the Beatles concert, ticket sales were a bit sluggish. The other hotels weren't initially supportive, and failed to sell the blocks of tickets Irwin had reserved for them and their guests. Increasingly worried, he placed ads in the Los Angeles Times under the bold headline "3000 Beatle Tickets," stating that tickets would be on sale at the Sahara Hotel's Los Angeles ticket agency. Irwin was hoping to draw fans from southern California and decided to make ticket-buying more convenient for people in that market. A few days before the concerts, empty seats were still plentiful, but then kids began begging their parents to take them to the concert. Soon, tickets became hard to find as high rollers, hotel guests, and Las Vegas residents demanded tickets from pit bosses, hotel employees, and even the Sahara box office itself. Both shows sold out, and Irwin was pleased that the results justified the risks he had taken.

The Beatles arrived from San Francisco at 1:35 a.m. on a remote runway at McCarran Field, about a mile from the main terminal, where many teenagers had been waiting for hours. Official vehicles were seen with their headlights off speeding toward the plane to pick up the group. The Las Vegas Review-Journal stated in its August 20 edition that the Beatles' arrival "was handled with the aplomb that would have pleased a secret service agent." Irwin, waiting on the tarmac at the bottom of the exit stairs, was first greeted by Paul, who extended his hand and said, "Hiya, boy!," much to the chagrin of the far older promoter. Paul probably didn't realize he was addressing Irwin. As the convoy sped off to the Sahara, cars filled with teenagers intent on catching a glimpse of the British rockers unsuccessfully tried to block their path.

Upon arrival at the hotel entrance, the Beatles' motorcade encountered a mob scene. The Sahara was pitifully understaffed and unsecured, angering Epstein and frightening the Beatles. Extra police, along with three police dogs, were called in to quell the near-riot. Reports stated that 2,000 people, mostly teenage girls, had been milling about the hotel property for days. They were now seen running

The Beatles pose high above the then infant Las Vegas Strip. The Sahara was one of the premier properties in the area, but newer development headed much further south down Las Vegas Blvd., including the MGM Grand, The Mirage and the Venetian. This photograph was shot on August 20, as the Boys prepared to perform two shows at the adjacent Las Vegas Convention Center at 4 p.m. and 9 p.m.

LAS VEGAS NEWS BUREAU (2)

The Fab Four rock the Convention Center as police officials ring the stage (above). An exterior picture of the Las Vegas Convention Center, often referred to as the "Rotunda" by locals (right). The venue was demolished in 1990 to make way for newer and larger convention facilities.

through corridors, riding elevators, and causing general havoc in their efforts to corner a Beatle. This was taking place in the wee hours of the morning as guests tried to sleep. One guest, perturbed by all the commotion outside, witnessed the Beatles being dropped off at the hotel's rear loading dock and commented to a newspaper reporter, "Ha, they're getting on the freight elevator, just like a load of garbage!" It was clear that not all hotel guests were happy the Beatles were there.

One newspaper reporter asked if the Beatles were able to leave their suite and enjoy the Vegas nightlife. Ringo replied, "No, we just stayed in our room and laughed at each other all night." While the band was imprisoned in suite 2344 in the Sahara's Alexandria Tower, hotel management helped break their boredom by bringing up a few slot machines. John was heard muttering, "Gambling is evil!" This unprecedented action would never be allowed today by the powerful Nevada Gaming Commission—not even at the insistence of the highest of rollers, entertainers, or sports figures.

Irwin assigned the Beatles a dressing room that he described as "massive" and complete with portable beds and saunas. Larry Kane was able to interview the boys before they hit the stage. It was during this interview that Kane asked some penetrating questions about segregation in America and the upcoming performance in Jacksonville, Florida. His exchange with Paul was remarkable for the times.

Kane: *What about this comment that I heard about from you, Paul, concerning racial integration at the various performances?*

Paul: *We don't like it if there's any segregation or anything, because we're not used to it, y'know. We've never played to a segregated audience before, and it just seems mad to me. Y'know, I mean, it may seem right to some people, but to us, it just seems a bit daft.*

Kane: *Well, you're gonna play Jacksonville, Florida. Do you anticipate any kind of difference of that opinion?*

Paul: *I don't know really, y'know, 'cause I don't know what people in America are like. But I think they'd be a bit silly to segregate people, 'cause y'know, I mean—I don't think colored people are any different, y'know, they're just the same as everyone else. But, y'know, over here, there are some people who think that they're sorta animals or something, but I think it's stupid, y'know.*

Kane: *Yeah.*

Paul: *You can't treat other human beings like animals. And so, y'know—I mean, I wouldn't mind 'em sitting next to me.... It's the way we all feel....*

As was the case at most of the 1964 tour stops, the Vegas concert began with the usual support acts: the Bill Black Combo, followed by the Exciters, the Righteous Brothers and Jackie DeShannon (all backed by the Bill Black Combo). Before the Beatles went onstage, they met Liberace and were quite excited about it. Eight-year-old Kelly Walsh attended the first of the two performances that evening and still remembers it being stupendous: "It was the loudest in terms of fan involvement—unrelenting." For her, it eclipsed subsequent shows she saw. She vividly recalls that, as she exited the convention center, scores of young girls were outside tearing at the grass in an effort to secure a keepsake from the event.

"The Rotunda," as the convention center was called by the locals, rocked and reverberated with poor sound quality during both shows. George humorously recalls seeing Pat Boone in the audience and relates in *The Beatles Anthology:* "I think the first four rows of that concert were filled up by ... his daughters. He seemed to have hundreds of daughters." The Beatles changed the standard set list, which they seldom did, adding "Till There Was You." Capitol Records used photos taken at the convention center for the picture sleeves of the singles "She's a Woman/I Feel Fine" and "Eight Days a Week/I Don't Want to Spoil the Party."

The press conference was held backstage at the convention center before the second of the two sold-out performances. Reporters asked such questions as, "What do you do with your money?," "What will you do when this fad is over?," and the rather insulting, "Do you regard yourselves as being musicians?" In addition to the press conference, Epstein organized an invitation-only cocktail

A worried Stan Irwin placed ads in the *Los Angeles Times* like this one, in hope of attracting Southern California teenagers to drive across the desert for the concerts. Other Las Vegas hotels had a difficult time getting behind Irwin's plan to present the group. Irwin, originally booked the hotel's Congo Room, but as the concert dates approached and ticket demand increased, he switched the shows to the larger Convention Center.

The performance contract that brought the Beatles to Las Vegas. The 8:30 p.m. show was later changed to 9 p.m. This contract was signed by Stan Irwin, the director of publicity for the Sahara-Nevada Corporation and NEMS's Bernard Lee who was given signing authority on such contracts by Brian Epstein. Note the ticket prices stated in line item 3.

640 Fifth Avenue
NEW YORK 19, N.Y.
Circle 7-7543

8 South Michigan Avenue
CHICAGO 3, ILLINOIS
STate 2-6288

9025 Wilshire Blvd.
BEVERLY HILLS, CALIF.
CRestview 3-2400

GAC GENERAL ARTISTS CORPORATION

Deposit *check*
Amt. Rec. $12,500.00
Date 5/1/64
O. K. *JD*

NOTE: ATTACHED RIDER HEREBY MADE PART OF CONTRACT

AGREEMENT made this ___27th___ day of ___April___, 19__64__,

between ___NEMS ENTERPRISES LIMITED___ (hereinafter

referred to as "PRODUCER") and ___Sahara-Nevada Corporation___
(hereinafter referred to as "PURCHASER").

It is mutually agreed between the parties as follows:

The PURCHASER hereby engages the PRODUCER and the PRODUCER hereby agrees to furnish the entertainment presentation hereinafter described, upon all the terms and conditions herein set forth, including those on the reverse side hereof entitled "Additional Terms and Conditions."

1. PRODUCER agrees to furnish the following entertainment presentation to PURCHASER:

___A show of approximately ninety minutes duration each, starring___
___THE BEATLES, plus additional supporting attractions to be selected___
___at the sole discretion of PRODUCER.___

for presentation thereof by PURCHASER:

(a) at ___Las Vegas Convention Center, Las Vegas, Nevada___;
(Place of Engagement)

(b) on ___Thursday, August 20, 1964___;
(Date(s) of Engagement)

(c) at the following time(s): ___Two shows: 4:00 P.M.   8:30 P.M.___

(d) rehearsals: ___to be advised___

2. FULL PRICE AGREED UPON: ___TWENTY-FIVE THOUSAND DOLLARS ($25,000.00) Guarantee___
___against 60% of gross admission receipts, after applicable admission taxes___
___have been deducted therefrom, for both shows.___

All payments shall be paid by certified check, money order, bank draft or cash as follows:

(a) $ ___12,500.00 (50%)___ shall be paid by PURCHASER to and in the name of PRODUCER'S agent, GENERAL ARTISTS CORPORATION, not later than ___immediately upon signing hereof___

(b) $ ___12,500.00 (50%)___ shall be paid by PURCHASER to PRODUCER not later than ___thirty days preceding actual play date.___;

(c) Additional payments, if any, shall be paid by PURCHASER to PRODUCER no later than ___All earned percentage, not later than intermission of performance covered herein.___

PURCHASER shall first apply any and all receipts derived from the entertainment presentation to the payments required hereunder: All payments shall be made in full without any deductions whatsoever.

3. SCALE OF ADMISSION ___7,500 seats at $2.00, $3.00, $4.00, $5.00; $47,000.00 net after taxes for both shows.___

___NEMS ENTERPRISES LIMITED___ (PRODUCER)

By___

___SAHARA-NEVADA CORPORATION___ (PURCHASER)

Return all signed copies to agent:
General Artists Corporation
640 Fifth Avenue
New York, New York
9025 Wilshire Blvd.
Beverly Hills, Calif.
Attn: Fred Dale

By___ V.P. ___Stan Irwin___

Address: ___Hotel Sahara___
___Las Vegas, Nevada___

Phone: ___

ALL COPIES OF CONTRACT MUST BE SIGNED ON REVERSE AS WELL AS FACE SIDE.

Form AA-1

party in between shows. Much to the disappointment of those in attendance, the Beatles didn't show. The convention center was evacuated shortly after the press conference due to numerous prank calls received by the Las Vegas Sheriff's Department, including a bomb threat.

During the Las Vegas visit, there was an alleged incident involving John that, had it been publicized and found to be true, could have derailed the entire tour. In his book, *Ticket to Ride*, Larry Kane recalls

LAS VEGAS NEWS BUREAU

that he was summoned from his sleep early in the morning by road manager Mal Evans, who requested his presence. He soon found himself in the hallway of the Beatles' floor with press officer Derek Taylor and the other road manager, Neil Aspinall, who were trying to address a dire situation. It appeared that underage twin sisters had been seen in John's hotel room. Kane was enlisted to calm the girls' frantic mother, who was pacing in the hotel lobby. He suggested to her that perhaps her daughters had found their way into John's room on a quest for autographs—an explanation that satisfied her and immediately eased her fears.

Persistent rumors surrounding the incident have circulated, including one claiming that a secret $10,000 blackmail payment was made. Taylor even went so far as to admit as much. There is no evidence that the matter was anything more than innocent, however. The Las Vegas police conducted a brief investigation, but nothing came of it—fortunately for the band, as such a lapse in judgment could have had severe consequences. Had a Beatle been accused of sexual misconduct with underage girls, the scandal not only could have ended the tour, but could have damaged the band's image enough to end their meteoric rise to fame.

Unused tickets for the Las Vegas concert are extremely rare, as both shows were sold out. The reason there are no seat numbers on the left-hand side of the ticket is because they were torn from a ticket book as they were sold, allowing the Sahara to accurately tally ticket sales. The Sahara later published an article about the concert in its *Saharan* magazine, which was sent to frequent guests of the hotel. This issue has since become quite collectible. Irwin recalls approaching Epstein to ask if he could license a necklace containing strands of the Beatles' hair—an idea that was politely rejected by the band's manager. Despite the money that could have been made, Irwin refused to cut up bedsheets and the like, noting that it wasn't his style. He believes the Sahara made $50,000 on the event.

Las Vegas has rarely seen the kind of commotion that was stirred up during its twenty-four hours of Beatlemania. The tour carried on as the group caught a flight to Seattle the next morning. Because Vegas didn't prove to be the experience they'd anticipated, they never performed there as a group again.

The Beatles walk onto the stage at the Las Vegas Convention Center to the delight of fans at the sold-out show. Stan Irwin, who gambled on presenting the group is shown with outstretched arms introducing the band.

SEATTLE

August 21, 1964
Seattle Center Coliseum
8 p.m.

The boys wave to the press and fans upon their arrival at Sea-Tac airport from Las Vegas. The plaid and checkered jackets make a statement of their own.

THE GIRL FELL SEVERAL FEET from an air conditioning vent and lived to tell about it.

According to opening act Jackie DeShannon, as the Beatles were returning to their dressing room after their Seattle press conference, a young fan fell out of an air vent onto the floor in front of Ringo. When the startled drummer asked the girl if she was okay, she turned away without saying a word and sprinted back into the Seattle Center Coliseum. It was a scene that was already becoming commonplace during the 1964 American tour. Beatlemania was in full swing as inventive teenagers devised whatever ploy was necessary to meet their idols.

After two wild shows at the Las Vegas Convention Center, the Beatles and company flew to the Great Northwest and descended upon Seattle. For the next twenty-four and a half hours, the group captured the hearts of young Seattleites while worrying their parents. According to Washington state historians, by 1964 "Seattle had begun what would prove to be a thirty-year evolution from a charming yet provincial hinterland to the bustling Pacific Rim city we know today." Since then, the city's been no stranger to rock 'n' roll despite its geographic isolation from the rest of the United States; well-known musicians and bands including Pearl Jam and Jimi Hendrix got their start there.

GEORGE CLARKONEN/THE SEATTLE TIMES

Seattle was also one of the first cities in the United States to hear Beatles music. KJR deejay Pat O'Day played "From Me to You" on the day of its release in the summer of 1963 and interviewed the Beatles by phone well before their debut on *The Ed Sullivan Show*. O'Day was also fortunate enough to introduce the group onstage at the Seattle Center Coliseum at both the 1964 and 1966 shows. He recalls George telling him how inspired he was by the music of the Wailers, a legendary band based in nearby Tacoma.

The Beatles' show on August 21, 1964, certainly continued to drive the musical revolution in the city. Prior to the group's visit, Woolworth's ran ads urging parents to succumb to the wishes of their teenagers with such taglines as "It's a mad fad, Dad" while filling their shelves with Beatles merchandise, from shampoo and nylons to toy guitars.

The city's famed Edgewater hotel was chosen by tour organizers to host the Beatles for one reason: no other hotel would have them. The now-historic inn, built for the Seattle World's Fair in 1962, gives its guests glorious views of Elliott Bay and the Olympic Mountains to the west. Today patrons can still stay

The Beatles fishing from a window in their suite at the Edgewater Inn. No one caught any fish from this staged photo-op.

Large mobs of fans greet the Beatles' limousine as it arrives at the Edgewater Inn, nearly bringing it to a halt. Police officers try desperately to create a barrier between the limo and the crowd. Note fans bending the car's radio antenna.

GEORGE CLARKONEN/THE SEATTLE TIMES

in the Beatles' suite (room 272—although it no longer has the original configuration) and even pretend to fish out the window, as the band was shown doing in several well-known photographs. Room 272 served as the band's living room, complete with a full bar, while rooms 274 and 270 had two beds each for the Beatles to sleep in. Over the years, the hotel has also played host to such groups as the Rolling Stones and Led Zeppelin.

During the Beatles' visit, the property was transformed into an impenetrable fortress by general manager Don Wright and public relations director Marty Murphy. A 350-foot-long barrier of barbed wire and plywood was erected along the hotel's picturesque waterfront setting. Local police arranged for the harbor patrol to comb the waters around the Edgewater for any suspicious activity, and were

ordered to keep anything and anybody from getting within ten feet of the hotel. Cops were stationed at every entrance and on every floor of the hotel to keep uninvited guests away.

Some recent high school graduates who had planned a summer trip and booked the hotel months in advance—long before the Beatles tour—found their reservations cancelled. Wedding party guests booked at the hotel were given special passes for entering and exiting.

The venue chosen for the Beatles concert was the Seattle Center Coliseum, located just yards from the world-famous Space Needle in the seventy-four-acre Seattle Center, site of the 1962 Seattle World's Fair. Constructed in the year of the fair, the venue was originally named the Washington State Pavilion and was considered an architectural wonder because of its hyper-parabolic shape. In 1964, the building

Fans welcome the Beatles to the Seattle Center Coliseum with their homemade poster, screams, and in one fan's case, her shoe!

was remodeled as a sports arena and reopened as the Coliseum. After a $74 million renovation in 1995, it was renamed Key Arena. This current incarnation hosts some 1.2 million patrons each year and, in addition to being a popular venue for professional sports, is considered one of the top concert venues on the West Coast.

The promoter for the concert was Northwest Releasing, a company founded by longtime Seattle impresario Zalmon "Zollie" Volchok and his partner Jack Engerman. The two men, who became associated while working for Sterling Theaters, would also promote the Beatles' 1966 Seattle show and their 1965 Portland appearance. Under the Volchok-Engerman partnership, Northwest Releasing became one of the largest talent booking agencies in America. But success didn't arrive overnight. Volchok began his career in the 1930s as an emcee and impresario for the Elsinore Theatre in his hometown of Salem, Oregon. He later helped launch the career of *Tonight Show* trumpeter Doc Severinsen.

The two promoters were also involved in roller derby, hosting events throughout the Pacific Northwest until finally hitting it big with Northwest Releasing. From 1953 to 1969, they booked the likes of

Frank Sinatra, Elvis Presley, and the Beatles. In 1979, under Volchok's leadership as executive vice president and general manager, the basketball Seattle SuperSonics won the NBA World Championship. In later years, Volchok fondly remembered that he'd provided the Beatles with only Coca-Cola in their dressing room in 1964. When they returned in 1966, it was stocked with beer.

In the early planning stages for the '64 tour, Beatles manager Brian Epstein offered Volchok two shows for August 21. Volchok was hesitant to accept because of the poor financial return he'd received earlier in the year from the closed-circuit telecast shown in local theaters of the Beatles' first American concert in Washington, D.C. Ultimately, Volchok refused the offer. Later, after seeing brisk

ticket sales in the weeks leading up to the concert, he made a $40,000 offer to Epstein for a second show. Unfortunately for Northwest Releasing and Seattle Beatles fans, the bid was too late. The tour schedule was already set in stone. The city would have to wait two more years before the Beatles would perform two shows.

The single performance on August 21 was a sellout. Tickets were impossible to find. Volchok remembered having to dip into his emergency reserve of tickets to pay off an old favor. The $5 tickets were being scalped on the streets for as high as $30 apiece.

The Beatles' fourth press conference in as many days was held just prior to their performance at the Seattle Center Coliseum. When George was asked, "How many more years do you think it will go on?," he replied simply, "Till death do us part." The press, having seen the photo of the boys fishing out the window of their hotel suite at the Edgewater, asked if they'd caught anything. Ringo humorously replied, "Someone on the other side of the lake kept shouting, 'There's no fish in here,' so I sort of got discouraged and pulled me line in." In an interview years later, Volchok confessed that the Beatles didn't

The Beatles take questions from journalists assembled as press officer Derek Taylor, looks on. The press inquired how much longer the group would be together, to which George responded, "Till death do us part."

Brings Teen-Agers To Store:

Beatles' Magic Carpet Has Grandmother Up At Dawn

GREATER LOVE has no grandmother than Mrs. Vivian Roberts, of Carnation, who sacrificed most of her Tuesday night slumber to help out her granddaughter and a friend.

Yesterday morning was the morning that MacDougall-Southwick put on sale pieces of the rug that graced the floor of the Edgewater Inn suite occupied last week by the Beatles.

MRS. ROBERTS, to make sure that her granddaughter Georgina Peterson, 14, and her friend, Nicky Montgomery, 16, visiting from Fairbanks, would not be done out of their share of the rug, brought them to the Pike Street entrance of the store at 3:30 a.m.

It was a long night, the girls said as they clutched their treasured pieces of the orange carpet and one they need not have endured actually.

For when the store opened at 9 a.m., 30 minutes early, there were exactly 60 kids, mostly girls, waiting to swoop down on the counter where the rug pieces were to be sold.

An early-arriving MacDougall's saleswoman, Miss Agnes Olsheski, who got to the store shortly after 8 a.m., was so struck by the patience of Nicky and Georgina that she bought and gave to the girls oversize color photos of each of the Beatles.

SHE SAID:

"It seemed to me that two kids who would wait

as long as they did to buy a piece of our rug should get something a little extra for their devotion."

There will be plenty of rug to go around, it woul appear. The rug will suppl pieces two inches square, eac neatly sealed in a plastic ba;

The carpeting was bougl by MacDougall - Southwic from the Edgewater for a undisclosed amount. The stoi also supplied new carpetin for the Beatle suite.

A portion of the procee will go to Childrens' Orthc pedic Hospital and Medic; Center.

Georgina yawned yesterda and said:

"I'm really going to slee tonight—with this Beatle rug under my pillow,"

Nicky said:

"Maybe we better get you grandmother one too."

A piece of carpet (above) from the Edgewater, walked on by the Beatles, made headlines the next day. The Seattle Health Department demanded it be sanitized before being sold. The iconic Edgewater Inn (below) sits on Elliot Bay.

really fish from their hotel window. It was strictly a photo op and nothing more. Even so, the image remains indelible.

The warm-up acts remained unchanged in Seattle. The Bill Black Combo, the Righteous Brothers, the Exciters, and Jackie DeShannon tried their best to satisfy a crowd that wanted little more than to see the Beatles. Still, the audience warmed up to DeShannon, who was celebrating her twentieth birthday that day. They serenaded the Kentucky-born singer with a chorus of "Happy Birthday," and in return she belted out her hit "Needles and Pins." Lan Roberts, one of the emcees, told the crowd that he had just shaken hands with Ringo, washed them, and let them drip into a bottle. This "Ringo secondhand water," he told them, would be given away on his show the next day. Suddenly, dozens of girls mobbed the police line at the front of the stage, shouting, "I want the Ringo water!" Needless to say, Roberts's phone was ringing endlessly the next day.

After the opening acts had finished their sets, Pat O'Day walked onstage to introduce the head-liners. In unison, 14,720 screaming fans welcomed the Beatles to Seattle. Some accounts place the crowd at 14,328 and others at 14,300, but Larry Kane, a journalist accompanying the Beatles on their tour, said a head count was irrelevant. The Seattle Center Coliseum reverberated as if 140,000 people were there. Kane actually covered his ears for the first time on the tour as the decibels reached the level of a fully ramped jet engine. Fortunately for the Beatles, a hundred Navy volunteers—along with police and firefighters—locked arms to restrain the onslaught of teenagers trying to rush the stage. Volchok, fearing that the kids could actually jump onto the stage, constructed a barrier higher than normal.

Journalists who were watching the events unfold onstage noticed that the Beatles looked extremely nervous and frightened by the frenzied crowd. Kane noted that John was sweating profusely. In addition to the usual bedlam, all the trappings of a Beatles concert were present: jelly beans, flashbulb pops, and smelling salts. One fan was carried out on a stretcher repeatedly screaming, "Paul, I love you!," despite pleas from the medical attendant to stay calm. Mary Swint (now Colovich), whose father, Jay Swint, worked for Capitol Records, was there with her brother Mark. She recalls emcee O'Day urging female fans to refrain from tossing their metal lipstick tubes onstage, as Ringo had been hit in the head with them at an earlier concert. George and Paul, she said, laughed throughout the show, perhaps amused by the madness all around them.

A *Seattle Times* reporter described the concert: "They came out like Brahma Bulls; they bounced to their places as the Coliseum let loose in one adolescent moan." For twenty-nine minutes, the Beatles raced through their hits: "Twist and Shout," "You Can't Do That," "All My Loving," "She Loves You," "Things We Said Today," "Roll Over Beethoven," "Can't Buy Me Love," "If I Fell,"

Edgewater Inn, Seattle

"I Want to Hold Your Hand," "Boys," "A Hard Day's Night," and "Long Tall Sally."

Then it was over. Lan Roberts remembers the concert as "a nonstop cyclone," adding, "I remember thinking while I was onstage, I'll never see this again; no one will." After the show the Beatles, unable to escape in their limousine, instead had to wait in their dressing room for over an hour while an escape plan could be hatched. Volchok decided to hire an ambulance to safely escort the group back to "Fort" Edgewater.

Hotel PR director Murphy, who can be seen sporting a tall beehive hairdo in archival footage, was on hand at the Edgewater throughout the Beatles' stay to fulfill any requests they made. In the early morning hours after the show, Murphy noticed several room service carts going in and out of the suite. Around 2:30 a.m., a representative from the Beatles' entourage summoned Murphy and informed her that the boys would like to speak with her.

Thinking she had done something wrong, Murphy entered room 272 and noticed John reading in bed in the adjoining room 274 and George sound asleep in room 270. Paul and Ringo hovered near the bar. She recalled that the room reeked of smoke, and the bassist and drummer were amped up and wanting to do something. Her first thought was that they could jump from the window into the bay and go for a swim, a suggestion that was met with howling laughter.

Out of desperation, she then called the Space Needle and talked with after-hours security, who approved her plan. With Paul and Ringo disguised, Murphy sneaked the two Beatles out of the Edgewater and into her 1957 Chevrolet, where they crouched down on the back floorboard. After an elevator ride to the tower's observation deck, the trio savored the early morning view from 520 feet up. As the group left the hotel for the airport several hours later, road manager Mal Evans presented Murphy with an autographed copy of their LP *A Hard Day's Night* as a token of their appreciation.

In the aftermath of the concert, the Beatles netted $34,569.96 and Northwest Releasing made a $10,147.17 profit. Some reviews in newspapers around the Northwest weren't too favorable. One reviewer, Lou Guzzo, wrote: "True talent trained in years of thankless effort goes begging for a hearing, while the noisy brigade of mediocrity counts its loot in millions." Dr. Bernard Saibel, a child guidance expert assigned to cover the concert, noted that "regardless of the causes or reason for the behavior of these youngsters last night, it had the impact of unholy bedlam, the like of which I have never seen. It caused me to feel that such should not be allowed again, if only for the good of the youngsters." He continued: "It was

A letter (above) to a lucky concert ticket winner of the Associated Grocers' jingle contest and a rare poster (left) produced by Royal Crown Cola.

ATLE TICKETS
oyal Crown
TLE CAPS ONLY

100 Beatle Tickets (to Aug. 21 Seattle appearance) will be auctioned singly Aug. 19 at Seattle Civic Center, not for money but for Royal Crown bottle caps! Drink R-C!

an orgy for teenagers ... frantic, hostile, uncontrolled, screaming, unrecognizable beings ... if this is possible—and it is—parents and adults have a lot to account for to allow this to go on."

Concert ephemera from the Seattle show are extremely rare. The typical generic North American program was used and, as of this writing, no posters or handbills have ever surfaced. In all likelihood they weren't produced, since the high demand for tickets eliminated any need for advertising. Only a few unused tickets, like the one shown in this chapter, have ever seen the light of day. This particular ticket, along with the accompanying letter, was won in a Beatles jingle contest sponsored by Associated Grocers. Even torn stubs from this show are rare. A fan was lucky if the usher returned the larger portion of the stub that showed the name "Beatles," the date, the price, and the venue name. Most fans were left with only a small stub featuring, at most, the date. Carpet squares from the Edgewater, purchased by MacDougall's department store, were cut up and sold, but only after being cleaned first, as mandated by the Seattle Health Department. Even though the sanitizing removed a bit of Beatles mystique, the squares are still quite collectible.

The Beatles would once again visit the Great Northwest on their last American tour, playing a pair of shows at the Seattle Center Coliseum on August 25, 1966. But for now they would put Seattle behind them, heading north to Vancouver, British Columbia, for their first concert on Canadian soil and the tour's first outdoor stadium show.

The Beatles were under constant police protection while in Seattle, even when being escorted to the stage for their performance in front of over 14,000 fans. Note the one fan peering over the whited-out windows of the coliseum to catch a glimpse of the group. Above, a fan's picture of the group on stage.

VANCOUVER

**August 22, 1964
Empire Stadium
8 p.m.**

THERE WERE PROBLEMS WITH CUSTOMS, A NEAR-RIOT, and a stop for nineteen-cent hamburgers—and the Beatles still hadn't reached Empire Stadium for their first concert appearance on Canadian soil. The date was August 22, 1964, and the place was Vancouver, British Columbia. The Beatles were hungry—and Canadian fans were thirsting for the group's concert that night.

The night before, the group had narrowly escaped the confines of the Seattle Center Coliseum after a particularly raucous show. From the venue, they'd ridden in the back of an ambulance to what looked like a military zone, but was actually the Edgewater Inn. After a good night and morning rest, the Beatles boarded their chartered aircraft for the short hop to Vancouver. But soon after the plane departed from Sea-Tac Airport and headed north, it suddenly banked and turned around. The pilot had been ordered back to Seattle after being notified that certain customs forms necessary to allow the Beatles into Canada were not correctly filled out. At a press conference shortly before the Empire Stadium show, John answered the burning question regarding their delay with his typically sardonic wit: "We had to be deloused."

The Beatles, along with Brian Epstein, arrive late at the airport in Vancouver, after having to return to Seattle to properly fill out customs forms.

Ever-present journalist Larry Kane noticed that the Beatles were not only excited by the prospect of their first North American gig in an outdoor stadium but also mesmerized by the transcendent beauty of Vancouver itself. Kane, noticing Ringo peering out the window as the plane descended into the city, asked the drummer how he felt. Ringo replied, "Man, it is just beyond great, isn't it?" The mood in the plane was definitely serene, but it would soon change as the calm devolved into a full-blown Beatles storm, with thousands of Beatlemaniacs testing the limits of Empire Stadium and the police force assigned to protect the band.

Back in the early spring of 1964, fans had queued up outside Toronto's storied Maple Leaf Gardens for the chance to get Beatles tickets for a September concert in that city. The Montreal Forum was also selected to stage two concerts. Even though Vancouver would trump those dates with an earlier concert, fans in western Canada had to wait until mid-June for officials to formally announce a Beatles concert for Empire Stadium. Manager Brian Epstein was initially concerned with filling the 35,000-seat venue and suggested to Norman Weiss of General Artists Corporation (GAC) that he find a venue of approximately 10,000 seats, which never materialized. Thus, Vancouverites were still able to lay claim to the first "Beatles" day in Canada: August 22, coinciding with the opening of the Pacific National Exhibition (PNE), an event created in 1907 to showcase Vancouver's economic potential.

Empire Stadium was constructed to host the track and field events for the 1954 British Empire and Commonwealth Games, but the building funds dried up before the project could be completed. A businessman named Jack Diamond stepped forward to organize and raise money privately to finish the stadium's roof. With the $360,000 he collected from business associates and friends, the venue was completed in time for the games. At its opening, it was considered Canada's largest sports facility. Ten years later, the Beatles would leave a mark on Empire Stadium that concertgoers would never forget. The stadium was demolished in the early 1990s, and the site served as a parking lot until being renovated for use as a multipurpose athletic field.

Planning for the Beatles' visit to Vancouver began months before their arrival. Ever mindful of the mania that accompanied the group's visit to other cities, local security personnel, city officials, and even the manager of the Hotel Georgia (where the Beatles had planned to stay) started mapping their strategy for dealing with the thousands of fans who would soon besiege the city. PNE officials were keenly aware of Elvis Presley's performance at Empire Stadium seven years earlier and the near-riot it caused. The *Vancouver Sun* called Elvis's visit "the most disgusting exhibition of mass hysteria this city has ever witnessed."

To get a feel for what his city would soon face, police superintendent Ben Jelley flew south to Seattle the day before to attend the Beatles' concert there. As a safety measure, Empire Stadium was ringed with four-foot-high crash barriers, layered four deep and aptly named "Beatle Baffles." Two hundred constables (100 more than originally planned) were assigned to the event, and PNE

DENI EAGLAND/VANCOUVER SUN (3)

When the Beatles arrived at each city, a long motorcade (above) would await to take them either to a hotel, or the venue where they would play. Due to their late arrival, the boys ate hamburgers and chicken wings in their limousine on the way to Empire Stadium. The group is shown in their limo (left) at the airport. Paul gives the "thumbs up."

officials added extra ushers and private security guards to patrol the venue and control the fans.

Hotel Georgia general manager Peter Hudson began his efforts to fortify the building early. In the weeks preceding the concert, he would lie awake at night and fret about how to handle the crush of fans while maintaining the excellent level of service his highbrow guests had come to expect. He decided to grant hotel access to those under the age of twenty-one only if they were accompanied by an adult. However, his mandate wasn't foolproof. For three days, a trio of girls eluded hotel security by hiding out on the premises—despite its sophisticated fortifications. Hudson also ordered plywood barriers to be erected that effectively blocked every door to the hotel except the main entrance. Barbed wire ringed the fire escape. In an act of desperation, the nervous manager even placed a call to his counterpart at the Beatles' Melbourne, Australia, hotel to get some much-needed advice on crowd control.

Fans line the street to greet the Fab Four, while some teenagers crane their necks out of a car window for a better view.

All of Hudson's worries, however, were for naught. The customs delay in Seattle forced Epstein to cancel the suites he booked at the Georgia. No one was more relieved than the hotel's nervous and sleep-deprived manager. A man of his word, Epstein paid $350 for the unused luxury suites as the Beatles' entourage raced to make the Empire Stadium show on time. For Hudson, the hero of the day was the customs official who had forced the Beatles' flight back to Seattle.

With a change in schedule, the Beatles and their traveling party were driven straight to Empire Stadium from the airport. Along the way, the caravan stopped at King's Drive-In to grab some nineteen-cent hamburgers. One can only imagine the surprise of employees and customers as the Beatles' three limousines and a police escort descended upon this small roadside restaurant. The band ate in the limo, arriving at their Empire Stadium press conference forty minutes late.

Vancouver's press (above) meets the Beatles. Empire Stadium (below) was the site of the group's first outdoor concert of the 1964 tour.

Meanwhile, back at the Hotel Georgia, legendary CFUN deejay Red Robinson pulled off an incredible stunt. As Robinson recalls: "We had a local band that had a drummer that looked like Ringo, so I added to a Beatles report that there was a rumor that someone looking like Ringo was seen outside the Hotel Georgia. I never said it was Ringo, but it was my job to build ratings and I thought that was a good way to get attention for the station, so I had this young man put on a hat and sunglasses and drive past the hotel. Within minutes, the police were there and the entire front of the Georgia was a mob scene. I took a lot of heat for that stunt and rightly so; it was a harebrained idea that could have gotten someone hurt. But, of course, I didn't think of that at the time; it just seemed like a good promotion and funny gag."

The Vancouver press conference was no different than the ones that would follow. Paul mentioned that they would be starting another movie soon. The quick-witted John added, "They have no actors for it yet." Another reporter asked if the Beatles were all Tories. John replied, "Whoever gives us the most money, y'know, we'll vote for them." Finally, a reporter asked Paul if the Beatles had time to date their fans. Knowing that the Vancouver visit would be short, McCartney replied with a wink: "It would have to be a quick one!" Robinson managed to secure a private interview with the group in a trailer located backstage. He broke the ice by giving the boys photos of their musical hero Buddy Holly. Robinson recalls their "incredible charisma."

With the obligatory press conference over, it was showtime. Once more, the support acts tried their best to win over the crowd. Jackie DeShannon was always a crowd-pleaser as she

DENI EAGLAND/VANCOUVER SUN

slinked onstage wearing a tight-fitting dress—singing, stomping, and gyrating her hips as she urged the audience to join in. It's unclear whether the crowd was frenzied because of her seductive moves and sensual voice or because they knew that their four idols were coming up next.

Finally, at 9:23 p.m., Robinson introduced the Beatles to an audience of 20,621. From the moment they hit the stage, insanity reigned at Empire Stadium. With the opening chords to "Twist and Shout," the security officials' worst nightmares were realized. According to newspaper accounts, 2,000 to 3,000 fans sitting in the field-level seats began to rush the stage. Another large group of fans who had failed to get tickets tried to tear down a gate. At the urging of the police and Epstein, Robinson climbed onstage in an attempt to quell the riot. John, dismayed by the deejay's sudden appearance, swore at him to leave

BILL CUNNINGHAM/THE PROVINCE

the stage, screaming, "No one interrupts a Beatles performance!" Pointing at the police and Epstein, Robinson yelled into John's ear: "They sent me up here!" John quickly cooled down. "Sorry, mate," he told Robinson. "Go ahead."

Robinson's plea to the fans survives on tape: "I hate to, ah … lookit, we got to back some of the people up; there's been two people crushed already. They'll have to cancel the show, they'll have to cancel the show. Hold it! Down, everybody down, or no show … the Beatles want to perform for you, but they can't do it if you don't sit down. Let's sit down, they want to perform for you. C'mon!" The police tried in vain

Police strain to hold barricades in place. The Fire Warden had to send in a special squad equipped with inhalators for fans who had passed out.

to control the crowd. First aid stations were packed with girls who were either emotionally overcome in the presence of their idols or trampled in the rush to the stage. The fire warden sent for a special squad equipped with inhalators to assist the hapless victims.

Gino Rossi, who was assigned to photograph the event, remembers his experience vividly: "As soon as the Beatles came onstage, within eight seconds all the fans emptied the seats and came onto the field. It was a mad rush and a constant movement that kept coming closer and closer to the stage. I was worried I was going to get trampled so I had to keep moving towards the stage until I was right on top of it. Fortunately, this was a stroke of luck because it allowed me the opportunity for some fantastic shots." Even Beatles publicist Derek Taylor was summoned to make an impassioned plea to fans, warning them once again that the concert would end if they didn't take their seats.

Larry Kane began noticing signs of a potential disaster. He recalls: "The police were standing in lines to blockade the fans, but those lines kept falling back under the weight of the crush. After the third song … John looked at Paul and they both shook their heads, signaling over the roar of the crowd that they would move from one song to another without waiting for the audience to react. No small talk or chit-chat in this concert … by the seventh song, there was hardly a pause for breath."

Twenty-eight minutes after they'd begun, the Beatles finished their set and made a mad dash for the motorcade. Kane further recalls: "They looked like they were in a 50-yard dash, their legs moving in long strides, their hair streaking behind their necks. Fear was written in their expressions." This was the first time Epstein realized the potential danger to the group at the hands of fans. He would later require promoters to hire special squads of security guards to suppress uprisings such as this. In the aftermath, 135 people were treated for various injuries, including broken bones and head trauma. Hundreds of shoes eerily littered the grass at Empire Stadium. The concert was an event that the Vancouver police wanted to forget. It had been the supreme test of their ability to maintain order in the midst of utter bedlam. Parents, concerned for their children's safety, were relieved it was over.

The Beatles were also visibly relieved as they entered the cozy confines of their chartered Electra aircraft, which left for Los Angeles at 11:40 p.m. They blew off steam by joking, engaging in a food fight, and talking about the wild night in Vancouver. The group would never return to the city again.

Considering the chaos, the group should have received hazardous-duty pay. Still, they managed to walk away with $48,000 ($108,412.01 gross) for the faster-than-normal twenty-eight-minute performance.

John adds some levity, while emcee Red Robinson tries to gain control of the crowd. Robinson threatened, "Everybody down, or no show!"

The next day, the headlines in the *Vancouver Sun* blasted the Beatles, proclaiming, "20,000 Beatle-maniacs pay so much for so little." Reviewer William Littler said: "As a music critic, I have had to subject my eardrums to more than a little of the cacophony which currently dominates the hit parade but the stuff shouted by these Liverpudlian tonsorial horrors left me particularly unimpressed." He concluded his review with a bold prediction: "I do not know how it came, why it came, and when it will go away, but go away the Beatle phenomenon will, and with it will go the Beatles. The day has yet to come and when it does music lovers everywhere can rejoice—yeah, yeah, yeah." Littler later had a distinguished career in both Vancouver and Toronto before retiring in 2005, but his estimation of the Beatles' staying power and legacy was clearly a bit off the mark.

Robinson had quite a different take on the group, stating, "Thank God for the Beatles! I was a true lover of rock 'n' roll and I'd like to think I was one of the guys who helped introduce west coast teens to rock 'n' roll back in the mid-1950s. Unfortunately by 1959 Buddy Holly was dead, killed in a plane crash, Jerry Lee Lewis was in legal trouble, and Elvis was in the army. Music companies started to manufacture less threatening music, Mickey Mouse music, and I was sick of it. Bobby this, Bobby that, seemed like everyone was named Bobby. After the Beatles appeared and launched the British invasion, we never had to worry about going back."

Much as with the Seattle show, only tickets and the generic North American program have found their way into collectors' hands. No posters or handbills have ever surfaced, though it's likely that PNE officials advertised the upcoming fair season and the Beatles' appearance in the local Vancouver papers.

A passed out audience member is removed by Vancouver Exhibition Officials as the Beatles play on. Support act member, Herb Rooney of the Exciters assists.

LOS ANGELES

**August 23, 1964
Hollywood Bowl
8 p.m.**

The Fab Four answer questions during a press conference at the Cinnamon Cinder, a teen nightclub co-owned by promoter Bob Eubanks.

AFTER A NEAR-RIOT IN VANCOUVER, the Beatles didn't know what to expect as their chartered plane descended into Los Angeles, the fifth stop on the 1964 tour. The original plan was for their flight to land at Burbank's Lockheed Airport, but fearing the chaos it would cause, airport officials denied landing rights and rerouted the flight to Los Angeles International, a move that delayed the band's arrival until 3:55 a.m.

The group was originally slated to stay at the historic Ambassador Hotel, but their reservations were cancelled days before their arrival. The hotel, which had hosted several Academy Awards ceremonies as well as Soviet leader Nikita Khrushchev, knew well that an army of teenage Beatles fanatics would tear the place down. General Artists Corporation's Roy Gerber was lucky enough to find a suitable replacement: the mansion of British actor Reginald Owen. Located at 356 St. Pierre Road, the home was leased for $1,000 and afforded the band much-needed rest and relaxation for the next three days. "It was very big, full of marble and glass and heavy carpets and a pool, which was very unusual," press officer Derek Taylor said of it. "Very few people have pools in England. When we arrived at the house, John and I went for a dawn swim." According to Taylor, the Beatles were up early. "Early, that is, for them—at about 1 p.m. We all spent the afternoon by the pool."

As with all the places the Beatles stayed, security was tight in Los Angeles, requiring the LAPD to muster all its resources to keep the situation safe. Streets were cordoned off, and Beatles seekers were turned away. The *Herald-Examiner* reported that damage to flowers and shrubs on the surrounding properties totaled $5,000, adding that the neighbors were extremely annoyed by the Beatles' presence. Many turned

PRIVATE COLLECTION

on their sprinklers to discourage the hordes of fans gathered in the area. Even so, Los Angeles would prove to be a great stop on this and subsequent tours, as the group was able to relax and bask for a few days in the warm California sun. Visiting the southland also enabled the band to party with the Hollywood elite and hang out with a who's who of the top pop music acts of the day. On the 1965 tour, they would meet their idol Elvis Presley.

Charles O. Finley reappeared in Los Angeles in his ongoing effort to persuade manager Brian Epstein to book the group in Kansas City. This time, however, Finley upped the ante, offering Epstein $150,000 for the appearance. Because the date Finley wanted them to play, September 17, was the group's only

rest day on the tour, Epstein interrupted their card game and asked what he should do. John, without even looking up, shrugged his shoulders and told the manager, "We'll do whatever you want." Finley finally got what he wanted. In turn, he made entertainment history with what was, at the time, the single-largest payout for a thirty-minute performance by the group.

The concert the Beatles would play in the City of Angels would go down in history as one of their most famous shows and the venue as one of the most recognizable: the Hollywood Bowl. Built in 1922, it is the largest natural amphitheater in the United States, with a seating capacity of 18,000 and an iconic shell that lends itself to unmatched sound. Over the years, noted architects such as Lloyd Wright (son of Frank Lloyd Wright) and Frank Gehry have contributed their skills to this architectural wonder. Surprisingly, it's not the Beatles who hold the attendance record at the Bowl. That honor goes to French opera star Lily Pons. Her performance on August 7, 1936, drew 26,410 paid admissions.

It's well known that Bob Eubanks presented the Beatles at the Hollywood Bowl in 1964, again on two consecutive nights in 1965, and at Dodger Stadium in 1966. But General Artists Corporation (GAC) first

The boys pose in front of a private home that tour management leased near Bel Air. The mansion was owned by British actor Reginald Owen.

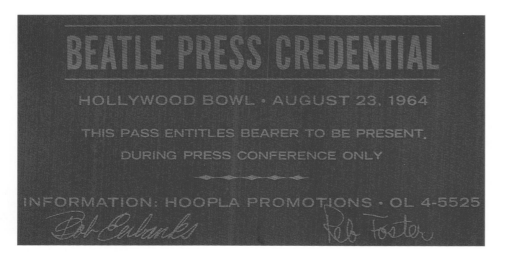

Promoters Bob Eubanks and Reb Foster (right) brought the Beatles to Los Angeles with Eubanks putting up his house as collateral to pay the group's guarantee. A press pass (above) to grant admission to the Cinnamon Cinder. Towels used by the Beatles (below) were cut up and sold as souvenirs.

gave two other promoters the chance to promote the group in Southern California. Lou Robin and Allen Tinkley were two heavyweights in the music business, and their Concerts, Inc. was one of the largest promotion companies on the West Coast. Their involvement with the Beatles began with the closed-circuit theater presentation of the group's first American concert at the Washington Coliseum. The two men, who worked for National General at the time, witnessed a poor financial return from the event.

So when GAC approached them to promote the Beatles at the Hollywood Bowl, they flatly refused. GAC wanted $25,000 plus 60 percent of the gross receipts. Robin and Tinkley considered this fee outrageous. Robin later recalled: "We didn't even pay Judy Garland that much and she was the hottest thing around!" GAC also demanded that the tickets be put on sale immediately. The two promoters had never done such a thing before and thought GAC was kidding. Robin later reminisced: "We thought that they were just another British group passing through, and we were afraid we would have an empty house and would be left holding the bag. The Beatles, at that time, were still considered a little unproven."

With Concert, Inc.'s refusal to promote the Hollywood Bowl show, Eubanks, despite great personal risk, was able to step in and take it. A hungry young promoter and popular KRLA deejay, Eubanks had the ability to recognize up-and-coming acts. He recalls: "Although I was a small fish in the pond of talent buyers, I had a sense of destiny I cannot explain. All I knew was that I was going to bring the Beatles to Los Angeles." Eubanks, along with partner Mickey Brown, had opened the Cinnamon Cinder nightclubs, which were patterned after New York's popular Peppermint Lounge. Eubanks and Brown regularly hired top acts such as Stevie Wonder, the Supremes, Chuck Berry, and Glen Campbell to play their North Hollywood and Long Beach locations.

Julie Steddom, who worked for the William Morris Agency and then at GAC, was instrumental in making the Beatles show a reality. Steddom was one of the only women working in the male-dominated talent industry. She felt loyal to Eubanks because of all the bookings they'd jointly made for the Cinnamon Cinder clubs. She personally handed his bid to her boss, Ed Green, who immediately rejected it. Eubanks was an unknown, Green told her, and he couldn't risk having a local deejay handle a show that even

Disney and the Feld Brothers were pursuing.

In early spring, a plan was unveiled to present the group at Los Angeles's iconic 80,000-seat Coliseum. The show would take place through a partnership with Disney, Dick Clark, or the Feld Brothers. Fortunately, Epstein didn't want to take the risk that his boys might be playing in a half-empty Coliseum. Undeterred, Steddom went over Green's head to GAC Chairman Buddy Howe. She spoke to him about Eubanks's loyalty to the William Morris Agency and their success in booking shows together over the previous two years. Howe agreed with Steddom, and Eubanks got the booking he wanted. Now the future game-show host had to raise the money.

Like Concerts, Inc., Eubanks was floored by the $25,000 guarantee required for the Beatles concert. He complained that even huge acts like Frank Sinatra commanded only $10,000 for a single performance. Desperate for a loan, Eubanks approached one bank after another and was repeatedly turned down. Finally, he visited a little storefront bank in Woodland Hills where a recently repossessed motorcycle was dripping oil onto the lobby floor. Fortunately for him, loan officer Elizabeth Miller had a son who was a big Beatles fan. She made the loan after Eubanks agreed to mortgage his own house as collateral. His final arrangements with GAC called for a guarantee of $25,000, with $12,500 due on signing the contract and the remaining $12,500 to be paid no later than thirty days preceding the actual concert date. GAC also required him to kick in 60 percent of the gross box office receipts over $50,000 after applicable admission taxes had been deducted. And so the deal was sealed for Eubanks to bring the Beatles to L.A.

His gamble paid off in early April, the moment tickets went on sale. The Bowl sold out in under four hours—a full four and a half months before the show. Terri Brown, one of Eubanks's assistants, helped with ticket requests from entertainment luminaries throughout Los Angeles. Brown remembers the line at the Hollywood Bowl: "I head down there and the line is unbelievably long, and I notice a small black girl standing in line with a chauffeur. I walked over and asked if I could be of help, and the chauffeur replied that he was picking up tickets for Nat King Cole. The little girl was, of course, Natalie."

Two hundred disappointed teenagers nearly caused a riot at Fred's Music Store in Rosemead when they were told no tickets remained. Two clerks were showered with apples, bottles, and paper as the other employees ducked for cover. It took six carloads of deputies to calm the small riot. Eubanks didn't save any tickets for the press, and even famed gossip columnist Louella Parsons was relegated to a seat in the last row. Local residents were upset that the Beatles would be playing the Bowl. One nearby resident wrote the Hollywood Bowl Association: "It is with regret that I learned the Bowl had been leased out for a Beatle performance at fantastically higher prices for tickets. It makes one ill to realize that

The historic Hollywood Bowl (above) is still in use today, and one of the country's premier outdoor concert settings. A letter to the Hollywood Bowl Association from a mother (left) complaining of scalpers getting a majority of the Beatles tickets and a warning of the mass-hysteria that would erupt on August 23.

Van Nuys, California
May 20, 1964

Hollywood Bowl Association
2301 N. Highland Ave.
Hollywood, 26, California

Dear Sirs:

For many years we have enjoyed the outstanding performances at the Hollywood Bowl, and it was with regret that I learned the Bowl had been leased out for a "Beatle" performance, at fantastically higher prices for tickets. It makes one ill to realize that such mediocrity can command such an increase over the really good performances.

It is even more sickening to know that so many tickets fell into the hands of those who would capitalize on this teen-age hysteria to the fullest.

Through a stranger at the Bowl, my daughter and her friends were directed to a ticket agent, Mr. Al Mutert in Sherman Oaks. There they were able to buy $7.00 tickets for $12.50 apiece! Needless to say, this was without my knowledge(a friend's mother was taking them around to try to buy tickets), because she never would have spent her baby-sitting money on a scalper's price had I known such things were going on.

She realizes now how wrong it was to deal with an agent like that, and for this I am grateful.

It is my earnest hope that a repeat of this performance never materializes, for the good of our teen-agers.

Sincerely,
L. C. Thompson

P. S. I hope you are completely prepared to cope with the mass hysteria on August 23rd!

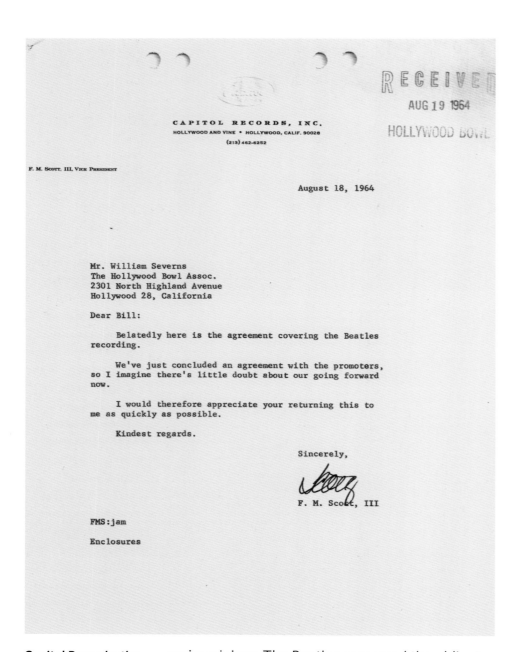

CAPITOL RECORDS, INC.
HOLLYWOOD AND VINE • HOLLYWOOD, CALIF. 90028
(213) 462-6252

F. M. SCOTT, III, VICE PRESIDENT

August 18, 1964

Mr. William Severns
The Hollywood Bowl Assoc.
2301 North Highland Avenue
Hollywood 28, California

Dear Bill:

Belatedly here is the agreement covering the Beatles recording.

We've just concluded an agreement with the promoters, so I imagine there's little doubt about our going forward now.

I would therefore appreciate your returning this to me as quickly as possible.

Kindest regards.

Sincerely,

F. M. Scott, III

FMS:jam

Enclosures

Capitol Records, the Beatles' American label, recorded the show, however George Martin deemed the sound quality as poor, likening it to putting a microphone by the end of a 747 jet.

such mediocrity can command such an increase in price over the really good performances."

Citing the huge demand for tickets, Eubanks tried to convince Epstein of the need for a second show that same evening. For weeks, Eubanks would awaken at 2:30 a.m. to place a call to London, knowing that Epstein would be available to chat only at 11 a.m. local time. Frustrated after failing to reach the Beatles' manager, Eubanks decided to fly a mutual friend, Jim Lee, who managed recording artist Chris Montez, to London to meet with Epstein in the hopes of arranging a second show. Epstein declined, feeling that a second show on the same night would not sell out. If word spread that the Beatles were not a success in Hollywood, Epstein said, it could derail the entire tour. Eubanks commented later: "When you sell an act out in three and a half hours, I can tell you it doesn't take a rocket scientist to figure out you can sell the next one in about four hours. There was that much demand." Eubanks recounted the simplicity of staging a Beatles show, saying that the group's only demands were an adequate sound system, a case of Coca-Cola, clean towels, and a television. He told GAC to get their own television.

The press conference was held at the Cinnamon Cinder at 11345 Ventura Boulevard, because Eubanks felt that his own nightclub would be a quieter place for reporters to interview the band. Word leaked out, however, and the once-secret press conference was soon mobbed by over 400 teens. One girl hurled herself in front of the Beatles' limousine and, fortunately, escaped serious injury. The Beatles answered the obligatory questions and then left to prepare for their show.

According to journalist Larry Kane in his book *A Ticket to Ride*, Ringo hovered behind the stage, watching people pass through the turnstiles. Kane mentioned to Ringo that he noticed "hundreds of older fans, men and women in their twenties and thirties." "No surprise," Ringo replied. "In time, you'll find out what we knew months ago. The music brings 'em in." Much to Eubanks's relief, the music and the mania did indeed bring the fans into the Bowl on that warm summer night of August 23, 1964—to the tune of 18,300 people.

As the group was introduced at 9:30 p.m., the crowd reeled in excitement. The four young men bounded onto the stage in matching dark suits to the now-famous cry by Eubanks: "And now here they are—the Beatles!" Jackie DeShannon recalls John acknowledging some enterprising teens who, to get a better and less costly view, had bravely climbed the trees that ringed the back portion of the Bowl. "Welcome to you in the trees!," he shouted moments before the first chords of "Twist and Shout" filled the venue. The crowd seemed better behaved and more reserved than previous audiences on the tour. Only three fainters were treated. Even so, Eubanks was tempted to quell the crowd by turning on the fountains in the reflecting pools that separated the masses from the stage.

One of the more interesting occurrences at the Bowl that night was Capitol Records' attempt to record the concert and further exploit the current wave of Beatlemania. George Martin, the Beatles' producer, made the recordings but shelved the project after he deemed the sound quality poor. "It was like putting a microphone by the end of a 747 jet," he later said.

640 Fifth Avenue
NEW YORK 19, N.Y.
CIrcle 7-7543

8 South Michigan Avenue
CHICAGO 3, ILLINOIS
STate 2-6288

9025 Wilshire Blvd.
BEVERLY HILLS, CALIF.
CRestview 3-2400

RIDER ATTACHED HERETO IS HEREBY MADE
PART OF THIS CONTRACT.

GENERAL ARTISTS CORPORATION

AGREEMENT made this ___16th___ day of ___April___, 19_64_,

between ___NEMS ENTERPRISES LIMITED___ (hereinafter

referred to as "PRODUCER") and ___ROBERT L. EUBANKS___
(hereinafter referred to as "PURCHASER").

It is mutually agreed between the parties as follows:

The PURCHASER hereby engages the PRODUCER and the PRODUCER hereby agrees to furnish the entertainment presentation hereinafter described, upon all the terms and conditions herein set forth, including those on the reverse side hereof entitled "Additional Terms and Conditions."

1. PRODUCER agrees to furnish the following entertainment presentation to PURCHASER:

A show of approximately two hours in duration starring the BEATLES, plus additional supporting attractions to be selected at the sole discretion of PRODUCER.

for presentation thereof by PURCHASER:

(a) at ___Hollywood Bowl, Hollywood, California___;
(Place of Engagement)

(b) on ___23rd August, 1964___;
(Date(s) of Engagement)

(c) at the following time(s): ___Concert performance commencing at approx. 8 p.m.___

(d) rehearsals: ___as required by PRODUCER___.

2. FULL PRICE AGREED UPON: Twenty five thousand ($25,000.00) dollars guarantee against 60% of the gross box-office receipts over fifty thousand ($50,000.00) dollars after applicable admission taxes have been deducted therefrom, which~ ~over amount is greater.~

All payments shall be paid by certified check, money order, bank draft or cash as follows:

(a) $ ___12,500.00___ shall be paid by PURCHASER to and in the name of PRODUCER'S agent, GENERAL ARTISTS CORPORATION, not later than immediately upon signing hereof,

(b) $ ___12,500.00___ shall be paid by PURCHASER to PRODUCER ~not later than~ Agent not later than 30 days preceding actual play date.;

(c) Additional payments, if any, shall be paid by PURCHASER to PRODUCER no later than _____
All earned percentage - not later than intermission of performance covered herein.

PURCHASER shall first apply any and all receipts derived from the entertainment presentation to the payments required hereunder: All payments shall be made in full without any deductions whatsoever.

3. SCALE OF ADMISSION $7.00, 6.50, 5.50, 4.50, 3.50, 3.00 - net after taxes $79,254.00.

(PRODUCER)
NEMS ENTERPRISES LTD.
By _Brian Epstein_

(PURCHASER)
ROBERT L. EUBANKS
By _Robert L. Eubanks_

Return all signed copies to agent:
General Artists Corporation
640 Fifth Avenue
New York, New York

Address: 5900 High Ridge Road
Calabasas, California

Phone: 340-6552

ALL COPIES OF CONTRACT MUST BE SIGNED ON REVERSE AS WELL AS FACE SIDE.

The official contract that brought the Beatles to the Hollywood Bowl. Eubanks wanted a second show but Beatles manager, Brian Epstein balked. Eubanks quipped, "When you sell an act out in three and a half hours, it doesn't take a rocket scientist to figure out you could sell out the next one."

Fortunately, with advances in sound technology, Capitol was finally able to release the album thirteen years later, in 1977. Simply titled *The Beatles at the Hollywood Bowl,* it used recorded material from both the 1964 and 1965 Bowl concerts. Fans who weren't able to attend a Beatles concert or were too young to do so at the time could now experience the sheer pandemonium that reigned at every performance.

An escape plan was needed for the Beatles after their performance. The Hollywood Bowl had only one narrow driveway next to the stage, so Eubanks made a deal with a local car dealer to borrow a 1964

HOLLYWOOD BOWL ASSOCIATION
LEASE

Dennis Bruton
1776 no Sycamore 1175ᵀ
#309-H050336 2350ᵀ
6500

THIS AGREEMENT entered into this ___15th___ day of ___April___, 19__64__, between the HOLLYWOOD BOWL ASSOCIATION, a California corporation, with its principal office at 2301 North Highland Avenue, Hollywood, California, (hereinafter called ASSOCIATION) and ___ROBERT L. EUBANKS and MICHAEL D. BROWN___

with its principal office at ___5900 High Ridge Road, Calabasas, California (Tel: 340-6552)___

(hereinafter called LESSEE).

WITNESSETH:

1. ASSOCIATION hereby leases to LESSEE the amphitheatre commonly known as the Hollywood Bowl, including the use of the appurtenances and equipment hereinafter specified, for the purpose of presenting the program entitled ___"The Beatles in Concert"___ and for NO OTHER PURPOSES WHATSOEVER on condition that the said program be promoted, advertised, and presented so as not to reflect unfavorably upon the acknowledged long standing cultural and civic reputation of ASSOCIATION, the said Hollywood Bowl or the "Symphonies Under The Stars" season of ASSOCIATION.

2. The term of this Lease shall be the period from ___8:00___ A.M. on ___Sunday, August 23___, 1964, until ___11:30___ P.M. on ___Sunday, August 23___, 19__64__.

3. In consideration of the foregoing Lease, LESSEE agrees to pay ASSOCIATION the following amounts:

   a. The sum of $___500.00___ (Five Hundred Dollars)
This sum is payable upon execution of this Lease.

   b. A sum equal to ___15___% of the gross receipts from the sale of tickets, exclusive of Federal admission taxes, and LESSEE guarantees that the amount to be received by ASSOCIATION under the provisions of this sub-section will not be less than $___1500.00___ (Fifteen Hundred Dollars). To assure compliance with such guaranty, LESSEE shall pay to ASSOCIATION the guaranteed amount upon the execution of this Lease.

   c. A sum equal to ___15___% of the gross amount of any collection that may be taken up.

   d. A sum equal to ___15___% of the gross receipts, exclusive of sales and other applicable taxes, from the sale of souvenir programs or booklets, music, librettos and other similar material.

   e. A sum equal to ___15___% of all monies that may be paid to LESSEE by reason of any radio or television broadcasts, motion pictures or recordings made in connection with or arising out of said program. No radio or television broadcasting or motion picture or recording rights are conferred by this Lease unless such rights are specifically set forth in Paragraph (2) of Additional Provisions V hereof.
   f. The sum of $5.00 as a night lighting charge for each hour or fraction thereof that the leased premises are used for night rehearsals or for other purposes requiring lighting either preceding or following the scheduled program, together with the cost of additional maintenance and/or policing personnel deemed necessary by ASSOCIATION in connection with the use described in this subsection "f".
   g. A sum equal to any costs incurred by ASSOCIATION in providing a PBX operator for rehearsals and performances, including operator's salary, necessary insurance and payroll taxes.

4. LESSEE agrees to deposit not less than 14 days prior to LESSEE's first use of the leased premises the sum of $___6500.00___ as security for the payment of the expenses for which LESSEE is or may become liable under the provisions of this Lease, including charges for insurance, salaries, equipment or services incurred by ASSOCIATION on LESSEE's behalf in connection with the program scheduled hereunder, or for the possible cost of removing from the leased premises any special stage settings, scenery, decorations, paraphernalia, or other equipment or property erected or placed on the premises by LESSEE which LESSEE may fail to remove within the period of this Lease. If all such expenses are not paid by LESSEE within 24 hours of the termination of this Lease, ASSOCIATION may deduct from such deposit an amount sufficient to pay all such expenses and shall at the expiration of sixty (60) days return the balance, if any, to LESSEE.

5. LESSEE hereby agrees to indemnify and to save and hold harmless the ASSOCIATION and the COUNTY OF LOS ANGELES, and their respective agents and employees, against all loss and/or damages to the leased premises, the buildings thereon and furnishings thereof, incurred while said premises are used by or are under the LESSEE's control, and against all claims by any person for personal injury and/or damage to property occasioned by and/or in connection with LESSEE's use of said premises. LESSEE shall, at its own expense, obtain and deliver to the ASSOCIATION not less than fourteen (14) days prior to LESSEE's first use of the leased premises, an insurance policy satisfactory to the ASSOCIATION, naming the ASSOCIATION and the COUNTY OF LOS ANGELES as additional assured and indemnifying the ASSOCIATION and the COUNTY OF LOS ANGELES against all such losses, damages and claims. LESSEE will provide the ASSOCIATION with evidence of an existing Workman's Compensation Insurance policy covering any person employed by LESSEE.

6. LESSEE agrees not to employ persons, purchase or rent supplies and/or equipment, or contract for services, or incur indebtedness of any kind in the name of ASSOCIATION, or use the name HOLLYWOOD BOWL ASSOCIATION in advertising or promoting the program and/or the LESSEE's productions, interests and activities.

7. LESSEE agrees that within 24 hours of the expiration, or any sooner termination of this Lease, any and all equipment erected or placed on the leased premises by LESSEE will be removed and LESSEE will quit and surrender the said premises, clean and in as good order and condition as when taken, reasonable wear and tear excepted.

8. LESSEE shall not have the right to assign this Lease or any part thereof or any of LESSEE's rights thereunder, or to sublet the whole or any part of the leased premises without ASSOCIATION'S written consent.

9. This Lease shall be deemed to have been made in the State of California and its validity, construction, performance, breach and operation shall be governed by the laws of the State of California applicable to contracts to be performed in California.

10. Time is the essence hereof. Each and every condition and covenant is a material part of the consideration for this Lease including those set forth in Additional Provisions Nos. I, II, III, IV and V attached hereto, and by this reference made a part hereof. LESSEE acknowledges that it has read all such Additional Provisions (the titles of which are not deemed to limit or extend said Provisions) and agrees to be bound by the provisions included therein. Any violation of any of the conditions or covenants by LESSEE shall entitle ASSOCIATION to enter upon the leased premises and remove all persons therefrom.

11. The terms set forth in this Lease constitute the entire agreement between the parties hereto. All prior negotiations and understandings have been merged herein. LESSEE represents that no person acting or purporting to act on behalf of ASSOCIATION has made any promises or representations upon which LESSEE has relied except those expressly stated herein. This Lease may only be altered by an instrument executed both by LESSEE and ASSOCIATION.

IN WITNESS WHEREOF, the parties hereto have caused this lease to be executed in Los Angeles, California, the day and year first above written.

LESSEE: ROBERT L. EUBANKS

By *Bob Eubanks*
(Title)

MICHAEL D. BROWN

By *Michael D. Brown*
(Title)

Address _____

Association (Lessor): HOLLYWOOD BOWL ASSOCIATION

By *J. W. Brown*
President

By _____
Secretary

Approved:
_____

THE HOLLYWOOD BOWL

SYMPHONIES UNDER THE STARS * HOLLYWOOD BOWL POPS

Robert L. Eubanks and Michael D. Brown
5900 High Ridge Road
Calabasas, California

August 27, 1964

STATEMENT OF CHARGES - LEASE OF HOLLYWOOD BOWL
Sunday - August 23, 1964

```
Stagehands
   Wages                                    $    536.42
   Vacation - 4.75% of $210.00                    9.98
   Health and Welfare 5% of $546.40              27.32
   Payroll Burden 10% of $573.72                 57.37    $    631.09 ✓

Crowd Control
   Ushers                                   $  1,366.20
   Police                                      3,186.80
   Guards                                      2,082.00
   Firemen                                       132.80
   Payroll Burden 10% of $6,767.80              676.78       7,444.58 ✓

Ticket Department
   Contract Fee                             $  1,250.00 ✓
   Sales Commissions (Mutual & Auto Club)      1,039.61
   Ticket Printing                               313.33       2,602.94

Use of 2 carbon arc spotlights and generators                 160.00 ✓
Insurance                                                      65.00
Parking - Press - 25 @ $2.00                                   50.00    $10,953.61
Less Hollywood Bowl Share of Police, Guard, and
   Firemen Services                                                    (2,700.80)
         Total Charges for Reimbursable Expenses                       $ 8,252.81

Lease Fee
   Fixed Charge                             $    500.00
   Rental 15% of $78,880.85                   11,832.13      $12,332.13 ✓
         Total due Hollywood Bowl                            $20,584.94

Less Amounts Paid
   Lease Deposit                            $  2,000.00
   Ticket Printing                               350.00
   Expense Deposit                             6,500.00      (8,850.00)
         Balance due Hollywood Bowl                         ✓$11,734.94

Ticket Statement                                            $85,085.00
   Less Federal Admissions Tax              $  6,204.15
         Amount due Hollywood Bowl            11,734.94     (17,939.09)
         Balance due Eubanks & Brown                                   $67,145.91

Paid on Hollywood Bowl Check #1391 - 8/23/64               $65,000.00
Paid on Hollywood Bowl Check #5236 - 8/27/64                 2,145.91  $67,145.91
```

2301 NORTH HIGHLAND AVENUE * HOLLYWOOD, CALIFORNIA 90028
BUSINESS OFFICE HOLLYWOOD 9-8171   TICKET INFORMATION HOLLYWOOD 9-3151

The statement of charges from the Hollywood Bowl Association. For their return engagement in 1965, Eubanks made more money than the Beatles did, through selling the promotion rights to KRLA.

Plymouth Valiant, a small compact car that could be easily parked next to the stage, out of the fans' view. Before the show, Eubanks pleaded with John not to say, "This is our last number," as he was worried about getting the group out of the Bowl safely. John informed the promoter that they always told the crowd it was their last number, but added, "When we put our instruments down, we will leave." Eubanks agreed to John's plan and had decoy limousines waiting with the doors open to foil fans. As promised, at the end of "Long Tall Sally," the group dropped their instruments and dashed to the waiting Plymouth, which raced out of the Hollywood Bowl to the freeway while fans practically destroyed the decoy limos.

Fans in the Bowl's famous box seats screaming their approval.

Eubanks also arranged for an armored car to be parked at Sunset and Van Ness to use in transporting the group to their rented Bel Air mansion. The car dealer promised Eubanks that if he could get a picture of the Beatles in his car, he would give it to Eubanks. Unfortunately, the photographer captured only the back of the vehicle and the backs of the Beatles' heads. Unsatisfied, the dealer immediately reneged on the deal. Safely ensconced in their rented mansion, the group threw a party for seventy-five invited guests that lasted until 7 a.m.

In an interview years later, Eubanks declared the Beatles' 1964 appearance at the Hollywood Bowl to be one of the most famous rock concerts ever—ranking it next to Woodstock. The promoter made $4,000 for his efforts and bemoaned the fact that he could have made more if Los Angeles Supervisor Kenny Hahn, who received several complaints from residents near the Bowl, hadn't bused in seventy marshals to protect the homes near the venue. When Eubanks asked Hahn who was paying for all this protection, Hahn told him, "You are." Ringo commented some years later that "the shell around the stage was great. It was the Hollywood Bowl. These were impressive places to me. I fell in love with Hollywood then." John remarked that the Bowl show was "marvelous. It was one we enjoyed the most ... good acoustics."

The day after the concert, the Beatles were asked to attend a meet-and-greet garden party hosted by Capitol Records president Alan Livingston at his mother-in-law's home in the Brentwood section of Los Angeles [See "The Garden Party" on page 86].

John, George, and Ringo later ventured down to the Sunset Strip's Whisky a Go Go nightclub, where such groups as the Byrds, Buffalo Springfield, and the Doors would become mainstays. Paul decided to

The Beatles on stage. John described the Bowl as one of his favorite venues of the tour.

PRIVATE COLLECTION (2)

stay at the mansion and entertain the comely Peggy Lipton (later of *Mod Squad*) before accompanying Derek Taylor to Burt Lancaster's home for a private viewing of *A Shot in the Dark*.

At the nightclub, the three Beatles were drinking and having a great time until Bob Flora, a photographer for United Press International, decided to take a close-up picture of George. The Quiet Beatle responded by tossing a drink into the photographer's face, inadvertently soaking actress Mamie Van Doren in the process. The incident elicited a front-page newspaper story featuring a photo of George with glass in hand. Ringo danced the night away, and the very married John was seen cuddled up next to buxom actress Jayne Mansfield.

Before leaving town, John, Derek Taylor, and photographer friend Ron Joy ventured out for some shopping at Beau Gentry. John bought a lightweight jacket and some cowboy shirts and then arranged for the store to send samples of clothing back to the mansion. The rest of the day was spent lounging by the mansion's lavish pool.

With the three-day L.A. stay completed and the band rested and sunbathed, they boarded a plane bound for the Mile High City—Denver, Colorado—to resume the tour. Always ahead of the story, newsman Dave Hull and deejay Jim Steck of KRLA actually entered the plane without boarding passes.

Attended by approximately 18,000 fans, the Beatles show wasn't the Hollywood Bowl's biggest crowd—that honor goes to French opera star Lily Pons who attracted 26,410 paid admissions in 1936.

They'd gotten caught up in the crush and excitement all around them and decided to just "go with it," something that was entirely illegal and ill-advised. Fortunately, KRLA flew them back to L.A. from Denver, with Hull carrying only seven dollars in his pocket and Steck penniless. They did, however, interview the group and watch the Denver performance from backstage.

Collectibles from this show are very rare, although the market is rife with the fantasy concert tickets featured on the cover of the Capitol album *The Beatles at the Hollywood Bowl*. Authentic unused tickets are virtually impossible to obtain, as the show was sold out. Stubs from the event show only the date and seating location, and consequently, many were discarded. Only the standard North American tour program was sold at the event. Passes from the press conference at Bob Eubanks's Cinnamon Cinder are rare but do surface from time to time. No posters or handbills were ever printed to advertise the concert.

As previously noted, Bob Eubanks would return the following year as promoter of two more Beatles shows at the Hollywood Bowl and, in 1966, as promoter of their Dodger Stadium concert, their next-to-last live performance ever.

Ringo (left) with his signature style, as the group rocks on stage to the delight of their many fans (above). The group rocked the Bowl and would return in 1965 for two concerts on consecutive nights.

The Garden Party

August 24, 1964
4–7 p.m.

THE DAY AFTER THE CONCERT, the Beatles were asked to attend a meet-and-greet garden party hosted by Capitol Records president Alan Livingston at his mother-in-law's home in the Brentwood section of Los Angeles .The party benefited the Hemophilia Foundation, attracting 500 invited guests and raising some $10,000. Livingston asked John if the band could perform, but he politely declined. Epstein was reportedly furious when Ringo appeared without a tie. Still, all went well as the Beatles sat in chairs and greeted the Hollywood elite that filed past them. Even hardened cowboy actor Jack Palance had something nice to say about the Beatles over a soda with Larry Kane in the kitchen of the Brentwood home: "Mostly, they're pretty decent guys. I don't go for the idolizing crap, but I'll tell you, the music is damn good!"

Entertainer Dean Martin's daughter, Deana (with tongue out) gets up close with the Fab Four. George and Ringo's expressions are priceless. Capitol Records' Alan Livingston (in suit) is at far left, while Neil Aspinall, Brian Epstein, Derek Taylor, and Mal Evans stand behind.

Invitees wait their turn (above) in the driveway of Alan Livingston's mother's home in the Brentwood section of Los Angeles. The invitation (left) that was sent to Livingston's fortunate friends.

R.S.V.P. Capitol Records, Inc. (Reservations & Information) HOllywood 2-6252, Ext. 270.

Admission by ticket only. Charitable contribution: Twenty-five dollars per person (each child, each adult). Make checks payable to The Hemophilia Foundation.

All children will meet and be photographed individually with The Beatles. Children must be accompanied by an adult; adults must be accompanied by children.

Alan W. Livingston
President, Capitol Records, Inc.
cordially invites you
to attend a
"Meet The Beatles"
Charity Garden Party
for the benefit of
The Hemophilia Foundation
of Southern California

Monday, August 24, 1964
4:00-7:00 p.m.
415 Avondale Avenue
Brentwood Park
Los Angeles 49, California

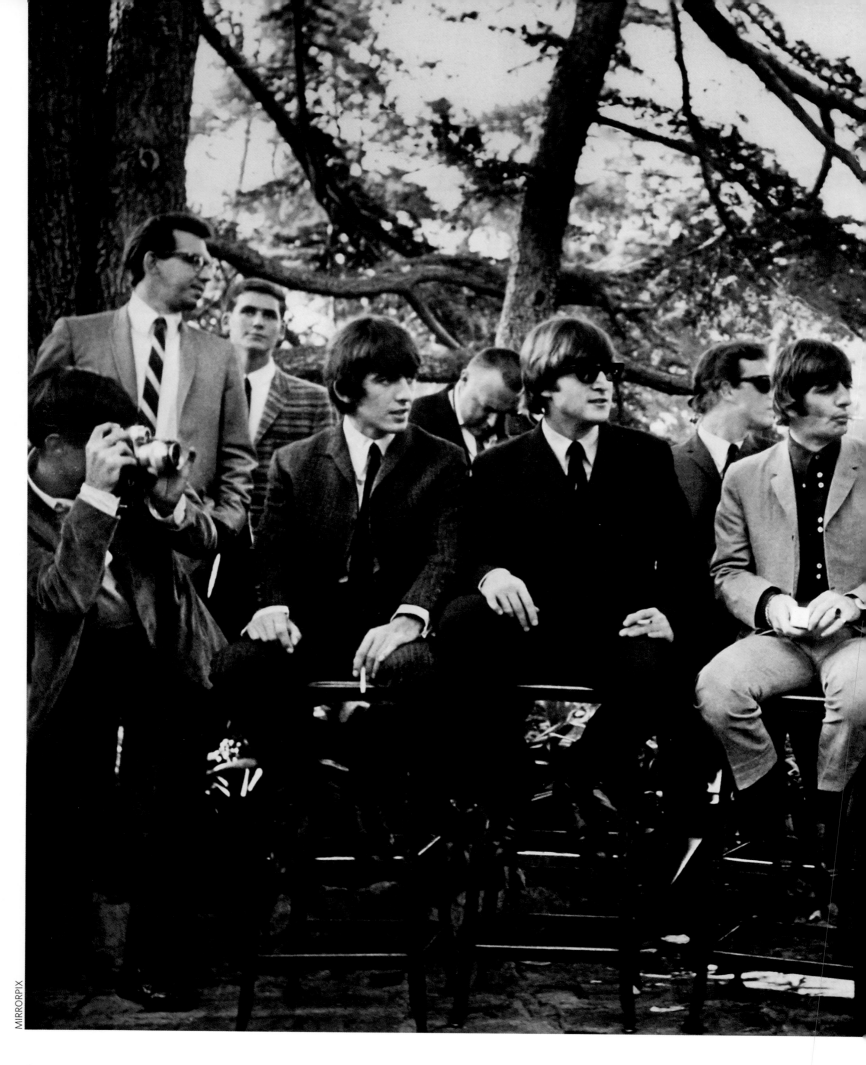

DATE   August 13, 1964
TO
OFFICE   Dept. Heads, Dept. Managers & Supervisors
       ☐ CRI   ☐ CRDC   ☐

FROM
OFFICE   Alan W. Livingston
       ☐ CRI   ☐ CRDC   ☐

☐ Scranton Plant
☐ 46th St. Studio—N. Y.
☐ 1730 Broadway—N. Y.
☐ L.A. Plant
☒ Tower—1750 N. Vine

MEMO

Capitol RECORDS

SUBJECT: BEATLES CHARITY GARDEN PARTY

As you may have heard, I am giving a charity garden party for the Beatles where children of invited guests will meet and shake hands with the Beatles and be photographed with them as well. Although this is being done in the interests of publicity and identification of Capitol with the Beatles to somewhat counteract the U-A tie-in, it also is being done for charity as specifically requested by the Beatles.

The party is by invitation only and each invited guest is requested to make a contribution of $25. per person to the Hemophilia Foundation of Southern California. I am not sending invitations to Capitol employees because I feel that in many cases the financial contribution would be a burden. Much as I would like to have Capitol employees as our guests, particularly those directly associated with the Beatles in regard to recording and sales, it would be impossible to accommodate the many people who will be coming. Rather than restrict such a Capitol guest list to only selected individuals, I feel the only proper thing to do is to treat all those wishing to come on the same basis.

If any Capitol Department Head, or persons associated with Beatles production or sales, wishes to attend, and bring his children on the basis of the above charitable contribution, he or she is, of course, very welcome. In such event, please call Ext. 270, and an invitation will be supplied.

Again, I am extremely sorry that we cannot have you on a different basis, but circumstances make it impossible if we are to adhere to the conditions laid down by the Beatles themselves.

AWL:cm   Alan W. Livingston

☐ INFORMATION COPY — READ AND DESTROY
☐ ACTION COPY — PLEASE HANDLE AS NECESSARY

SIGNED:

FORM 1669CL REV. 10 11/60   P   X   C   61   62   63   64   65   66   67   68   69   ☐ COPY SENT TO CENTRAL FILE

Paul holds the granddaughter of actor Edward G. Robinson as the other three Beatles look on. The memo from Alan Livingston (above) regarding the upcoming "Meet the Beatles" garden party that would benefit the Hemophilia Foundation of Southern California.

The Fab Four patiently shake the hands and greet the large group of party attendees, showing class and professionalism.

Brian Epstein (far right, above) fields a question from John while one partygoer (in the white dress) points perhaps asking which Beatle is which? Famed gossip columnist Hedda Hopper (left, with hat) was a powerful force in the celebrity culture of Los Angeles.

DENVER

**August 26, 1964
Red Rocks Amphitheater
8:30 p.m.**

The Fab Four say hello to Denver. The Mile-High City was the band's sixth stop on the tour.

ON AUGUST 26, 1964, AFTER A THREE-DAY LAYOVER IN LOS ANGELES, the Beatles made their way east for their sixth stop on the tour, touching down in Denver. Much like Las Vegas, Denver was years away from being the sprawling metropolis it is today. It was, in fact, one of the least-populated centers on the tour. Several mysteries still shroud this concert, such as the final attendance tally and the alleged availability of oxygen tanks should group members have needed to be revived while performing in the thin air of the Mile-High City.

The Beatles' plane landed at 1:35 p.m. in a remote area of Stapleton Airport, with a crowd estimated at over 10,000 waiting to greet the band. City officials extended their welcome by literally laying out a red carpet. Also on hand was Don Martin, the news director of the concert's sponsoring station, KIMN Radio. Martin remembers that the noise generated by the fans completely drowned

©NICHOLAS DESCIOSE

out the roar of departing planes. He saw the group board the waiting limousines, which then exited one of the airport's back entrances en route to downtown Denver. As the motorcade whisked the Beatles to their hotel, thousands of fans lined the streets as if President Johnson were paying a visit. Martin, who was in the Beatles' caravan, recalls forcing the vehicles of competing stations off the road in order to maintain KIMN's presence. All the KIMN deejays handed out record surveys and albums to the kids along the motorcade route.

Arrangements had been made for the group to stay at the historic Brown Palace Hotel. Opened by Henry C. Brown in 1892, the imposing red sandstone hotel has been in operation ever since. Brown spent $2 million of his own money to build the beautifully appointed structure, which included steel-frame construction, indoor plumbing, elevators, and electricity. The building also contained its own power plant and had two artesian wells that supplied fresh water, making it one of Denver's premier properties. The hotel was already in its seventieth year of operation by the time the Beatles stayed there. Thankfully, it survived Beatlemania despite the nearly 5,000 fans camped near the front entrance.

Because the reservation had been booked under another name, hotel manager Karl Mehlmann didn't know that the Beatles would be staying at the hotel until two days before their arrival. He remembers

The choice in 1964 was between Lyndon Johnson and Barry Goldwater, but this fan's pick for president was clear.

...STORIC MEMENTO OF THE BEATLES TRIP TO ... ENCLOSED MATERIAL, IS A PART OF THE CARPET SPREAD AT THE FOOT OF THE STEPS LEADING FROM THE BEATLES CHARTERED ELECTRA JET WHEN IT LANDED IN DENVER, ON THE 26TH OF AUGUST 1964 AT 1:35 P.M. THE BEATLES, JOHN, PAUL, GEORGE AND RINGO, WALKED OVER THIS MATERIAL WHEN THEY FIRST SET FOOT ON DENVER SOIL!

KIMN-DENVER

The Historic Brown Palace Hotel (top) where a guest can still stay in suite 840 and place the same room service order as the Beatles did—grilled cheese sandwiches and fries. KIMN and airport officials laid-out the red carpet for the group, then had it cut for resale (above).

groups of parents showing up with screwdrivers and pliers to snap up anything the Beatles had touched, including doorknobs.

The band stayed in suite 840 and ordered room service. Hotel worker Tom Baines delivered five grilled cheese sandwiches, fries, and soda pop. When John saw the plate of food, he rudely exclaimed to Baines, "Bloody America with your chips all over the place." Ringo quickly defused the situation by adding, "Pay him no mind. We're here on the road. There's no rest. You can't imagine what it's like." If one visits the Brown Palace Hotel today, suite 840 is still available and, yes, room service will deliver the same food the Beatles ordered.

Joan Baez, who was in town for a gig, visited the group backstage prior to their concert and was talked into traveling with them for a few dates. Baez was often seen as part of the entourage in successive tours, and in August 1966 she would join the Beatles in their dressing room at Candlestick Park just prior to their last-ever concert.

The promoter for the Denver concert (along with sponsor KIMN Radio) was Verne Byers. Denver born and raised, Byers was a fixture in the city and a former big-band leader. "Verne Byers and His Orchestra" was billed as the "band that sings and swings." He later formed a promotions company named Lookout Attractions and admitted he'd never even heard of the Beatles before booking them to play in Denver. Byers thought the Beatles' unique haircuts were a clever way to separate themselves from other touring acts such as the Beach Boys.

Byers received an unexpected call from Chicago shortly after *The Ed Sullivan Show*. The caller, a General Artists Corporation (GAC) representative, informed the promoter that the Beatles wanted to play Denver if the price was right. Byers assumed that the booking fee was $3,000 until the caller told him, "Go get a chair and I'll tell you." Byers was shocked to learn he would have to ante up $20,000. He almost rejected the offer on the spot. The businessman reasoned that, to turn a profit, he would need to charge $6 a ticket—twice his usual price. Byers had just recently charged $3 a ticket for a performance by Igor Stravinsky, who at the time was considered the world's greatest living composer. However, Byers had a "feeling," he later said, that he should book this new band from Liverpool, England.

Speculation abounds regarding the venues considered by Byers and GAC for the Beatles' concert. Primary sources reveal that GAC presented manager Brian Epstein with two choices: the 22,000-seat Denver University Stadium or the 9,500-seat Red Rocks Amphitheater. On the sourced document, Epstein boldly checked "Red Rocks." He felt it was too great a risk to try to fill a 22,000-seat venue in a lower-population market. The deal wasn't final until well-known attorney Tom Clancy (no relation to the best-selling author) put the deposit down on Red Rocks in April 1964. This closely followed Byers's refusal of a $50,000 offer from Charles O. Finley to cancel the show and move it to Kansas City. It was also reported that the famous beer-brewing Coors family, and especially their children, were counting on a Beatles show in Denver. So it was that Red Rocks, an open-air venue set among natural rock formations twenty miles west of Denver, was selected for the show.

Much like the Hollywood Bowl with its outdoor setting, Red Rocks provided a beautiful natural backdrop. Here, performers were flanked by towering three-hundred-foot red sandstone monoliths that dated back some 700 million years. Anyone daring to venture to the top of the venue would be treated to the distant lights of the Denver skyline. The 818-acre Red Rocks Park, originally known as the "Garden of Angels," was once considered one of the seven natural wonders of the world.

Then, at the beginning of the twentieth century, a visionary named John Brisben Walker began producing musical events at the park, later convincing the city of Denver to purchase the land, develop the area, and maintain it as a first-class musical venue. The actual amphitheater itself, completed in 1941, was built by the Civilian Conservation Corps (CCC) and the Works Projects Administration (WPA) during Franklin D. Roosevelt's administration and was a product of the president's New Deal.

Byers wisely advertised two Denver establishments he owned on the back of the admission ticket. One was the Baja, a local club that was, in

DENVER PUBLIC LIBRARY

A peek into a fan's bedroom (above) and KIMN's promotion of the show (left). Glen "Boogie" Bell introduced the group on stage—he is pictured on far left, three photos down.

his words, "the home of the biggest names in show business." The other was the picturesque Robin's Nest, an upscale restaurant set atop a mountain peak and known for its slogan, "A Taste, A Steak, and All That Jazz." The number of actual tickets printed remains a mystery to this day. Attorney Clancy admitted that "the printing of tickets for shows at Red Rocks was a guessing game between the promoter and city officials due to the lax rules concerning the general admission seating policy. The Beatles got the balance of their money on the day of the show, but we printed more tickets than we sold."

Jay Mack of KIMN Radio recounts that Byers chose the station to sponsor the show because it was the dominant player in the Denver market. Mack recalls that "there were twenty-two radio stations in the Denver area and they were splitting only 40 percent of the market share. With 5,000 daytime watts and 1,000 at night, KIMN could be heard as far away as North Dakota." KIMN

©NICHOLAS DESCIOSE (2)

never had to put up any money to bring the Beatles to Denver because of its promotional power.

On August 18, Byers contacted the local field office of the FBI after receiving an anonymous postcard that threatened death to the Beatles if he didn't cancel the show. According to the note, a hand grenade would be tossed into the audience if the concert went on as scheduled. After a thorough investigation that even involved FBI director J. Edgar Hoover, the note was deemed an extortion attempt. Three weeks after the concert, on September 21, the case was officially closed.

This was not the first time that Epstein feared for the Beatles' safety, nor would it be the last. Many more threats would follow the group as they toured the world. In the book *The Beatles Anthology*, Beatles producer George Martin, commenting on the Red Rocks concert, recalls that "Brian [Epstein] and I climbed up on a gantry overlooking the stage, and we looked down at the Boys below during the performance; and the amphitheatre is such that you could have a sniper on the hill who could pick off any of the fellows at any time—no problem. I was very aware of this, and so was Brian, and so were the Boys."

Denver area Beatles fans wait for the show to begin at Red Rocks outdoor amphitheater. The natural setting provided a dramatic backdrop for the concert.

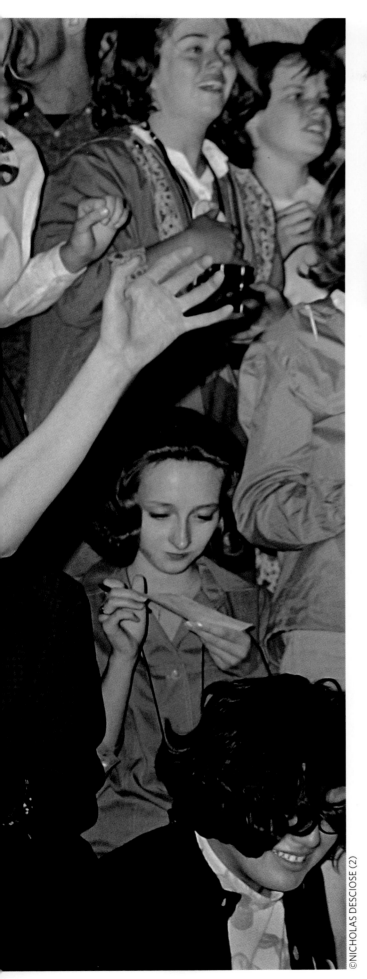

©NICHOLAS DESCIOSE (2)

The day before the concert, fans began camping near the venue as Beatles music from their transistor radios echoed among the rock formations. With local weather forecasters noting a high probability of rain, Byers briefly considered moving the concert indoors to the Denver Coliseum.

The Beatles show at Red Rocks gave the venue the opportunity to test a new ordinance that banned alcoholic beverages, cans, and bottles from the premises. This new rule was enacted after a Ray Charles concert where rowdy fans had hurled beer cans at the singer. On the morning of the show, the *Rocky Mountain News* printed a strongly worded editorial that read: "Attention, teenagers of Denver. You have the opportunity of attracting worldwide attention today! Don't be rowdies. Don't throw things. Don't try to smuggle beer or liquor into Red Rocks Theatre. Don't kick and elbow. Gird on the self-discipline that is the mark of a true American citizen."

Just before the group made its way to the venue, the customary press conference was held backstage at Red Rocks. Intrigued by the Old West and the Native American culture, the Beatles—and John in particular—turned the tables on reporters by posing their own questions on the subject. The local chapter of the Jaycees presented them with western-style vests embroidered with their names. KRLA's stowaway deejay from Los Angeles, Dave Hull, was able to secure a private interview with the group before being given a stern warning and put back on a plane to L.A. after the concert.

Before the show, Byers checked the audio system with the sound engineers and noticed

Screaming for the Beatles: This pandemonium (left) followed the group wherever they went in America. Red Rocks appears to be nearly full in the images above. Some speculate that there were 2,000 empty seats in the 9,450 capacity venue in Morrison, Colorado.

The "Mile-High" Beatles rock and roll. John screams into the mic as Paul, George and Ringo back him up.

On stage at Red Rocks: Note the fans and officials watching in the wings. Rumor had it, that oxygen tanks were brought in to help the group with the thin air. Photographic evidence shows this was unlikely. Opposite page: Ringo in motion— his signature style made him stand out amongst rock drummers.

that Ringo didn't have a microphone. "Don't worry about it," the drummer said. "They won't hear me anyway."

Glen "Boogie" Bell, the program director and morning man at KIMN, had assigned the station's Jay Mack to introduce the Beatles. Unfortunately, Mack was in a car accident a week before the show. With Mack out of action, the Beatles' introduction fell firmly back onto the promoter. Bell remembers driving up to Red Rocks and entering the backstage area to find Jackie DeShannon and the Beatles sitting in a very sparse waiting room. After introducing DeShannon, he remembers returning to the "ready room" to make small talk with the group.

At 9:30 p.m., promoter Verne Byers introduced the group, which was greeted by a boisterous but polite audience. On his way to the stage to prepare for the concert, a young nineteen-year-old photographer for the teenybopper magazine *Tempo* was able to shoot five impromptu frames of the group next to a giant American flag prior to their donning of stage suits. Nicholas DeSciose's finished product eventually appeared in *Life* magazine and launched his career. After Byers made his brief introduction with Bell watching in the wings, the deejay strolled to his car, drove home, and went to bed. His kids still can't believe their father never bothered to watch the show or get autographs from the band. He received a flat fee of $50 for his night's work, later confessing that he was "more of a Sinatra fan."

Singer-songwriter Joan Baez, and *Denver Post* entertainment editor, Barry Morrison. Baez met the group early on into the tour, and traveled with them for a few dates, and on subsequent tours.

Most historians and firsthand observers claim that 7,000 fans attended the show, with 2,000 seats left unoccupied. They blame the low attendance figures on the lack of public transportation and the twenty-mile distance from downtown Denver. According to other accounts, however, including those of police officers and photographer DeSciose, the house was full. They claim that a few of the ushers allowed people in without taking their tickets.

Others remember lax security making it possible for some to sneak into the venue. Colorado State University student Ted Scott, along with three other friends, simply jumped the turnstile when DeShannon hit the stage. Because all the seats at Red Rocks were general admission, concertgoers could leave their seats to move closer to the front. While security and ushers were preoccupied with trying to control the movement of the crowd, many outside the amphitheater were able to enter undetected. Photos from the Denver daily newspapers and others taken by DeSciose seem to show a full house. At this point in history, any estimation of the crowd size would be purely speculative.

Lillian Walker Moss of the Exciters was devastated by the behavior of the fans at Red Rocks. She recalled that when her group went onstage, some fans booed and yelled, "Niggers go home!" Offended, Moss ran off in tears. Herb Rooney, the group's only male member, encouraged the girls to return to the stage and give the performance of their lives. They completed their set to a standing ovation and two encores.

The late Bobby Hatfield, the tenor half of the Righteous Brothers, loved the vibe at Red Rocks. But for Hatfield and his musical partner Bill Medley, the Denver concert was the beginning of the end. The duo's hits were better known in the western part of the United States. As the tour traveled eastward, their popularity waned, forcing them to quit. Their last performance as a supporting act was four days later, on August 30 at Atlantic City, New Jersey.

During the Beatles' performance at Red Rocks, Epstein noticed what appeared to be deejay Jim Staggs from Cleveland recording the show. According to Larry Kane, Brian angrily confronted Staggs about it. The bewildered deejay replied, "Now why in the hell would I do something like that?" Kane realized then that "Brian would do anything to protect the artistic sanctity and profitability of his Beatles."

As the concert progressed, the Beatles appeared a bit out of breath due to the high-altitude conditions. Many people over the years have confirmed that oxygen tanks were available on each side of the stage so the group could "refresh" themselves. While the oxygen may have come in handy for a lengthier show, the Beatles' Red Rocks performance lasted only thirty-five minutes. Nevertheless, eyewitnesses

©NICHOLAS DESCIOSE (2)

recall that halfway through the first song, the group seemed out of breath. That said, no evidence exists that the group ever took a "hit" of oxygen. In a later interview, Paul commented on the Denver show: "We were told it was high above sea water, altitude ... we got there, and we started finding it was a little hard to breathe, because we weren't used to it. I remember singing 'Long Tall Sally' and thinking, 'Hey this is great—hyperventilation of the highest order! Well, Long Tall Sally, wheeze, wheeze ...' I was sweating, but I got through it. It was an interesting experience, physically."

With the Denver concert finished, the group retreated to the Brown Palace Hotel, sacrificing a night on the town for some much-needed rest and relaxation. They flew out the following morning, bound for their first stop east of the Rockies: Cincinnati, Ohio. They would never play Denver again.

Memorabilia from this show is exceedingly scarce. Just a few unused tickets have surfaced over the years, giving credence to the notion that Red Rocks was, indeed, a sellout. The oversized tickets are nice keepsakes for those lucky enough to find one. Even ticket stubs from this show are seldom seen. A hit parade survey from sponsoring station KIMN featured a handbill/ticket order form, but these are extremely rare. No posters are known to exist, and only the generic 1964 tour souvenir program was sold at the show.

A final bow at Red Rocks—the band would never return to Colorado.

CINCINNATI

**August 27, 1964
Cincinnati Gardens
8 p.m.**

Cincinnati Gardens was modeled after Toronto's Maple Leaf Gardens. The Beatles held the attendance record for just thirty-two days until a rally held by presidential candidate, Barry Goldwater.

WHEN THE BEATLES AWOKE IN THEIR HOTEL ROOMS at Denver's Brown Palace Hotel, they were about to face the most grueling day of their 1964 North American tour. After arriving at Denver's Stapleton Airport, they would take an afternoon flight to Cincinnati, Ohio, where they would be driven to the venue, conduct a press conference, perform a concert, and then board a late-evening flight, arriving in New York at 3 a.m.

For the Beatles, it was all in a day's work. No one could ever accuse the group of slacking off as they logged thousands of hours together. At the Cincinnati press conference, John was asked, "What will you do when the wave of Beatlemania subsides?" He wisecracked, "Count the money." With the largest cash advances in U.S. entertainment history, this particular tour would indeed rake in a fortune, but not without exacting a heavy toll on the boys and their entourage. The Cincinnati stop epitomized the stress

30—Cincinnati Garden, Cincinnati, Ohio

and toil of touring as the group endured oppressive heat in excess of 100 degrees while awaiting their turn onstage in an auditorium packed to the walls with fans.

The Cincinnati date was engineered by five enterprising radio personalities from WSAI Radio—Dick Purtan, Steve Kirk, Bob Harper, Dusty Rhodes, and Mark Edwards—collectively known as the Good Guys. Purtan was having dinner with the program director of Indianapolis radio station WIFE, and the pair began to discuss the Beatles. The executive told Purtan that they were trying to nail down a date for the group to appear at the annual Indiana State Fair. With his interest piqued, Purtan placed a call to General Artists Corporation (GAC). He was informed that six or seven dates were still open and that a Beatles concert would require an arena that could accommodate 10,000 to 13,000 fans.

For the August 27 date, GAC's Norman Weiss had given manager Brian Epstein the choice of playing in Cincinnati, now that there was interest; Evansville, Indiana; or Allentown, Pennsylvania. When GAC gave the nod to Cincinnati, Purtan immediately placed a call to Cincinnati Gardens and reserved it for August 27. He then needed to come up with a $12,500 deposit to book the Beatles. After discussing the situation with his wife, Purtan decided he would approach the other jocks at WSAI to participate, asking each to invest in the effort to bring the Beatles to Ohio. The five deejays put up $2,500 apiece and the contract was cemented. Dusty Rhodes remembers going to his bank to borrow the money and being pleasantly surprised when his banker was

The group arrives in Cincinnati, the first stop on the East Coast swing of the tour.

more than happy to help—provided, of course, that Rhodes supply his family with tickets to the show. The contract with GAC was signed by WSAI's Bob Harper on April 16. With a signed contract in place, the Good Guys (who had never promoted concerts before) turned to Dino Santangelo to help consult, produce, and promote the show.

The first mention of a Beatles concert in Ohio appeared in the *Cincinnati Post* on April 14, 1964. By April 20, the Good Guys at WSAI, along with Santangelo, had harnessed the power of radio to incessantly advertise the show. As in other tour cities, all advance ticket sales were done by mail order, with purchasers sending in cash or checks and a self-addressed stamped envelope. The *Post*

Due to confusion over which airport the Beatles' plane would land, only three hundred fans turned up at Lunken Airport. This plane would later crash in 1966, killing American Flyers owner Reed Pigman and 83 passengers and crew.

THE JACK KLUMPE SAFETY NEGATIVE COLLECTION, AV 3 AND THE OHIO HISTORICAL SOCIETY

CONFIDENTIAL   BEATLES SCHEDULE   CONFIDENTIAL

        PM - Arrival at Lunken Airport
             Bus and Police Wagon

        PM - Short press conference at airport on runway area.

        PM - To bus or Patrol Wagon.
             (Dino, 5 jocks, Walt Burton, Beatles, Bess Coleman, Ida Sidelle) (1 jock
             with other acts)

        PM - Arrival at Vernon Manor (Pre-register) Police Contact - Capt. Reis
             (Same group as above usher Beatles to room)
             (Booze, flowers, cigarettes in rooms)

        PM - 3 jocks leaving Vernon Manor
             2 jocks remaining with Beatles
             (Walt Burton stays at Vernon Manor)

5:30   PM - 3 jocks and Dino at Gardens

6:30   PM - 2 jocks and Beatles leave Vernon Manor in Patrol Wagon for Cincinnati
             Gardens
           - Bus leaves Hotel with other acts and instruments.

7:00   PM - Arrive Gardens - (driver will use special entrance) - 2 jocks and Beatles
             meet Dino and 3 jocks at Gardens undercroft, Police Guard will escort
             whole group to dressing rooms.

7:30   PM - Dressing room - Press Conference
             All 5 jocks will be present till 7:50 PM (Entrance to Press Conference is
             by Press Badge only.)

7:50   PM - 5 jocks meet backstage and plan for MC duties

8:00   PM - Jocks introduce first act.

CONFIDENTIAL   AFTER SHOW   CONFIDENTIAL

        - Beatles will take curtain call.

        - 5 DJ's on stage leading the applause

        - Ask people not to leave their seats -- the Beatles will come back.

        - Upon hearing police sirens, announce to crowd that Beatles have left
          left the Gardens under police escort for the airport.

        - 5 jocks assemble backstage.

        - Have wives, etc. assemble with you backstage.

        - ** Have everyone you know spread rumor that Beatles have left the building.

          * Stay backstage until Dino calls for you and escorts you to Beatles
            dressing room.
          * Bus and police wagon will take Beatles back to hotel.

The itinerary (above) for the WSAI DJ's. John and Paul along with Derek Taylor and Neil Aspinall (upper right) head to the press conference.

reported in its May 9 edition that all tickets had been sold, requiring WSAI to return over $30,000 in unfilled orders to devastated fans. Cincinnati Gardens manager Alex Sinclair, who had never witnessed an event as popular as this, met the demand head-on by extending the capacity of the arena by over a thousand seats. Sinclair figured that WSAI (which had announced the sellout to prevent further ticket requests) could have easily filled the Gardens to capacity several times over. Purtan pleaded with GAC to add another show, but his request was turned down. Officials made sure that all tickets being sold were legitimate, and the *Post* reported in its April 15 edition that "to avoid any chance of counterfeit tickets, a special printing job on bonded paper with a code identification would be utilized." Ticket prices were $5.50, $4.75, $4.00, and $2.75.

Police were tough on scalpers, even sending out the vice squad to apprehend offenders. A woman named Joyce Dallas tried placing an ad in a local newspaper to sell her ticket at an inflated price, for instance. City officials set up a sting by placing a call to meet with her as prospective buyers. After she offered the $5.50 face-value ticket to plain-clothes police for $15, Dallas was promptly cited and fined for selling a ticket without a license. After Judge Robert Wood heard her plea of guilty and the $25 fine was paid, he ordered the "evidence" to be handed over by the police. Dallas also had to plead guilty regarding having previously sold another ticket. Judge Wood then asked that the ticket be given to the General Protestant Orphan Home, where it was thrown into a hat and a winner randomly chosen. Ida Ante, a ward of the state and the home's biggest Beatles fan, won the prized ticket. She vowed she would bring George Harrison back with her after the show.

In the months leading up to the concert, trouble began brewing between the Gardens and the local Musicians Union. WSAI jock Dusty Rhodes remembered that the dispute had nothing to do with promotion of the show by the radio station or the Beatles playing there. Instead, the union used the concert to pressure Gardens management to sign a contract that specified the number of musicians required for certain events at the venue. The union threatened to have the Beatles show cancelled. With only a month before the August 27 concert, both sides were still at an impasse.

WSAI urged Beatles management to move the concert to another venue, suggesting Louisville, Kentucky, or Columbus, Ohio. They even met with officials from Cincinnati's Crosley Field, home of the Cincinnati Reds baseball team. John Murdough, the Reds' business manager, stepped up to the plate and announced to the local press that he "would be delighted to have the Beatles play at Crosley." Even Beatles fans got into the act as fifteen-year-old Sue Sportzilli and sixteen-year-old Pat Fox circulated petitions to pressure the union to settle. They secured 157 signatures, including those of Reds

The Beatles at the press conference with the WSAI "Good Guys" DJ's who put up their own money to bring the group to Cincinnati. From left, behind the Beatles: Derek Taylor (NEMS), Bob Harper, Dick Purtan, Dusty Rhodes and Steve Kirk (Mark Edwards not pictured).

Venue officials around the nation told teenagers to "sit down and behave!" The message didn't get through to these Cincinnati fans standing on their chairs.

Every fan usually had their favorite Beatle, and let it be known with homemade signs.

ballplayers Pete Rose, Mel Queen, John Edwards, and Sam Ellis. Epstein and GAC refused to move the concert to an outdoor setting. Fortunately for all involved, the dispute was settled and the Beatles' show was allowed to proceed as planned.

The Beatles' plane arrived at Cincinnati's Lunken Airport at 5:05 p.m. There was some initial confusion about their airport arrival. The Cincinnati metropolitan area was served by two airports—Lunken Airport and the Greater Cincinnati Airport (in northern Kentucky)—both equal distance from the city. It was assumed that they'd land at Greater Cincinnati and, as a result, that's where most of the diehards gathered. One enterprising fan had phoned the control tower in Denver and got the scoop on Lunken, but it was too late to spread the word to his fellow Beatlemaniacs, so only 300 people were on hand to greet the group. Upon exiting the plane, Ringo was asked about the flight. "Yes, the flight was great," he replied. "And no one got sick."

The original plan was for the group to stay over at Cincinnati's famed Vernon Manor Hotel, where the entire eighth floor was reserved for them. As word leaked out, however, girls packed the lobby, with the crowd soon swelling to about two hundred. Unfortunately, their vigil was in vain. It was decided that

the group wouldn't stay overnight in Cincinnati, but instead would fly out of the city as soon as they could board the plane after the concert. The Vernon Manor rooms were canceled because of a request from the New York City Police Department. They'd implored tour organizers to have the Beatles arrive in the city between midnight and 6 a.m. to avoid a potential riot.

The motorcade from the airport arrived at Cincinnati Gardens around 6 p.m. The Beatles were ushered to their dressing room, which was marked with a 4. Upon arrival, the boys rested on cots and George reunited with his sister Louise. He told her that the homes he had seen in America were enormous compared to his own, chatted with her about security, and wondered why such great lengths were taken to protect the group and their whereabouts kept such a secret. His sister tried to explain, but George remained unconvinced, replying, "Why, Louise? It's just us."

At 7 p.m., they dined on a meal provided by the Colony Restaurant of Swifton. Consisting of New York strip sirloin steak, French fries, and tossed salad with Thousand Island dressing, it was topped off with iced tea, which none of the group touched. They preferred the Coca-Cola that had been supplied by WSAI's Good Guys.

Fans compete for George and John's attention and hope for an acknowledgment from the stage.

The Beatles played in oppressive heat at Cincinnati Garden that was in excess of 100 degrees. as promoters filled every nook and cranny with seating.

Following dinner, the press conference took place. For thirty-five to forty minutes, the Beatles fielded the typical flurry of questions. One reporter directed a question at George: "What would you have done if you had not become Beatles?" George wasted no time with his reply: "We would just have been bad entertainers."

It's been said that the group talked with Elvis Presley before the show, but there's no evidence to support the claim, not even in the newspaper accounts of the day. Current sources state that the group's dressing room was burglarized and personal effects stolen, but again, no evidence exists. Though not quite as dramatic, it *is* true that the Beatles were made official Kentucky Colonels in Ohio, as reported by the *Cincinnati Post* on August 28.

THE JACK KLUMPE SAFETY NEGATIVE COLLECTION, AV 3 AND THE OHIO HISTORICAL SOCIETY (2)

Police treat a girl who had fainted outside Cincinnati Gardens.

Because promoters overbooked Cincinnati Gardens, concessioners had to work overtime to accommodate the overflow crowd. They busily went about readying 5,200 hot dogs, 5,200 buns, 2,000 pounds of popcorn, and 20,000 soda cups. The Gardens, which was modeled after Toronto's famed Maple Leaf Gardens, was built in 1949 at a cost of $3 million. The arena was (and still is) owned by the city of Cincinnati. During the 1964 season, the Gardens housed the Cincinnati Royals basketball team, which featured the young and talented Oscar Robertson and Jerry Lucas, and was also home to the Xavier University Musketeers basketball team. At the time of its opening, it was the country's seventh-largest indoor arena. Surprisingly, the Beatles don't hold the record for the best-attended single event at the arena. That honor goes to former Arizona senator Barry Goldwater, who attracted 16,025 supporters to a presidential campaign rally at the Gardens just thirty-two days after the Beatles' performance.

The boys once again dazzled the assembled crowd with rousing renditions of their hits. The *Cincinnati Enquirer* reported that when the group walked onstage, the "mob exploded into a maelstrom of sound—screaming, stomping, crying, begging, moaning—every imaginable sound a human is capable of making ... the screaming was so loud for ten minutes that the Mormon Tabernacle Choir and the Marine Corps Band would have been drowned out."

When the concert ended, the boys dashed for their waiting cars and headed toward Lunken Airport, where their chartered turboprop stood ready for their flight to New York City. Dino Santangelo, the show's producer, remembers that the Beatles left the Gardens so quickly that the fans couldn't believe they were actually gone. He recalls letting one skeptical girl inside the Gardens to see for herself: "She checked all over, she looked under a corner of the stage, she even picked up the corner of some matting. She even looked in and under cars that were parked in the vicinity of the dressing room door. It was like she was looking for a mouse." The *Post* reported in its August 29 edition that some interesting items were abandoned by fans inside the Gardens, including an adjustable wrench, a screwdriver, two hacksaw blades, and a variety of handbags.

The Beatles made approximately $36,000 for the performance. The cots they used backstage (which were provided by L. Lodge Weber of Cincinnati Hertz Rent-a-Car) were later donated to a Christmas fund drive. Dick Purtan and Dusty Rhodes claim to this day that they have a dollar bill signed by all four Beatles. Purtan still remembers it taking only three phone calls and thirty minutes to book the biggest act of all time. As he puts it, "Right place, right time!"

According to police officer Ted Bird, the fans in Cincinnati "conducted themselves like young ladies and gentlemen. They screamed, yelled, and panted, but there was no other sign of disorder. They were a credit to Cincinnati." This was a far cry from what lay ahead at some of the venues on the tour. In Cleveland, Ohio, for instance, where the band would play almost three weeks later, the show would be nearly halted by police because of disorderly conduct by fans. This "drop-in" date at Cincinnati was perhaps such a success because the city had only six hours of Beatlemania to endure.

No Cincinnati concert posters or handbills are known to exist, and only the generic 1964 U.S. tour program was sold at the show. Radio station WSAI produced an "after-show" flyer that featured photos from the concert and a small write-up of the day's events. Unused tickets from this show are rare. The group would return to the city in 1966, but would play at Crosley Field instead.

The aftermath of the sold out performance. The group would play Cincinnati again at Crosley Field on the 1966 summer tour.

NEW YORK

August 28 and 29, 1964
Forest Hills Tennis Stadium
8:15 p.m.

Ringo gets a kiss from sixteen-year-old, Angie McGowan (below), who returned his St. Christopher medal lost earlier when she accidentally ripped it from his neck in the hotel lobby.

IN THE WEE HOURS OF FRIDAY, AUGUST 28, New York City welcomed the Beatles for the second time in six months. The group was set to play two massive shows on two consecutive nights at the Forest Hills Music Festival. The city once again found itself bracing for Beatlemania. The group had just completed one of the most difficult stops on the tour, spending nearly seven hours in Cincinnati, where they'd performed amid oppressive heat and overcapacity conditions at Cincinnati Gardens. They had literally laid down their instruments and dashed for a waiting car, only to be whisked to the airport and flown to the Big Apple. They arrived five minutes ahead of schedule, touching down at JFK Airport at 2:55 a.m., to the delight of the 3,000 fans who had waited long into the night to see them.

Tour organizers had decided against allowing the group to stay over in Cincinnati, instead responding to a plea from New York City police to have them arrive in the very early hours of the morning. By doing so, they hoped to avert the bedlam that always accompanied the band's arrivals. Still, dedicated followers began staking out spots at JFK Airport as early as 6 p.m. Thursday. Back in the city, the NYPD called in a hundred officers—eighteen mounted on horseback—and twelve private security guards to protect the group's hotel, the Delmonico on Park Avenue. Their assignment was to block entrance to anyone under the age of twenty. An additional hundred policemen manned barricades between Fifty-Ninth and Sixtieth Streets to keep fans at a safe distance.

Teenagers kept vigil during the early-morning hours and screamed with excitement when anyone at the Delmonico peered out a window. Police actually had to resort to bullhorns to implore hotel guests to stay away from their windows, fearing chaos would erupt in the streets. Twenty or more girls tried storming the hotel entrance, but swift and decisive action by New York's Finest quelled the disturbance. Similar episodes continued through the next day.

After the ride from JFK, the group arrived at the Delmonico. Other area hotels, having witnessed the pandemonium at the Plaza in February, had denied requests from Beatles management for lodging in the city. It took TV host Ed Sullivan, who lived at the Delmonico, to intervene on behalf of the group and assist in booking the hotel.

Like many of the hotels where the Beatles stayed, the Delmonico was historic in its own right. The thirty-two-story building has marked the northern end of the commercial section of Park Avenue since it was built in 1929. It was originally called the Viceroy and later the Cromwell—until the famed

A John Lennon fan expresses herself across the street from the Hotel Delmonico.

Delmonico's restaurant opened on the ground floor on October 1, 1929, just a few weeks before the stock market crash.

Despite serious breaches by teenagers trying to get to the Beatles (and one mother who had to be rescued from a heating duct), the hotel survived Beatlemania and is today owned by billionaire Donald Trump, who, not surprisingly, has renamed it Trump Park Avenue.

Sixteen-year-old Angie McGowan, her mom, and three teenage girlfriends were in the hotel when the Beatles arrived from the airport. As the group crossed the lobby, McGowan was able to throw her arms around Ringo's neck to kiss him, but was shoved back, ripping the drummer's beloved Saint Christopher's medal from his neck and into her hands. The fan was amazed by her newfound treasure.

In their hotel suite, the Beatles entertained journalists and radio personalities such as WABC's Cousin Brucie and Scott Muni until finally settling into bed around 6 a.m. The pace of the tour had indeed picked up, and the few days of rest spent in Los Angeles a week earlier seemed like a distant memory. The boys rose from their beds at around 2 p.m. and dined on a late breakfast of corn flakes, orange juice, and soft-boiled eggs.

HOTEL *Delmonico*

502 Park Avenue
New York

Ringo, understandably upset at the loss of his Saint Christopher's medal, went on a radio program being broadcast from the hotel and pleaded for its return, noting that it meant everything to him and had been in his possession for a few years. McGowan heard the broadcast and wanted to give back the medal, but first she had to convince officials she actually had it. Apparently 150 other girls were making the same claim. After it was verified that the medal was indeed Ringo's, McGowan and her three friends were allowed to present it to the drummer in a highly secured setting. Photographers captured every conceivable angle of McGowan planting a kiss squarely on the lips of the relieved (and grateful) Beatle, who rolled his eyes at the gesture.

The Beatles' two concerts would take place on Friday and Saturday night at the Forest Hills Tennis Stadium. Founded in 1892 with thirteen members, the West Side Tennis Club grew over the years and eventually moved to the Forest Hills area in 1912. The land was purchased for $2,000 and, soon after, a 14,000-seat horseshoe-shaped stadium was built. The venue hosted the U.S. Tennis Open for more than six decades and helped to advance the sport of tennis in the United States.

The West Side Tennis Club also began a music festival each summer in 1960. The first show, by actor and folksinger Theodore Bikel, was rained out. As the Sixties progressed, however, the venue began to attract top acts such as Frank Sinatra, Bob Dylan, and Jimi Hendrix, who opened for the more popular Monkees at a show there in 1967. The stadium's capacity was not enough to accommodate the growing interest in tennis, and a new facility was built in nearby Flushing Meadows. The U.S. Open moved there permanently in 1978. In 2010, Forest Hills was saved from the wrecking ball when West Side

Tennis Club members voted to reject a plan by developers to replace the storied venue with condos.

The promoters for the Forest Hills shows were Ron Delsener and Don Friedman, who partnered with radio station WMCA and its "Good Guys" (who emceed the event). After a stint as a surveyor in the army, Queens native Delsener followed his dream of being in the entertainment business. He got a job at the Forest Hills Tennis Stadium, making $75 a week working for two promoters. In 1964, he struck out on his own and booked the Beatles to play two consecutive evenings at the venue. Delsener reasoned that by doing an outdoor show, he wouldn't have to pay for heat or air conditioning. More important, kids would still be on summer vacation, looking for something to do.

Later, with the sold-out Beatles performances (over 32,000 seats) under his belt, Delsener convinced Thomas Hoving of the New York City Parks Commission to stage concerts in Central Park, initially at the Wolman Skating Rink. A great marketing man, Delsener was able to secure sponsorship for the concerts from companies such as Ford and Rheingold Beer, and eventually attracted such diverse artists as Led Zeppelin, the Who, and Diana Ross. Because these sponsorships laid the groundwork for today's multi-million-dollar tours, Delsener is credited as being the "Father of the Outdoor Concert." He once said that some of the "sweetest bouncers [I've] ever known are six-foot-seven-inch ex-cons" and that "the only way to prevent ticket scalpers is to hire nuns."

The contract for the Beatles to play Forest Hills was signed on April 17, 1964, between NEMS Enterprises Limited and Delsener's Trans Nations Productions for the guaranteed cost of $40,000 plus 60 percent over $80,000. At NEMS's request, Delsener also agreed to an addition to the tour rider: "Purchaser (Trans Nations Productions) will supply Producer (Nems Enterprises) at Purchaser's sole expense, two chauffeur-driven 1964 Cadillac Limousines, August 28 and 29, and will pay for five

Fans keep vigil behind barricades and scream with excitement at any movement behind a hotel window. Police officials resorted to bullhorns warning hotel guests to stay away from their windows fearing that chaos would erupt in the streets.

The Beatles face their ninth press conference in as many days (above), and when asked about leisure time, John shot back, "What leisure time?" A poster (right) that was displayed at the Forest Hills ticket offices informing fans the series of concerts had been sold out.

deluxe one-bedroom suites at a New York Hotel of Producer's choice, August 28 and 29. Both suites and limousines will be charged directly to purchaser." During the planning for the tour, Norman Weiss of the General Artists Corporation (GAC) had given manager Brian Epstein the option of playing the Indiana State Fair on August 28 and 29, but Epstein opted for the New York appearance.

WMCA was one of New York's finest radio stations—an independent with no affiliates. Owned by the Straus family, the station was strictly talk until its format was changed to Top 40 in the late '50s. In late 1960, program director Ruth Meyer consolidated the station's format, instituting the "team radio" approach, which had the on-air personalities working together as a unified group. Once the Good Guys concept was fully implemented in 1963, the station shot to the top of the ratings. The Good Guys were known individually as Joe O'Brien, Harry Harrison, Jack Spector, Dan Daniel, B. Mitchell Reed, Johnny Dark, Ed Baer, and Frank Stickle.

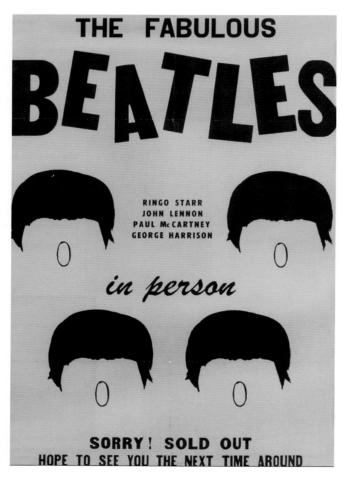

THE FABULOUS

BEATLES

RINGO STARR
JOHN LENNON
PAUL McCARTNEY
GEORGE HARRISON

in person

SORRY! SOLD OUT
HOPE TO SEE YOU THE NEXT TIME AROUND

These jocks relentlessly promoted the shows not only at Forest Hills, but also at other New York venues where the Beatles performed. Much of the time, the promo spots they produced featured the group's actual voices. In one spot, the opening strains of "She Loves You" are heard just before a familiar voice chimes in: "This is John Lennon, and on behalf of all the Beatles, I'd like to thank the WMCA Good Guys for introducing the Beatles sound and Beatlemania to America. Thanks!"

In one of their most notable promotions, Meyer came up with the idea of giving away a lock of Ringo's hair, but never got permission from the drummer. Good Guy Joe O'Brien was assigned the task of obtaining the lock during the group's first visit to America in February. With scissors in hand, O'Brien approached Ringo at the Plaza Hotel. The startled drummer refused to give up a piece of his precious mane until

John intervened. "Oh, Ringo," he said. "Give him a piece of your *#&%-in' hair!" WMCA ran the contest and received over 85,000 entries.

The Good Guys always wore matching suits, sported the same haircuts, and made personal appearances together. Most WMCA listeners from the day will remember the "We're the Good Guys" theme song that was played constantly. WMCA made a commitment to its audience to play the newest releases and even had sources in the United Kingdom to secure records before their official release dates. WMCA couldn't compete with the rising popularity of FM radio, however, and revived its talk radio format in 1970.

Back at the Hotel Delmonico's Crystal Ballroom, the Beatles sat down for a press conference that began at 5:30 p.m. just prior to their first night's performance (August 28). The usual superficial questions were asked.

> **Reporter:** *What do you think of topless bathing suits?*
> **Paul:** *We've been wearing them for years!*
> **Reporter:** *What do the Beatles plan to do with their leisure time while they're here in New York?*
> **John:** *What leisure time?*

And of course there was the obligatory question: "If your fame subsides, will you cut your hair?"

Press officer Derek Taylor fielded complaints from legitimate journalists who were seeking to ask important questions but were overshadowed by teen magazine reporters, fan club members, deejays, and VIPs, all of whom were clamoring for attention.

Meanwhile, in an upstairs suite, Weiss was desperately trying to formulate a route the Beatles could take from midtown Manhattan to Queens. He realized that traveling through the Midtown Tunnel could spell disaster if the limousine motorcade became stuck or delayed in any way. His solution? A helicopter. Officials at the West Side Tennis Club balked at the idea of a landing on their sacred tennis courts, however, at least until the NYPD interceded and adopted Weiss's plan.

The entourage traveled to the Wall Street Heliport, but the takeoff was delayed because the pilot hadn't received permission to leave with his precious cargo. At the same time, another crisis was brewing at the venue. GAC tour manager Bob Bonis arrived ahead of the Beatles only to learn that their dressing room was an empty tent behind the Forest Hills stage. An angry Bonis confronted promoter Delsener about the lack of accommodations and informed him that the Beatles were to use the West Side Tennis

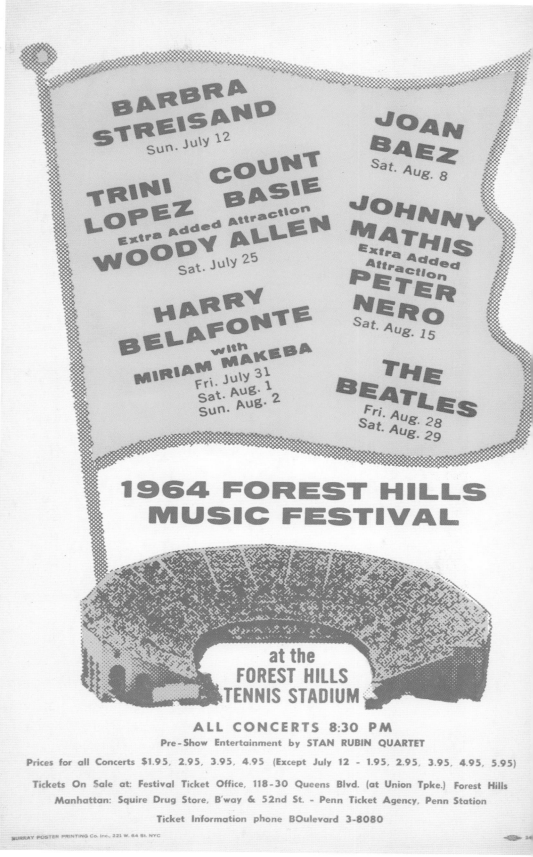

A poster advertising the 1964 Forest Hills Music Festival summer concert lineup.

A predominately female fan legion lines up at the Forest Hills ticket office located on Queens Blvd. near the Union Turnpike, waiting for tickets to go on sale. Only two young men can be seen in the picture.

Club's opulent locker rooms. The promoter told Bonis that the club wouldn't allow the use of the club-house, fearing that the group might damage it. Unrelenting, Bonis threatened to radio the helicopter with instructions to turn around unless proper dressing rooms were provided. Delsener quickly arranged the use of the club in time for their arrival.

Due to the flight delay, the Beatles arrived late at the venue, much to the dismay and consternation of the Righteous Brothers, who were onstage at the time. As the copter appeared in the sky and circled the venue, all eyes and cameras were diverted skyward. At that moment, no one cared what Medley and Hatfield were singing. This may have been the proverbial last straw for the Brothers, as they abandoned the tour after performing in Atlantic City two nights later. In *The Beatles Anthology*, George Harrison even commented on the pair's displeasure at the Beatles' dramatic entrance. Despite the great exposure the duo was getting on the Beatles tour, they were paid only $750 a week compared to the $500 a night they were making on the West Coast (where they were far more popular).

Shortly before the group went onstage for the first night's concert, they were briefly visited by legendary bandleader Benny Goodman and his two college-age daughters. The conversation was strained as the musical legends from different generations sought to find common ground.

The Beatles' safe arrival at the venue was by no means the end of Weiss's problem with the helicopter transport. Apparently no one had asked the pilot to wait. Instead, he flew his craft back to Manhattan. A harried Weiss frantically called the air service, demanding that the copter return before the Beatles hit the stage. Even though the concert was delayed almost an hour, the Beatles took the stage at 9:50 and gave one of their finest performances, much to the relief of officials and the audience of 17,000.

A dramatic appearance onstage by two young girls at the August 28 show demonstrated the effects of Beatlemania. The story below is retold firsthand by Mary Smith, at the time a seventeen-year-old fan from Connecticut who arranged the stunt. The accompanying pictures depict the chaos that ensued onstage.

My friend and I sent away for tickets to see the Beatles on August 28 at Forest Hills Tennis Stadium. For us, it was the summer between eighth and ninth grade and we were in love with everything Beatles. Finally, the tickets arrived and we began to develop a plan. We would run up on stage, my friend to Ringo and I to George. We would dress conservatively so we would be less conspicuous. Babysitting would be the cover story for our parents, and that was it. Pretty simple and direct. In fact the couple we were to be babysitting for was actually in on the deal. They had graciously agreed to take us to Forest Hills and then bring us home after the concert. They were great!

All went as planned. But once inside the stadium, my friend and I were disappointed to see how far from the stage we were seated. We had to change that fast and we zeroed in on the VIP section. It was on the court, very near the stage, and there were folding chairs. We casually walked down to that section and just sat there,

The Beatles, along with their management, GAC representatives, and promoters exit the helicopter that flew them from Manhattan and landed adjacent to the Forest Hills Tennis stadium.

MIRRORPIX

Seventeen-year-old Mary Smith, grabs a startled George during the Friday evening concert as Paul and Ringo look on.

as if we belonged. There were a few stairs at the side of the stage near John Lennon. At some point, while the Beatles were playing, we walked towards the stage and then simultaneously started running towards our favorite Beatle. My friend, on her way to Ringo, was stopped by security and pulled from the stage. I continued on, passing in back of John Lennon. He saw me and I said, "Don't worry, I'm going to run to George," and John took a little step forward, as if to clear the way, still playing! I think it was "I Want to Hold Your Hand." He seemed to be amused by my presence.

I'm not sure George saw me coming, so when I put my arms around him, he was at once surprised, terrified, and seemed to be screaming. As you can imagine, this was not the response I had ever considered. I thought, what am I doing? I want to hug him, not hurt him. Next thing I knew, security pulled me away and took me from the stage, back to court level. I think I must have been in shock. I don't clearly remember much after that or the remainder of the concert. The security guards were kind enough to let me and my

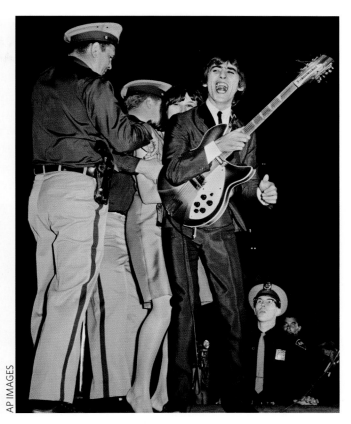

Police intervene to escort Mary Smith from the stage, as a bemused George tries to free himself from the young fan's grasp.

friend stay for the rest of the performance. I think they understood we weren't a threat; we were just kids. I guess when I was approaching the stage, my shoes fell off. It wasn't until after the concert that I became aware and obsessed about those shoes. How was I going to explain to my parents that I lost my shoes babysitting? In the parking lot after the concert's finish, I overheard some other kid's transistor radio. The station they were listening to was playing an interview, with me begging for my shoes. I didn't remember that interview even taking place! I called the radio station from a pay phone, explained who I was, and asked them not to play that interview. Unbelievably, they agreed, and I was relieved. It was then that I felt I could safely hide the entire episode from my parents. Minutes later, someone returned my shoes to me, though I wasn't sure how.

The wonderful young couple who drove us to the stadium picked us both up at the gate and drove us back to Connecticut. My friend and I were in a sort of dazed state. I don't think we said a word on that drive. We didn't mention our experience to the couple and we never mentioned anything to our parents about it. It all seemed a bit embarrassing and we weren't sure if it was a mishap or an adventure. Either way, it seemed private. The morning after, I took down all my Beatles posters and pictures from my wall. All my adolescent love for them no longer existed. It was a strong moment of maturity. I still loved the Beatles, but in a different way. The most satisfying aspect of the whole experience was that I set out to run on stage and hug George, and I did! John Lennon was interviewed the next day: "One last night got George. I could hear all these wrong notes and he was trying to carry on playing, you know, and the girl hanging on his neck. It was funny."

Following the final bow, the group ran offstage and into the waiting helicopter that whisked them back to Manhattan. They quickly retreated to the safety of their Delmonico suite. The four Beatles, along with Epstein and road managers Neil Aspinall and Mal Evans, enjoyed a quiet dinner in one of the back bedrooms while an exhausted Derek Taylor was entertaining journalists and guests in the hospitality suite. Among the luminaries present were DJ Murray the K as well as Peter Yarrow and Mary Travers (of Peter, Paul and Mary fame).

One group of visitors decided to bypass the hospitality room entirely and go directly into the group's suite. It was here that the Beatles met singer-songwriter Bob Dylan for the first time. He was accompanied by his road manager, Victor Mamoudas, and writer Al Aronowitz. After some introductions and Dylan's request for a glass of cheap wine, pills were passed around the living room. This was a common practice among musicians, as pills were used quite regularly to survive the rigors of playing and touring. Certainly the Beatles had popped their share of pills during their formative years in Hamburg, Germany, to help them endure the long stints they would spend onstage—up to twelve hours a night.

AP IMAGES

The group belts out their hits during a two-day stint at the horseshoe shaped tennis stadium. Roadie Mal Evans (far left in glasses) keeps a watchful eye on the crowd.

Dylan then offered something a bit more organic: marijuana. It wasn't the first time the Beatles had tried the weed. They'd used it in Germany, albeit a less powerful version that had little effect on them. Dylan, assuming the Beatles were familiar with the consequences of grass, began to quiz John about a line in one of their songs about getting high. A puzzled John told Dylan that he'd incorrectly deciphered the words to "I Want to Hold Your Hand"—the phrase was "I can't hide," not "I get high."

At Dylan's suggestion, the lights in the suite were dimmed and towels were stuffed under the doors. The folksinger then proceeded to roll a few joints. The first was handed to John, who immediately passed it to Ringo, whom he called his "official taster." With all eyes on him, Ringo proceeded to smoke the entire thing. Waiting for a reaction, he burst into laughter. With that, John, Paul, and George, along with Epstein, Aspinall, and Evans, all indulged. Later, they would claim that the drug had elevated them to new levels of enlightenment and consciousness. History has shown the profound effect the experience had on their future musical direction.

The next morning, the siege continued at the Delmonico as the crowd shouted, "Show your faces!" The hotel's switchboard operators were flooded with calls—some 200,000 since the group had arrived. In the late afternoon before the second show at Forest Hills, the group ate Nathan's Famous Hot Dogs and salami sandwiches brought in from Coney Island. As performance time approached, they were once again ushered through a side entrance of the hotel onto the streets of Manhattan, with NYPD officers on either side as they walked to the waiting limousines and then traveled to the heliport.

The sold-out performance on Saturday, August 29, was a repeat of the previous night's concert. This crowd seemed much more determined to storm the stage, forcing the NYPD to employ their elite tactical force to support the more than 150 officers and 100 private security guards. As the Beatles finished their set, they ran to the safety of the helicopter while being pursued by some fifty fans who had broken through the police barriers.

MIRRORPIX

The elite West Side Tennis Club and its hallowed courts had survived the onslaught of Beatlemania for two wild nights, and the Beatles had been introduced to a substance that would dramatically change their lives. Rather than return to Manhattan, the Beatles' helicopter flew over Queens, turning south along the Atlantic seaboard towards Atlantic City, New Jersey, where they alighted around midnight for the next stop on their tour.

The Forest Hills concerts and the Hollywood Bowl performances the following year are the only occasions when the Beatles played two shows over two consecutive nights in the same North American city. During planning for the 1964 tour, Weiss had advised Epstein to have the group play Freedomland in New York City over a three-day period, with three shows daily, at a ticket price of $1 to $2 each. The suggestion was soundly rejected by Epstein, who settled on the safe option of Forest Hills.

In terms of collectibles, the Forest Hills Music Festival produced a poster for the scheduled summer of shows that announced the Beatles along with Barbara Streisand and Joan Baez. The generic American tour program was sold at the event, and stubs and unused tickets for both shows are rare. No handbills were produced to advertise the shows.

Singer-songwriter, Bob Dylan, (in center of photo) along with writer, Al Aronowitz, (to the left of Dylan) arrive at the Delmonico Hotel to visit the Beatles after their show at Forest Hills.

ATLANTIC CITY

**August 30, 1964
Convention Hall
8:30 p.m.**

Steel Pier Presents at
ATLANTIC CITY
CONVENTION HALL
In Person
THE **BEATLES**
Show
Sunday, August 30, 1964 - 8:30 P. M.
MAIN FLOOR $3.90

The Beatles sit for the last press conference in August (below) while enjoying Coca-Colas. Opposite page: The boys pose with New York's WTRY DJ's.

IF THERE WAS ONE VENUE IN AMERICA THAT DESERVED A SLOT ON THE BEATLES' whirlwind 1964 North American tour, it was the famous Steel Pier in Atlantic City, New Jersey. Known as "the Nation's Showplace," the pier was *the* place to catch the top acts of the day. It hosted such legendary entertainers as Charlie Chaplin, Benny Goodman, Bob Hope, Amos 'n' Andy, and the celebrated "Diving Horse." It was also home to the most famous beauty contest of them all—the Miss America Pageant, which staged a run on the "Wooden Way" for eighty-four consecutive years. As the years passed, the pier fell into disrepair—until Donald Trump built the Taj Mahal Resort and Casino and returned the Atlantic City icon to its former glory.

On Sunday night, August 30, 1964, the pier continued its string of successful acts by presenting the Beatles at the Atlantic City Convention Hall to an oversold audience of 18,000 spectators. After two wildly

PRIVATE COLLECTION (2)

successful concerts on two consecutive evenings at New York's Forest Hills Tennis Stadium, the Beatles boarded a helicopter for the short flight into New Jersey, landing late in the evening at Bader Field. Upon arrival, the Beatles entourage was stunned to find only two limousines waiting for them, no fans, and not even a police escort. The stretch limos were occupied by promoter George Hamid Jr. and his children. George Harrison wryly commented, "What's happened? Do they hate us in Atlantic City?" What the Beatles didn't understand was that the controlled reception was emblematic of the Hamid family's powerful influence on the seaside city.

George Hamid Sr. was born in Lebanon in 1896. At the age of ten, he'd immigrated to the United States as a member of Buffalo Bill's Wild West Circus. A skilled acrobat, he won the world acrobatic championships at Madison Square Garden and was taught to read and write by famed sharpshooter Annie Oakley. By the mid-1920s, he had become successful in booking talent and had created the world's largest talent agency for circus performers. At one time he owned the New Jersey State Fair, and in 1945 he acquired control of Atlantic City's Steel Pier. He also owned the largest chain of movie theaters in New Jersey.

Hamid and his son, George Jr., were respected talent buyers in Atlantic City, so it was only natural that General Artists Corporation (GAC) would give them the opportunity to book the Beatles. George

Atlantic City's Convention Center (top) sits at the end of the famed Steel Pier. The LaFayette Motor Inn (above), where the group spent three nights. They passed the time writing songs, playing monopoly and simply relaxing. Promoter George Hamid's Steel Pier program (right) for the 1964 season.

Jr. recalls: "My friend Norman Weiss, who was booking the tour, called me in early 1964 and asked me to present the Beatles." Weiss wanted George Jr. to book the Atlantic City Convention Hall on a date that immediately followed the Democratic National Convention. (It's interesting to note that the group played San Francisco's Cow Palace in August just days after the Republican National Convention had been held there.)

During the initial planning stages of the tour, manager Brian Epstein had rejected the idea of holding a concert in New Jersey. Weiss had first suggested the August 30 date at the Convention Hall, but wanted the group to perform three shows in a single day. The ticket price would be $1.25, and Hamid would offer $25,000 plus 50 percent of the gate. Adamantly opposed to the notion of three shows in a day, Epstein bypassed New Jersey.

Ultimately, Weiss and Epstein decided the Beatles would play just one show on August 30 in Atlantic City and then take a couple of days off until the Philadelphia booking on September 2. Interestingly, Weiss had also suggested to Epstein that another concert take place in between Atlantic City and Philadelphia on September 1, at Bowden Stadium in New Haven, Connecticut. He told Epstein that an outdoor venue could hold 19,000, and tickets could sell for between $3 and $5, with an offer from the promoter for a guarantee of $20,000 and 60 percent of the gross. In the margin of his before-tour planning sheet, Epstein wrote "Yale Bowl for Aug. 30." At that point in planning the tour, he was not satisfied with the terms of the August 30 date for Atlantic City. But according to New Haven officials in 2012, no venue named Bowden Stadium existed in 1964 or ever. Weiss must have contacted Epstein, noted his mistake, and then suggested the Yale Bowl; but with that venue holding in excess of 80,000, Epstein understandably passed and gave his boys a day off.

Convention Hall's capacity at the time was 16,500 seats and, until the Houston Astrodome was built in 1965, it boasted the largest free-standing roof without pillars in the United States. In 1964 the Liberty Bowl, a college football game, was held there. Because the Democratic National Convention had vacated the building just prior to the Beatles concert, entire sections of chairs were still set up. George Jr. instructed workers to leave those chairs intact and arrange a thousand more along the sides of the arena to further accommodate the crowd. Recalling a 1958 Ricky Nelson

The Beatles are escorted to the stage of the Convention Center by a bevy of police. Note George's glance (below) toward the assembled police officers.

John prepares to walk on stage. Note his set list taped to the top of his Rickenbacker guitar.

concert that had gotten a bit out of control, George Jr. placed his vendors and friends in the front rows at the front and sides of the hall, hoping their good behavior would quell any potential uprising.

Upon arrival in New Jersey, the Beatles were whisked away in limousines from the sedate Bader Field and driven to their hotel with the promoter's children in tow. George Jr., well aware of the mania that had besieged each city on the tour thus far, decided on a diversionary tactic. In the days just prior to the band's arrival, he falsely leaked to a local radio deejay that the Beatles were booked to stay at the Shelbourne Hotel. Only the promoter and one other person knew the truth.

The other person was Frank Gravatt, the owner of the Lafayette Motor Inn, where the group was booked to occupy the entire sixth and seventh floors. Weiss informed George Jr. that he would call him the minute the helicopter left Forest Hills so the group could be picked up. To avoid any chaos, the promoter asked that no police be involved.

The secretive plot was short-lived, however. Once word spread that the group had arrived, it was only minutes before the Lafayette was surrounded by fans. Newspaper accounts estimated the crowd to be around 200, but by 11 a.m. the next morning that number had swelled to over 2,000. With the crowd repeatedly singing, "We love you Beatles, oh yes we do...," the Sunday church service taking place across the street from the hotel was disrupted, forcing the minister to cut short his sermon. This prompted him to write a scathing letter of rebuke to Gravatt. The motel owner attempted to make a sizable donation to the church, but the gesture didn't seem to satisfy the preacher who was upstaged by the shaggy singers from Liverpool.

MIRRORPIX (2)

With the Beatles scheduled to appear at a press conference at Convention Hall, a plan had to be devised by hotel management and George Jr. to deliver them safely to the venue. Given the lack of security, however, all hell threatened to break loose. As the group approached the entrance to the hall on Pacific Avenue, a group of around 3,000 fans awaited their arrival. George Jr. had requested only four or five policemen to escort the group inside the arena. He recalled that police almost resorted to nightsticks to calm the crowd and that Ringo was nearly overtaken by the overzealous throng. Press officer Derek Taylor, commenting to journalist Larry Kane, summed up the chaotic scene: "This is the biggest thing that's ever happened. There's no question about it. It's like nothing before it, not like Presley, it's not like Sinatra, it's not like the late President Kennedy, it's the Beatles, and they are without precedent." George Jr. limited the press conference to about seventy people, all of whom he knew and could count on for good behavior. It lasted fifteen minutes.

Although it was customary for the deejays from sponsoring radio stations to introduce the Beatles at their concerts, George Jr. decided to personally handle the task. That proved awkward. Standing uncomfortably erect onstage, he announced to the capacity crowd that the national anthem would be sung before the Beatles hit the stage. The audience responded with stony silence. He then told the fans that the British

Paul prepares for the stage, while John—with poor vision—squints to see what lies ahead.

A typical concert pose for police officers across North America. Some officers resorted to putting bullets in their ears to quiet the screams.

national anthem would be sung at the conclusion of the concert. Hearing this, they went wild.

Another city, same gig: the Beatles belted out the standard set list of songs, following the usual opening acts, with one unique aspect—this concert marked the last performance of the Righteous Brothers with the tour. As George Jr. had pledged, the show concluded with the fans singing "God Save the Queen." This was done not in a fit of British pride, but rather as a way to give the Beatles' handlers enough time to escort them to a police van waiting in the basement of Convention Hall. At road manager Neil Aspinall's urging, police officials allowed the van to drive the wrong way down a one-way street onto Pacific Avenue on its way back to the Lafayette.

The Beatles now had two days off—until September 2—before their Philadelphia show. Still, the boys remained prisoners in their hotel room and unable to relax on the beach. Noise from the fans stationed around the hotel was incessant and annoyed guests and journalists alike, including a British newsman who had just finished covering the Democratic National Convention and sought a little rest and relaxation. In his interview with the group, the journalist mentioned that his days off had been wrecked by the commotion and noise. George Harrison advised him to simply "put the air conditioning on and close the windows and that's it, away you go." Newspaper accounts from the day after the concert declared that the Beatles were given a more enthusiastic reception than Lyndon Johnson had received at Convention Hall a week earlier.

Since the boys were sequestered in their room, American tour manager Bob Bonis went in search of amusements to keep them happy. Since they were in Atlantic City, he thought of the famous board game Monopoly, which features various sites in and around the seaside city—including Pacific Avenue, where the Lafayette was located. Soon, pictures appeared of the group playing the game with Jackie DeShannon.

In the course of locating a Monopoly game for the boys, Bonis caught a glimpse of the seedier side of the rock 'n' roll scene. As he made his way to the Lafayette's front desk, he overheard a mother instructing her daughter in an apparent blackmail scheme, directing her to make her way up to the Beatles' suite and scream "Rape!" when she saw John. "Then," as the mom put it, "we'll be rich!" After hearing this, Bonis gave strict orders to hotel security: "No one gets in. Period!"

The view from behind the stage at the Convention Hall. The venue played host to the Democratic National Convention just three days earlier. Organizers decided to leave up temporary chairs to accommodate more requests for Beatles tickets.

Paul had a phone conversation with Elvis Presley arranged by a *New Musical Express* reporter, in which the two men stammered through a short conversation. Knowing that road manager Mal Evans was an Elvis devotee and a card-carrying member of the singer's fan club, Paul slipped him the phone so he could chat with the superstar.

As in several other cities during the tour, the Beatles spent some of their time composing new songs. In Atlantic City, Paul wrote "What You're Doing" for inclusion on a new album, but carelessly left the lyrics behind. They were found by a maid and given to George Jr. for safekeeping. Another song, "Every Little Thing," was also worked out. The band was also treated to a screening of their recently completed film *A Hard Day's Night* and were photographed holding a twenty-inch submarine sandwich from the famous White House Sub Shop.

©CURT GUNTHER COURTESY STEVE GUNTHER

George takes the lead (above) on "Roll Over Beethoven" as a cop shields his ears. Opposite page: George plays Monopoly in his hotel room, as Neil Aspinall hands him a list of requests.

As the group was preparing to leave Atlantic City on September 2, George Jr. had to concoct yet another ruse to get them to the bus they were to take to Philadelphia. He arranged for the hotel's restaurant to bring in a few vehicles, including a fish truck. The bus was parked miles away, so the promoter cleaned out the truck as best he could and brought two vans around to the front of the hotel to distract the fans. Once the diversion was on, George Jr. placed the boys, along with Aspinall and Evans, in the smelly truck and instructed them to lie flat. The truck rendezvoused with the bus, and the Beatles were on their way out of Atlantic City and the care of George Jr. They would play Philadelphia that same evening and then fly immediately to Indianapolis, Indiana, where they would play the following night (September 3).

It was in Atlantic City that the Beatles first heard psychic Jeane Dixon's dire prediction that their plane would crash en route from Philadelphia to Indianapolis. Until they'd survived that late-night flight out of Philly, neither the group nor their entourage would rest easy.

The promoter had only to print tickets and supply the generic U.S. tour program for this concert stop. No posters, flyers, or handbills were needed. There may have been a four-ticket minimum purchase, and that may explain why several unused tickets have surfaced over the years. Press conference invitations were sent out to around seventy individuals, yet none have appeared in the collectibles market.

PHILADELPHIA

September 2, 1964
Convention Hall
8 p.m.

Philadelphia's
Convention Hall,
where the group
played one sold-out
performance.

THE FIRST CASUALTY OF THE BEATLES' EPIC FIRST TOUR OF NORTH AMERICA was the duo of Bill Medley and Bobby Hatfield. The Righteous Brothers had indeed "lost that lovin' feeling" after they left the cozy confines of the western states, where their music was more popular. They became discouraged as fans repeatedly chanted "We want the Beatles" as they played, then felt completely upstaged when the Beatles' helicopter hovered noisily above the stage during their set at Forest Hills. They were making $750 a week on the tour, far less than the $500 a night they earned back home. Manager Brian Epstein understood their predicament and released them from their contract.

Their replacement was Clarence "Frogman" Henry, who'd scored a Top 10 hit in 1956 with "Ain't Got No Home." The Frogman remained a supporting act for the rest of the tour. Henry, New Orleans born and raised, styled his act after the likes of Fats Domino and Professor Longhair and was able to whip up his audiences with his fused jazz and blues that turned into rock 'n' roll.

After switching over from a foul-smelling fish truck to a more comfortable touring bus, the Beatles left Atlantic City on September 2 for the hour or so trip to Philadelphia and their concert that evening. Known as the City of Brotherly Love and the birthplace of *American Bandstand,* Fabian and Frankie Avalon, Philadelphia was still reeling from the late August race riots that had decimated parts of North Philly. The police were not taking any chances with their high-profile visitors: the Beatles' bus entered the city accompanied by a police motorcade and didn't travel to the Warwick Hotel, where the group had originally been booked to stay downtown. As in Vancouver, Epstein had sensed trouble and cancelled the band's Warwick reservations, deciding to make Philadelphia another five-hour drop-in visit.

Despite the fact that the hotel cancellation was announced in the newspapers, a few girls still had to be removed from the Warwick's closets and freight elevators. Other major hotels around the city were also besieged by fans certain that the band was staying in the city. Instead, the Beatles' motorcade and bus drove directly to Philadelphia's Convention Hall and into a surprisingly vacant underground garage. Like Atlantic City, this was one of the simplest, least dramatic arrivals on the tour. Fans were seen holding banners that read "City of Beatle Love," an obvious take on the moniker "City of Brotherly Love." Upon their arrival at the hall, the group was escorted without incident to their dressing room.

Philadelphia's Convention Hall, constructed in 1931, was located adjacent to the University of Pennsylvania campus. Originally known as Municipal Auditorium, it earned the name Convention Hall after hosting numerous political conventions. Just four days prior to the Beatles concert, President Lyndon Johnson had given a speech there. Convention Hall also hosted the 1960 NBA Basketball All-Star Game, and the Jackson 5 played their first official concert as Motown artists at the arena.

The booking for the Philadelphia concert

FELIX G. GERSTMAN & MOE SEPTEE Present

IN PERSON! — **IN CONCERT!**

THE BEATLES

WIBG's
HY LIT, m.c.

Wed., Sept. 2, 8 pm · CONVENTION HALL

All Seats Reserved: $5.50, 4.50, 3.50, 2.50
TICKETS ON SALE TOMORROW (MON.) 4:30 TO 10:30 PM
AT CONVENTION HALL BOX OFFICE — NO MAIL ORDERS

A group of lucky fans (above) get up close and personal with their idols, presenting them with homemade trinkets. Felix Gertsman and Moe Septee were the promoters for the show in Philadelphia, and ran this ad in the newspapers (left).

was handled by two well-known local promoters and a popular deejay at WIBG. Hy Lit (born Hyman Aaron Lit) was the number-one afternoon radio personality in the Philadelphia metro area. When he first heard the band earlier in the year, he desperately wanted to book them. He mined his contacts at Capitol Records but was informed that someone else had beat him to the punch. That man was Moe Septee (born Moses Septytor), a longtime impresario in Philly. Devoutly religious, Septee had studied to become a rabbi before he caught the show business bug and embarked on a long and illustrious career that included founding the Philadelphia Pops Orchestra. For the Beatles concert, Septee teamed up with longtime partner Felix G. Gerstman, who was far more familiar with theater productions. Gerstman's

WIBG's Personalities JOE NIAGARA and HY LIT... with THE BEATLES

A flier (right) produced by WIBG Radio 99, which sponsored the concert. Popular local DJ, Hy Lit, helped introduce the band on stage. This lobby poster (below), was one of only a few that were printed and displayed around Convention Hall to advertise the upcoming concert.

Photographs taken at party given in honor of The Beatles at Plaza Hotel in New York City on Monday, February 10, 1964

name appears on the press and official passes issued for the concert, and he signed the performance contract calling for a $20,000 payment against 60 percent of the gate.

Hy Lit informed Capitol executives that he would not play another Beatles record until he was given the name of the individual who had stolen his thunder. Lit finally made connections with Septee and offered a dual promotion of the concert that would harness both his huge radio presence and Septee's savvy as a promoter. The deal was done with a handshake, and both men split the $20,000 contract fee. Tickets went on sale in early May and sold out in 90 minutes.

Lit recalls making announcements that tickets would go on sale at 3:30 p.m. This was done to prevent kids from playing hooky from school to stand in line. When they started queuing early in the day anyway, police ordered ticket sales to begin immediately. The students who remained in school were understandably upset when they failed to get tickets. Lit also regrets that tickets weren't sold on a limited-order basis, as area ticket agencies quickly snapped

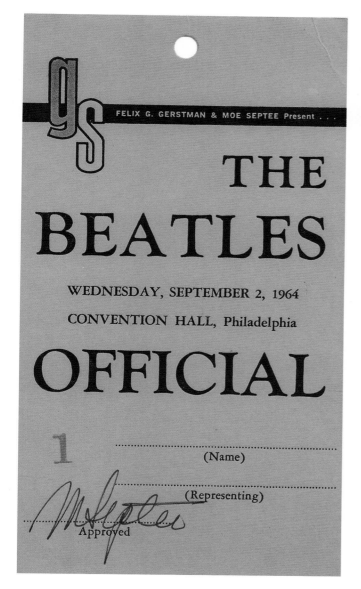

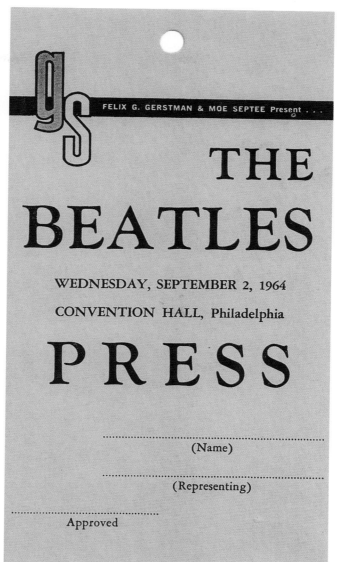

PRIVATE COLLECTION

"Officials" and "Press" passes (left) that were issued by promoters, Septee and Gertsman. High-ranking Philadelphia police officials (below) pose with the Beatles before the group hit the stage.

them up. One group purchased 1,500 at a time.

Lit also remembers that Philadelphia's legendary future mayor Frank Rizzo, who at the time was a high-ranking police official, called the deejay requesting front-row tickets for his kids as well as a personal meeting with the Beatles. Lit demanded to know how Rizzo had gotten his unlisted number. Rizzo didn't mince words, telling the deejay in no uncertain terms that "Frank Rizzo can get anything he wants!"

Quietly ensconced in their dressing room, the Beatles were plied with scotch and Coke by Hy Lit. They also munched on fish and chips from Philly's famed century-old Bookbinder's Restaurant. For an hour, starting at 6 p.m., the band endured the usual press conference drill that included twenty-five reporters, twenty-five VIPs, a small group of teenage girls and fifty policemen. Hy Lit gave exclusive radio coverage to WIBG and refused to return calls from competing stations that might jeopardize this exclusive sponsorship. The press conference took place without a hitch, but some of the Beatles' cheeky answers had to be amended, by each other, for damage control. One reporter asked John, "When you were here last February, you said you found American girls too forward. What do

Promoters Septee and Gertsman received a fairly good deal to bring the Fab Four to Philly—they only had to produce a $20,000 guarantee. Hy Lit shared half the fee. The show sold out in 90 minutes.

640 Fifth Avenue
NEW YORK 19, N.Y.
CIrcle 7-7543

8 South Michigan Avenue
CHICAGO 3, ILLINOIS
STate 2-6288

9025 Wilshire Blvd.
BEVERLY HILLS, CALIF.
CRestview 3-2400

RIDER ATTACHED HERETO IS HEREBY MADE PART
OF THIS CONTRACT

H

GENERAL ARTISTS CORPORATION

AGREEMENT made this ____17th____ day of ____APRIL____ , 19__64__ ,

between _____NEMS ENTERPRISES LIMITED_____ (hereinafter

referred to as "PRODUCER") and ____FELIX GERSTMAN, INC._____
(hereinafter referred to as "PURCHASER").

It is mutually agreed between the parties as follows:

The PURCHASER hereby engages the PRODUCER and the PRODUCER hereby agrees to furnish the entertainment presentation hereinafter described, upon all the terms and conditions herein set forth, including those on the reverse side hereof entitled "Additional Terms and Conditions."

1. PRODUCER agrees to furnish the following entertainment presentation to PURCHASER:

____A show of approximately two hours in duration starring the BEATLES, plus additional supporting attractions to be selected at the sole discretion of PRODUCER.____

for presentation thereof by PURCHASER:

(a) at ____Convention Hall, Philadelphia, Penn.____ ;
(Place of Engagement)

(b) on ____Wednesday September 2, 1964____ ;
(Date(s) of Engagement)

(c) at the following time(s): ____Concert performance commencing at aprox. 8.p.m.____ ;

(d) rehearsals: ____As required by PRODUCER____ .

2. FULL PRICE AGREED UPON: ____Twenty thousand dollars ($20,000.00) against 60% of the gross box-office receipts after applicable admission taxes have been deducted therefrom, whichever amount is greater.____

All payments shall be paid by certified check, money order, bank draft or cash as follows:

(a) $ ____10,000 (50%)____ shall be paid by PURCHASER to and in the name of PRODUCER'S agent, GENERAL ARTISTS CORPORATION, not later than ____Monday April 20, 1964____ ;

(b) $ ____10,000 (30%)____ shall be paid by PURCHASER to PRODUCER ~~not later than~~ 's agent not later than ____ ____thirty days preceding actual play-date.____ ;

(c) Additional payments, if any, shall be paid by PURCHASER to PRODUCER no later than _____ ____All earned percentage - not later than intermission of performance covered herein.____

PURCHASER shall first apply any and all receipts derived from the entertainment presentation to the payments required hereunder: All payments shall be made in full without any deductions whatsoever.

3. SCALE OF ADMISSION ____House to be scaled to not less than $45,000.00 after taxes. Ticket prices not to exceed $5.00 including tax unless increase approved by PRODUCER.____ NEM ENTERPRISES (PRODUCER)

By ____[signature]____

FELIX GERSTMAN, INC. (PURCHASER)

Return all signed copies to agent:
General Artists Corporation
640 Fifth Avenue
New York, New York

By ____[signature]____

Address: ____180 West 42nd Street,____ ____New York 36, N.Y.____

Musicians' Union
27 JUL 1964

Phone: ____LO4-6990____

ALL COPIES OF CONTRACT MUST BE SIGNED ON REVERSE AS WELL AS FACE SIDE.

Form AA-1

you think of them now?" John replied, "Forward? No, backward!," to which Paul and the others quickly added, "Oh, they're great. We think they're great."

At the appointed hour, Septee and Lit introduced the Beatles to a wild Philadelphia audience. Lit received permission from Septee to stage his own coup. The deejay managed to place center stage and behind the group a huge sign that read "A WIBBAGE WELCOME FOR THE BEATLES." The word

The Beatles perform their set at Philadelphia's Convention Hall. WIBG placed a huge banner behind stage that read, "A WIBBAGE Welcome For The Beatles."

"WIBBAGE" was the pet name for WIBG, and the sign couldn't have made the concert's sponsorship more obvious. When the Beatles strode onto the stage, the arena lit up. Bill Medley of the Righteous Brothers, recalling his time on tour, had often wondered why the house lights would come on when the Beatles appeared on stage. Watching from the wings at a previous concert, he soon realized it was actually a barrage of flashbulbs. As the screams hit a crescendo, one policeman, fresh from riot-torn North Philly, yelled to another, "Take me back to Columbia Avenue!," the epicenter of the uprising.

Some accounts of the Philadelphia concert suggest that it was attended by a "mostly white audience," but this may have been sensationalism. Speculation has abounded that police, fearing another riot, took extra precautions to prevent a recurrence, but in fact any Philadelphian, regardless of race,

COURTESY OF GINA SMITH

was allowed to buy tickets when they went on sale in early May. The Beatles' contract rider detailed their refusal to play before segregated audiences, and on August 20 in Las Vegas Paul spoke about it to reporters and also commented on plans by the promoter of their upcoming Jacksonville, Florida, concert to segregate the venue, the Gator Bowl.

With the concert finished and no plans to stay the night, the group was ushered to their plane at the North Philadelphia Airport. They were headed to America's Heartland for a show at the famous Indiana State Fair in the city of Indianapolis.

The entire group had anticipated this flight with some degree of dread. Just a few days before, while the Beatles were in Atlantic City, popular psychic Jeane Dixon had predicted that their plane would crash en route from Philly to Indianapolis. Dixon had accurately foretold the assassination of JFK, so there was cause for concern. John had secretly obsessed about the death of his music hero Buddy Holly in a plane crash. George became so concerned that he phoned Dixon for some reassurance, later commenting to journalist Larry Kane, in true British fashion, "Just hope for the best, keep a stiff upper lip, and away we go, y'know. If you crash, you crash, don't you? When your number's up, that's it." Ringo later remarked: "A lot of people would like to think we were scared into saying a prayer. What we did actually was drink."

While Dixon's forecast clearly proved inaccurate, there was some substance to her eerie claim. One of the two American Flyers Electra turboprops (Tail # N183H) used on the Beatles' tour did crash two years later, in April 1966, killing eighty-three military personnel and civilian crew members. American Flyers founder Reed Pigman Sr., who hosted the Beatles & Co. at his Missouri ranch at the end of the 1964 tour, had a heart attack at the controls and was among the casualties. The accident still stands as the worst in Oklahoma aviation history.

Moe Septee continued to book acts into Convention Hall until 1975, when he changed career directions and became a Broadway producer. He passed away in 1997, at the age of seventy-one. Despite a grassroots effort to save Convention Hall, it was demolished in 2005. The Perelman Center for Advanced Medicine now occupies the site.

Memorabilia from this concert are few. Promoter Moe Septee didn't have to do a lot of advertising for the show, as it sold out in under two hours. No handbills or flyers were printed, but two types of press passes were generated for officials and members of the media. A lobby poster was printed, perhaps by Convention Hall, and displayed there to promote the show just before tickets went on sale in May. As at other venues, the official North American tour program was sold. Philadelphia concert tickets are extremely rare in any form, stubs or unused.

John, Paul, and Ringo wave from the back of a limousine after the show. The car was headed to the airport for a late-night flight to Indianapolis.

INDIANAPOLIS

September 3, 1964
Two Shows
Indiana State Fairgrounds Coliseum, 5 p.m.
Grandstand, 9:30 p.m.

INDIANAPOLIS, INDIANA, HOME TO THE FAMED INDY 500, would now take its turn hosting the Beatles. How would America's heartland embrace the music of the Brits? The true test would be their performance at the famed Indiana State Fair, noted more for the grading of cows and apple pie competitions than for concerts by long-haired musicians from across the Atlantic. It was also in Indianapolis that perhaps the strangest tale in Beatles touring lore occurred when Ringo, accompanied by Indiana state troopers, decided to slip away before dawn one morning for a tour of the countryside.

Published accounts stating that the Beatles spent the night before the Indianapolis concert at deejay Hy Lit's home in Philadelphia are most certainly untrue. And indeed, accounts of the Beatles' whereabouts during the American tours were routinely exaggerated. A similar story surfaced claiming that the group, between shows at the Las Vegas Convention Center, had dinner with a family who were friends of promoter Stan Irwin. Further, the Beatles reportedly asked if they could go for a swim in the

The Beatles arrive from Philadelphia in Indianapolis after midnight—their eleventh stop on the 1964 tour.

INDIANA STATE ARCHIVES

family's pool, only to discover that they hadn't brought their bathing suits. The problem was allegedly solved when the family lent the boys their son's white bun-hugger underwear. Family members even claimed to have snapped pictures of the event, but they've never surfaced. Such was the nature of the tall tales from reporters and fans alike.

Shortly before 1 a.m. on September 3, the Beatles' chartered Electra glided into Indianapolis's Weir Cook Airport, eliciting a collective sigh from its famous passengers. After all, this was the flight that psychic Jeane Dixon had doomed in a plane crash. As the plane taxied within sight of yet another waiting crowd of fans, John mocked Dixon's prediction with his own: "A big cop will grab me by the arm and take me to a waiting car." John proved to be a more apt psychic than Dixon because, of course, his comical forecast came true moments later.

Fortunately for the Beatles, Indianapolis would not be a drop-in date like the previous day in Philadelphia. The group and entourage were booked to stay at the Speedway Motel. This caused some concern for the security team, as the motel had an open layout with outdoor hallways and plenty of

The Fab Four take a gander at "Miss Indiana State Fair," Cheryl Lee Garrett (above), and sit for yet another press conference to John's obvious boredom.

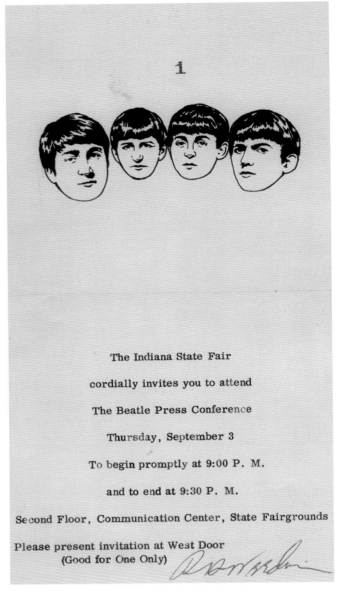

The Indiana State Fair

cordially invites you to attend

The Beatle Press Conference

Thursday, September 3

To begin promptly at 9:00 P. M.

and to end at 9:30 P. M.

Second Floor, Communication Center, State Fairgrounds

Please present invitation at West Door
(Good for One Only)

The Indiana State Fair Coliseum (top left) played host to the 5 p.m. show. An invitation (upper right) to the press conference that was held shortly before the evening show at the racetrack. The Speedway Motel (above) has hosted Indy car drivers, as well as the Beatles.

places where determined fans could hide and wreak havoc. One such enterprising young man, dressed as a waiter complete with a room service tray and glasses, made it past the tight security before his ruse was discovered. The teen later found himself in an Indianapolis police station, where he was issued a stern warning.

The Speedway Motel, while not among the more luxurious places the Beatles stayed during the 1964 tour, did cater to many notables over the years. Opened in 1963, the motel was adjacent to Turn 2 at the famous Indianapolis Motor Speedway and hosted such guests as actors Jim Nabors, James Garner, and Paul Newman (who filmed scenes of his 1969 movie *Winning* at the motel). In fact, many an Indy race-car driver preferred the comforts of the motel over the motor homes they drove to the track each year.

Word had spread that the Beatles had plans to stay in downtown's Essex House Hotel, but it was decided that all four of the boys would occupy a single room at the Speedway Motel. (The single-room claim has been disputed over the years, as some sources cite four rooms—228, 230, 232, and 234—one for each Beatle.) Even though the Essex House Hotel reservations were cancelled, determined fans still removed doorknobs and even lifted off some of the wallpaper.

During the Beatles' two-day stay in Indianapolis, some 40,000 to 50,000 phone calls were received by the Speedway Motel and the fairgrounds. One of the calls was a bomb threat stating that either "a gun or explosion" would injure the group. This particular call was received by Robert H. Weedon, the fair board's entertainment director, who immediately called on the police to address this and any other potential threats.

August 3, 1964

Hon. Melvin Price
Member of Congress
1234 New House Office Building
Washington, D. C. 20515

Dear Congressman Price:

In reply to your letter of July 31st, addressed to the ticket office Indiana State Fair, please be advised that all tickets for the "Beatles" show have been sold for several weeks.

Our house only seats 12,500, and we had demands for at least 20,000.

We regret we are unable to oblige.

Very truly yours,

Hal L. Royce,
Secretary-Manager

HLR:bj

GENERAL ARTISTS CORPORATION
640 FIFTH AVENUE
NEW YORK 19, N.Y.

August 10th, 1964

Mr. Robert Weedon
Indiana State Fair
Indianapolis, Indiana

Dear Mr. Weedon:

With reference to the engagement of THE BEATLES, we would appreciate very much if you would have in their dressing rooms, prior to their arrival, a supply of clean towels, chairs, a case of cold Coca Cola, and if at all possible, a portable TV set.

Also, please make sure the dressing rooms and lavatory are clean.

Thank you for your cooperation.

Sincerely,

IRA SIDELLE
Company Manager

IS//jm

COLISEUM

THE TENNESSEE ERNIE FORD SHOW
WITH JERRY VAN DYKE

Sat. - Aug. 29 - 5:00 & 8:00 p.m.
Sun. - Aug. 30 - 2:00 & 8:00 p.m.

Boxes: $3.30
Side Mezzanine: $3.30-$2.65-$2.45
End Mezzanine: $2.00
Arena Seats: $3.30-$2.45
General Admission: $1.00

FLAT SADDLE HORSE SHOW

Mon. - Aug. 31 thru Fri. - Sept. 4
7:30 p.m. Nightly except
Thur., Sept. 3 at 8:00 p.m.

Boxes: $2.40
General Admission: $1.00

THE BEATLES   *SOLD OUT*

Thurs., Sept. 3 - 5:00 p.m.

$5.00-$4.00-$3.00

THE ANDY WILLIAMS SHOW
WITH THE OSMOND BROTHERS

Sat. - Sept. 5 - 5:00 & 8:00 p.m.
Sun. - Sept. 6 - 2:30 & 8:00 p.m.
Mon. - Sept. 7 - 4:30 & 7:30 p.m.

Boxes: $3.30
Side Mezzanine: $3.30-$2.65-$2.45
End Mezzanine: $2.00
Arena Seats: $3.30-$2.45
General Admission: $1.00

WESTERN HORSE SHOW

Tues. - Sept. 8 & Wed. - Sept. 9
7:30 p.m. Nightly

Boxes: $2.40
General Admission: $1.00

GRANDSTAND

TOMMY STEINER'S
(Rodeo Cowboys Association Approved)
WORLD CHAMPIONSHIP RODEO

Admission to Grounds
Adult or Car 75¢
CHILDREN (12 and under) FREE
(when accompanied by adult)
Advance Gate Ticket—Adult or Car 50¢

TENNESSEE ERNIE FORD . . .

Ole' Ern has plenty of "pea-pickin'" friends in Indiana. This is his fifth visit to the Indiana State Fair. One of his famous songs, "Sixteen Tons" was first sung from the Coliseum stage during his 1958 appearance.

THE BEATLES . . .

England's popular rock 'n roll singers, John Lennon, Paul McCartney, Ringo Star and George Harrison, are scheduled for one appearance on the Coliseum stage during their tour of the United States. This is the only State Fair included in their late summer itinerary.

WORLD CHAMPIONSHIP RODEO . . .

All of the favorite events associated with a Championship Rodeo — bareback bronc riding; saddle bronc riding; calf roping; Brahman bull riding; steer wrestling and grand entry are in-

ANDY WILLIAMS . . .

Andy is a newcomer to the State Fair but not to the TV screens in this area. This popular recording star and TV personality will feature a group of young singers, The Osmond Brothers, on the show. Another TV personality, Mark Wilson, star of the show, "The Magic Land of Allakazam," is also scheduled to entertain the entire family.

FLAT SADDLE and WESTERN HORSE SHOWS . .

Two big horse shows are scheduled for the big tanbark arena. An "honor-rated" show—the Indiana State Fair horse show is known nationally. (For the highlights of each horse show, check the daily judging schedule under entertainment.)

JACK KOCHMAN'S HELL DRIVERS . . .

A favorite with State Fair visitors for the past several years, Kochman's daredevil drivers give the spectators a fast moving show with their feats of auto driving. Now featured at the World's Fair, this

Even an Indiana State Congressman (above left) couldn't obtain a ticket to the 5 p.m. show. GAC's request (above right) for clean towels and Coca Cola in the dressing room. The Fair's program of events (left).

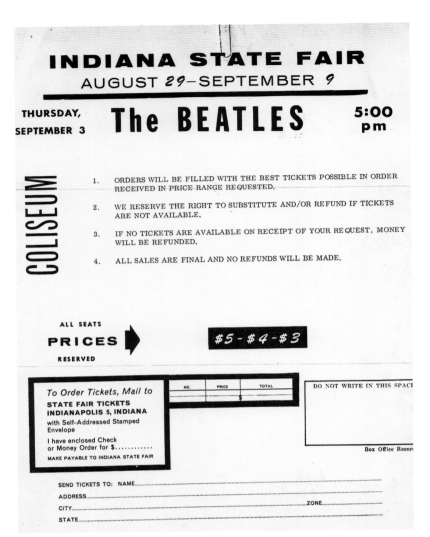

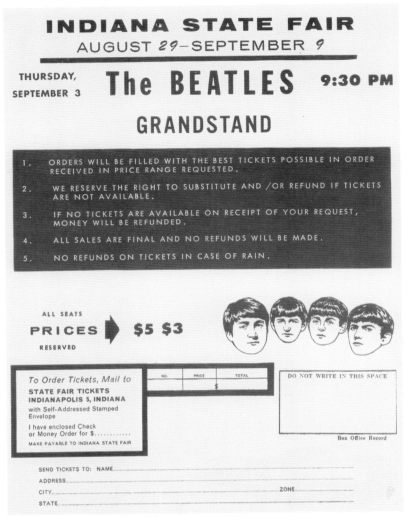

Ticket order requests for the 5 p.m. and 9:30 p.m. shows. The nighttime show was added in early August, and was later moved to the Fair's horse track.

The booking for the concert was done by the Indiana State Fair Board Commission in early May 1964. Norman Weiss of General Artists Corporation (GAC) had originally given Beatles manager Brian Epstein the choice of playing either New York's Forest Hills Tennis Stadium or the Indiana State Fair over two consecutive nights, August 28 and 29. Epstein chose the former. The Indianapolis shows then were set for September 3, a date that had until then been tentatively reserved for a show at Boston's famed Fenway Park. Although the September 3 show in Boston was scrubbed, the city would remain on the Beatles' tour agenda; a September 12 performance at the Boston Gardens was later added to the tour schedule.

The commission was desperately hoping to book two performances for the evening of September 3, but word came back from GAC that the group disliked performing two shows on the same day. Up to that point, only the appearance in Las Vegas had afforded fans a double show; the group wouldn't begin doing two shows in a day on a more regular basis until later in the tour.

Undaunted, the commission refused to give up. One member of the commission, Estel L. Callahan, recalls it going back to GAC with an offer of 80 percent of the gross to add a second show. GAC readily accepted. Documentation indicates that the second show, at 9:30 p.m., was added rather late, in early August, which might explain its failure to sell out. To make matters worse, the later show wasn't listed in the official fair program.

The Beatles' 5 p.m. show was played in the Coliseum, while the 9:30 show took place at the racetrack due to a scheduling conflict in the Coliseum with the Flat Saddle Horse Show. This would be the only instance in the Beatles' North American touring history when they'd play two different venues in the same city on the same day. In 1966, the band would play two different cities in one day—Cincinnati on Monday afternoon (due to a rain-out the previous night) and then 320 miles away in St. Louis that same evening.

On August 6, after the second concert was announced, one opportunistic fan named Connie Dieren made an impassioned plea to the commission to arrange a meeting with the Beatles between shows:

The group walks towards the stage of the Coliseum for the 5 p.m. show (left) while fans begin to take their seats (below) in the grandstand area of the racetrack for the evening show.

"I wrote to you last month, asking you if you could arrange for me to meet the Beatles because I had written a movie for them. It was just reported on the radio that they will be giving two shows. You know now how they get mobbed wherever they go, I'm sure you won't be letting them leave the Coliseum between shows. So wouldn't that be a perfect time to let me meet them—between shows? I don't have to talk to all of them. John is really the one I want to talk to since he is my favorite and he is an author too. But I'd love to talk to Ringo. George will do fine too. If Paul is the only one who'll see me, I'll talk to him although he rates last with me." Connie then made one final request: "I'd like to ask another favor. Could my sister and two friends come along?" So much for Connie's screenwriting career.

Numerous letters requesting tickets to the Indianapolis shows still exist in the Indiana State Fair Board Commission files. One such letter sums up the ingenious ways fans tried to get tickets. Eighteen-year-old Joyce Kirsch wrote to Congressman John Brademas: "Please HELP me! I need two tickets

On stage at the Coliseum. Although more than 20,000 ticket requests were received, the venue only held 12,500 seats.

to the Beatles performance at the Indiana State Fair. Could you use all the influence you can possibly muster to obtain these tickets for me? My sister wrote me that a large volume of tickets have been held back for government officials. Since you're a Democrat, I know you will take an interest! I'll cry a lot if you can't help me get the tickets and you wouldn't want that now, would you?"

It's unlikely that Congressman Brademas was able to procure tickets to the sold-out show, as evidenced by a letter from the fair board to an actual member of Congress. Representative Melvin Price (a Democrat from Illinois) was denied tickets by fair board manager Hal L. Royce, who mentioned in his reply to the congressman: "All tickets for the Beatles show have been sold for several weeks. Our house only seats 12,500, and we had demands for at least 20,000." That said, radio stations WIBC and WIFE were able to secure several thousand tickets each to use in promotions and giveaways.

Finally, it was time for the Beatles to make the twenty- to twenty-five-minute drive to the fairgrounds from the motel. Over 200 police officers were summoned to maintain order. Shortly before the show,

GAC manager Ira Sidelle sent a letter to the commission requesting that the Beatles' dressing room "have a supply of clean towels, chairs, a case of cold Coca-Cola and, if at all possible, a portable TV set."

The commission tapped WIFE morning deejay Jerry Baker (professionally known as Jack Sunday) to emcee the 5 p.m. show. Baker relates that WIFE was the number-one station in Indianapolis at the time, having begun its Top 40 format only in January of that year. WIBC's "Bouncin' Bill" Baker (no relation) emceed the second show.

At 6:21 p.m., the Beatles kicked off their first show after the usual warm-up acts (the Bill Black Combo, the Exciters, Clarence "Frogman" Henry, and Jackie DeShannon). Jerry Baker recalls the experience: "It was the only time in my career that I was scared. It must have been written on my face, because Paul very calmly walked by me onstage and looked at me as [if] to say, 'What are you doing here?' You could feel the electricity in the building, enough to light up the city. It became so loud that it almost

became quiet, if that makes any sense. It just went to another dimension and everything was surreal. I can't explain the noise, but it just sucked all the air out of the Coliseum and it just took my breath away." Dairymen at the fair began to worry about whether their prized cattle would drop from fright. WIFE recorded the first show and planned to air it the following week, but legal issues nixed those plans.

Following the first concert, the Beatles were whisked by car, still sweaty in their stage clothes, to the fair administration building. Here they changed clothes and endured yet another press conference, preceded by the presentation of various gifts and a photo op with Miss Indiana State Fair. During the briefing, the group lauded the harmonies of the Beach Boys as well as the Detroit Sound (or, as Paul referred to it, "American colored groups").

The second performance, in front of the outdoor grandstand, was as raucous as the first, but the constant screaming, contained by a roof at the first show, was more muted as it drifted off into the Indiana night sky. When the performance ended, officials tallied up the damage: thirteen cases

John screams to Paul's delight, as the Fab Four rock the Coliseum.

Karen Marks
11 yrs old
1964

JAN · 64

Jack + Doyne
Marks'
Farm house +
barn that
Ringo visited.
1964

NOV · 64

Karen Marks
with younger
brothers and
sister.
1964

The
Versatile
MORGAN

Eleven-year old Karen Marks (above) and her horse, home, siblings, and an autograph of Ringo Starr (right). Marks was shocked when her State Trooper father brought home a Beatle.

COURTESY OF KAREN MARKS

of hysteria and an arm gash suffered by a young man who'd been pushed through a glass door. Even the former governor's daughter-in-law, Mrs. Henry F. Schricker, received aid after being pushed to the ground by crazed fans. Even so, fair officials declared the concert a security success, attributable to the efforts of extra fire officials; state, county, and city police; Sea Scouts; civil defense personnel; and even local Boy Scout troops.

The group would depart for Milwaukee, Wisconsin, the next day, but not before a good night's sleep at the Speedway Motel. It was during this last night's stay in Indianapolis that Ringo, finding it difficult to sleep, emerged in the early morning hours from the room he was sharing with the others. He approached a trio of Indiana state troopers and talked them into giving him a city tour in their police cruiser. Appearing on the *David Letterman Show* in 1989, Ringo talked about how one of the troopers, Jack Marks, allowed him to briefly drive his cruiser. According to Ringo, they were then chased by another officer (who had obviously seen the long-haired driver) and escaped by ducking into an alley and cutting off the lights.

Trooper Marks denies Ringo's claim that the drummer was handed the keys to his cruiser. The three troopers, however, did take Ringo past the governor's mansion and other landmarks before heading to Marks's farmhouse in Noblesville, some twenty-five miles north. The trooper walked Ringo out to the barn, where his wife was busy preparing her horses to be shown at the fair. She gave the drummer barely any notice.

Inside the house, eleven-year-old Karen Marks was up early with her seven- and nine-year-old brothers. "I can't believe Dad brought home a Beatle!" was her first thought when she saw her dad's special guest. Her two brothers scattered to the barn, and Marks brought Ringo inside the house for a cup of instant coffee. He introduced Karen to Ringo, who later gave her an autograph and a kiss on the cheek. Just as the group was leaving on their return trip to the Speedway Motel, Mrs. Marks's veterinarian arrived with his trailer to help transport the horses to the fair. Marks introduced the drummer to the vet and several stunned kids who were along for the ride. Ringo gave a kiss on the cheek and an autograph to one of the other girls and waved good-bye.

On the way back into town, Marks stopped his car for breakfast at the Iowan Restaurant, at the junction of Highways 31 and 431, just north of Carmel. Sleepy-eyed diners were shocked to see a Beatle in the tiny roadside establishment. Ringo was branded an imposter by one customer, who commented, "Did you see that jerk with the Beatle wig on?" A family seated at the diner recognized the famous drummer, however. They'd driven all the way from Kalamazoo, Michigan, in an unsuccessful attempt to secure tickets to the concerts. Happily, all was not lost as they were able to shake hands with Ringo, chat him up, and score autographs, along with several other patrons.

This entire incident has been documented in several books and, though it seems unreliable, the *Indianapolis Star* published a photo of a calendar page showing Mrs. Marks's handwritten entry about the visit. Ringo's *Letterman* appearance corroborated the story as well. Mr. and Mrs. Marks pleaded with their daughter not to tell anyone of the visit, for fear of teenagers coming to the farm and tearing up the place, so Karen kept it to herself until she entered college and was able to share it at long last. She can honestly say that Ringo Starr was the first boy to kiss her!

Before the Beatles left Indianapolis, fair officials allowed their Cadillac to drive the famed Indy 500 track. George commented, "It was fantastic. I couldn't believe how long the straightway was, and to be on the banking and see all the grandstands was great!" (Of course, he would later become a passionate Formula 1 racing fan and a familiar face on the racing circuit.) The group also raced slot cars on a tiny set in their motel room and posed with golf clubs for photographers on the motel's putting greens. The press later noted that the Beatles were better musicians than golfers.

The band left Indianapolis $85,232 richer. Still, their visit was marred by a dispute with the owner of the Speedway Motel. Beatles management refused to pay for five of the twelve rooms, contending that it was the fair board's responsibility to pay for those used by security personnel. The board felt it was the Beatles' responsibility. Ultimately, the $150 tab at the center of the dispute was paid by the board, citing the tremendous success of the shows.

The Beatles' flight left Indianapolis early in the afternoon, bound for the city of Milwaukee, Wisconsin. During the flight, Paul was spotted wearing a "To Hell with the Beatles" button he'd borrowed from the plane's flight engineer, perhaps as a comedic protest of the motel dispute. An Indianapolis fixture for forty-six years, the Speedway Motel was demolished in 2009.

Memorabilia from the Indianapolis shows are very uncommon. For reasons unknown, unused tickets from the sold-out 5 p.m. show are plentiful, while full tickets from the 9:30 p.m. show, which didn't sell out, are almost nonexistent. Other items from this show have surfaced in recent years, including ticket order forms, press passes, and the original Indiana State Fair program for the 1964 season, which was given to attendees at the fair entrance as they walked in. The fair program, although printed in large quantities, is difficult to find and lists only the Beatles' 5 p.m. show, proof that the 9:30 show was added much later. The generic 1964 Beatles concert program was sold at both shows. Although some collectors claim that a concert poster was printed, that has never been fully verified.

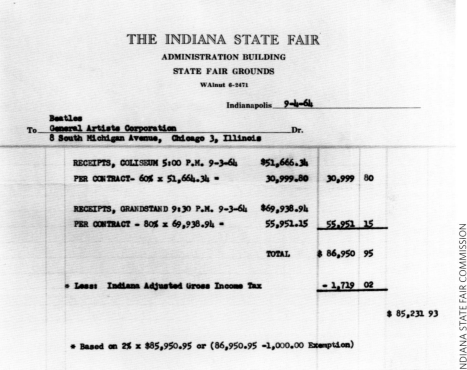

INDIANA STATE FAIR COMMISSION

Payment to General Artists Corporation for the Indianapolis stop. The Beatles netted more than a million dollars while on tour in North America during 1964.

MILWAUKEE

**September 4, 1964
Milwaukee Arena
8 p.m.**

"The Threetles" at the press conference in Milwaukee. John skipped because of a sore throat.

MILWAUKEE, WISCONSIN, WAS THE TWELFTH STOP on the Beatles' tour of North America. The September 4 performance would be their fifteenth in the seventeen days since their opening show at San Francisco's Cow Palace. The stress and strain of touring was starting to show. The band members were exhausted by the frantic pace, so much so that they were given antibiotics in their hotel room after the Milwaukee show to help them forge ahead. John was nursing a sore throat after the previous day's double performance in Indianapolis, Indiana, and would have to skip the Milwaukee press conference in order to rest up for the evening's concert at the Milwaukee Arena.

It was in Milwaukee that the group experienced the first seriously negative incident of the tour. When their chartered plane landed at General Mitchell Field at 4:20 p.m., roughly 700 fans had been patiently waiting to see them, some for up to twenty hours. Usually the group was given the opportunity to wave to fans before being whisked away in limousines. In Milwaukee, however, the plane taxied to the new National Guard headquarters on the far side of the field, out of the fans' view. Moments later, the Beatles boarded their waiting cars and departed for the hotel, leaving the masses distraught at not having even seen their idols.

A blame game quickly ensued between Beatles management and Milwaukee police. The fans blamed the police, feeling that the sixty-five police officers and thirty-two sheriffs' deputies on hand were enough to keep the crowd under control and the group safe enough for a closer debarkation. The police shot back, informing the media that it was the Beatles' management that had directed the plane to a remote area. The airport snub became the focal point of the press conference, supplanting the usual questions about hair length, pimples, and what the boys ate for breakfast. With John absent, the three remaining Beatles were relentlessly grilled. Paul vehemently denied any Beatles

PRIVATE COLLECTION (2)

involvement. "The police told us we couldn't go past [the fans]," he told the press. "It's mean not to let them have a wave. It's a lousy deal—a dirty trick." When the press blamed Beatles manager Brian Epstein for the decision to land farther away, Paul came to his defense. "It's a lie," he said. "Our manager wasn't even on the plane." George added, "It was a dirty lying policeman who said that."

The promoters for the Milwaukee concert were Franklin Fried of Chicago-based Triangle Theatrical Productions and Nick Topping (born Nick Topitzes), the company's Milwaukee representative. Fried

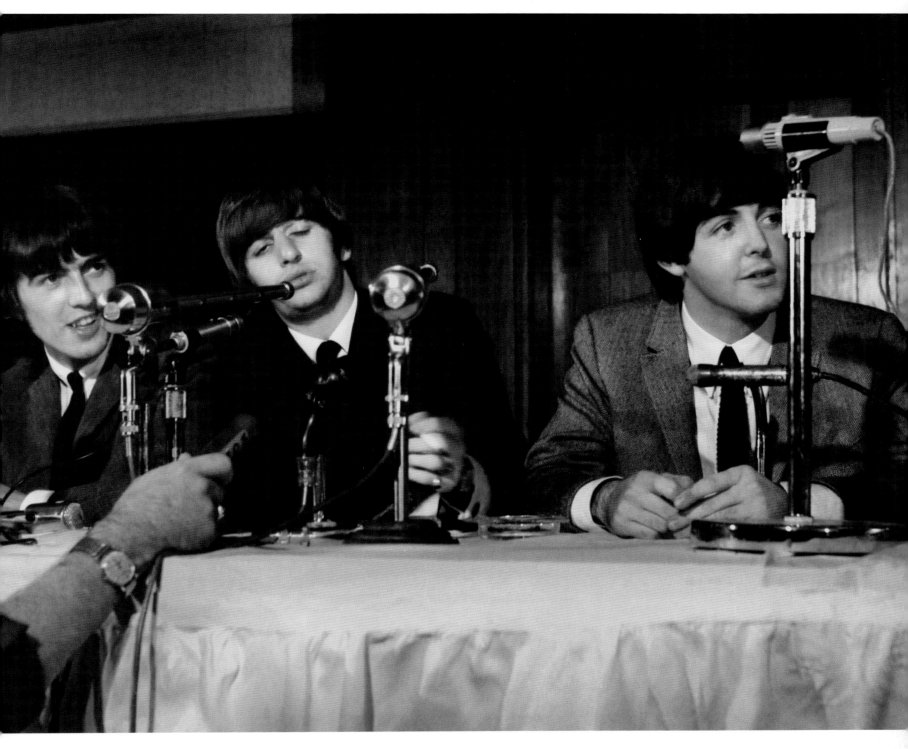

began his career in the entertainment business after becoming unemployed as a welder. Fortunately, he was a good friend of Al Grossman, who later managed the careers of Bob Dylan and Peter, Paul and Mary. Grossman needed a gofer, and Fried took the job. Later, with some much-needed experience under his belt, Fried launched Triangle Theatrical Productions.

Topping, the son of Greek immigrants, ran an import store on Milwaukee's south side for more than fifty years. He began promoting ethnic and folk music concerts in the 1950s and '60s, and brought to Milwaukee such diverse acts as South Africa's Miriam Makeba, Pete Seeger, and Mikis Theodorakis (composer for the film *Zorba the Greek*). After the Beatles' appearance on *The Ed Sullivan Show*, Fried contacted Topping about booking the Beatles into Milwaukee. Topping, later a well-known activist in the peace and civil rights movements, liked the fact that the Beatles supported peace and equality.

On April 17, 1964, Fried's Triangle Theatrical Productions signed a contract with NEMS Enterprises to present the Beatles in the city. The group was guaranteed $20,000 plus 60 percent of the gross. On

George, Ringo and Paul take questions from the Milwaukee press. It was the band's fifteenth concert in seventeen days, and Ringo's face shows the effects of touring.

West Wisconsin Avenue at 19th

MILWAUKEE'S PRESTIGE MOTOR INN

that same day, Fried signed another contract to present the group in his hometown of Chicago on the night following the Milwaukee concert (September 5).

Bob Barry, the evening personality for radio station WOKY, was asked by Fried to emcee the show. He initially turned down the opportunity after learning he wouldn't be paid for it. Hearing of his decision, music director Arline Quier told the deejay that "he was out of his mind" and convinced him to accept, but by then, Fried had already asked the number-one deejay from WRIT to do the honors. With Barry's

Milwaukee Auditorium — Sept. 4 — Milwaukee

Promoter Franklin Fried printed a special souvenir program for the concert in Milwaukee, as well as for the Chicago show the following night.

persistence, however, backed by an impressive following on WOKY, Fried was persuaded to relent and give him the job. With Barry at the helm, WOKY was the only station allowed to do a live broadcast of the group's arrival at General Mitchell Field.

Barry was also able to interview the group at the hotel, but the recorder containing the tape was stolen. The WOKY news department broadcast a public plea for its safe return, and an anonymous caller soon revealed its exact location: on the fourth pew in the chapel at St. Francis Convent on

The Milwaukee program contained an error switching the names of John and George underneath their respective faces. The similar program for Chicago the next night was corrected

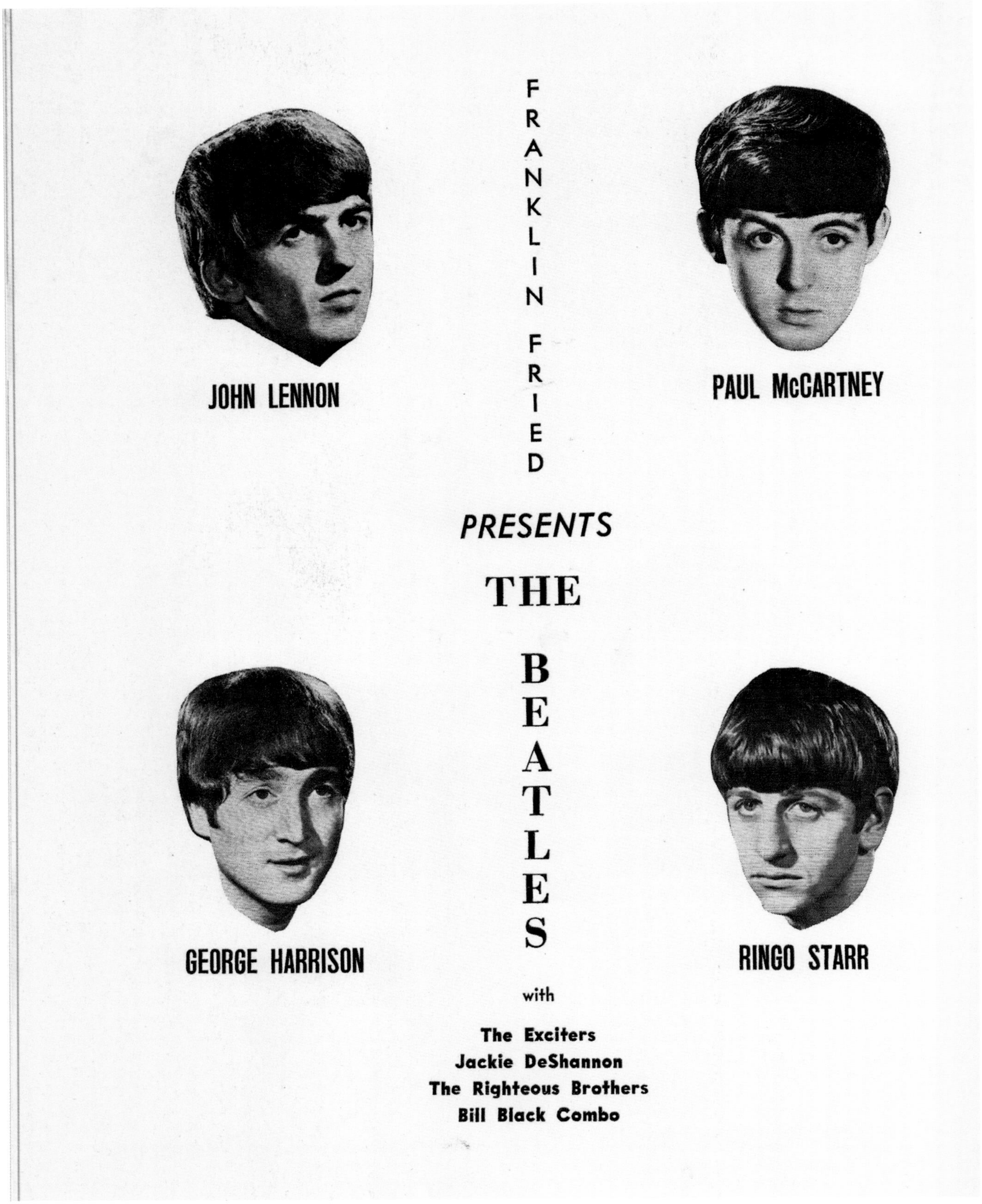
FRANKLIN FRIED
PRESENTS
THE
BEATLES
JOHN LENNON
PAUL McCARTNEY
GEORGE HARRISON
RINGO STARR
with
The Exciters
Jackie DeShannon
The Righteous Brothers
Bill Black Combo

South 27th Street in Milwaukee. Fortunately for Barry and WOKY, it was precisely where the informant said it would be.

The Beatles' Milwaukee accommodations were on the seventh floor of the Coach House Motor Inn at 1926 West Wisconsin Avenue. Because of the hotel's cutting-edge design, the Beatles' rooms had views to the east, south, and west. As usual, Pinkerton guards had a notable presence at the hotel and blocked entry to anyone unable to produce a room key.

PRIVATE COLLECTION (2)

WOKY'S Bob Barry (left) at General Mitchell Field, laden with gifts from fans for the Fab Four. Barry again poses (below) with Paul at the Coach House Inn the day after the show. He was a popular local DJ who introduced the Beatles on stage.

The venue chosen for the Beatles' one and only Wisconsin appearance was the Milwaukee Arena. Built in 1950, it was one of the first arenas to accommodate broadcast television, and the Beatles were the first big entertainment act to rock its halls. Seating for the concert was 12,000, though the arena had a usual capacity of 10,000 people. Those who attended the concert still recall the intense volume inside the building that night. The arena later served as home to the NBA's Milwaukee Bucks from 1968 to 1988.

When the Beatles left the Coach House for the concert, they found security tight in and around the Milwaukee Arena. About 150 police officers were on hand, including twenty assigned to guard the perimeter of the stage. Arena manager Elmer Krahn was so nervous about the concert that he decided to close all the concession stands in an effort to keep the corridors clear, despite the financial beating he would take with the loss of concession revenue.

As the doors to the arena opened at 6:30 p.m., several ticketless fans desperately tried to gain entry. One enterprising young man with Beatle-length hair tried to convince police he was Ringo's brother and demanded to be let inside. When denied, he became belligerent and was arrested. Later, at his court appearance, he was reprimanded by the judge, who told him to "go and get a haircut."

In between the press conference at the Coach House and the concert at the arena, reporter Larry Kane had the opportunity to conduct a backstage interview with the group. Of all the journalists who covered the tour, Kane posed some of the most thought-provoking questions. In this particular interview, he asked a few inane questions about the origins of jellybean throwing and George's opinion about cornflakes, but he also covered some serious topics: the mixing of entertainment with politics, the safety standards of American cars versus imports, the Beatles' opinions of presidential candidate Barry Goldwater and how to prevent war. Kane made the Beatles feel comfortable and, in turn, his line of questioning gave the public more reason to love the group. They would soon be regarded not only as musicians but as spokesmen for a generation striving to make its mark as a powerful political and social force.

Finally at 9:10 p.m., the Beatles took to the stage in blue silk suits. Bob Barry recalls the moment: "Jackie DeShannon finished her set, and I was told it would be about fifteen minutes before the Beatles were ready. I told every Beatles story I could think of and got a huge cheer just for mentioning their name. As soon as I brought up the airport, I was hit by boos from all over the arena. I quickly changed the subject, then finally got the signal that they were ready and I shout[ed], "The Beatles!"

PRIVATE COLLECTION (2)

Reporter Bernice Beresh of the *Milwaukee Sentinel* was assigned to cover the concert. She likened the stage entrance by the group to a "nuclear explosion" as the mostly younger crowd screamed their approval. As Bob Barry told it: "I was sitting right next to the stage and when the screams subsided momentarily, the music would cut through for ten or fifteen seconds and they sounded great! But being able to hear the group immediately reinvigorated the screamers and they'd drown them out again." Throughout their customary half-hour set, the boys were pelted with everything from hair rollers to flashbulbs. When it was over, they were whisked away by a black limousine that had been stationed by the east stage door at North 4th and West State Street.

One curiosity was the promoters' decision to stage another concert next to the Milwaukee Arena, during the Beatles' concert, so that fans without Beatles tickets could be entertained instead by several local bands. Nearly 3,000 teens, failing to see the Beatles, bought tickets to see bands such as the Galaxies, the Seven Sounds, and Mojo Man and the Pharaohs. A fight broke out at 10:45 p.m., however, causing police to shut the event down.

As the Beatles returned to the relative security of the Coach House Motor Inn, approxi-

The group leaves the Coach House Inn to catch a flight to Chicago, the next stop on the tour.

mately 450 raucous fans gathered outside, screaming to get the attention of any group member brave enough to wave from a window. It took a police-enforced midnight curfew to finally quell the crowd. The next day, local newspapers carrying the headline "Beatles Conquer City!" deemed the concert an overwhelming success. The frustrations surrounding their airport landing had already been forgotten. The press had a field day with the fuss and attention surrounding the group, wishing that Milwaukee Braves baseball fans could be as passionate in their efforts to keep the team from moving to Atlanta.

Before leaving town, Paul further captured the hearts of local fans with an act of kindness. Hearing about a fourteen-year-old girl who was hospitalized and unable to attend the previous night's performance, he picked up the phone and called her. Christine Cutler, surrounded in her room by hospital staff, took the prearranged call and was able to ask the bassist any question she wanted.

Early in the afternoon, four black limousines escorted by ten motorcycle cops drove the Beatles past nearly a thousand fans who had gathered at the Coach House to say their good-byes. As the motorcade

faded from view, scores of fans scurried into the hotel to find any souvenirs that may have been touched by a Beatle: cigarette butts, scraps of food, paper—at least until hotel personnel had the building cleared. Today, the Coach House serves as a dormitory for Marquette University students.

Arriving at General Mitchell Field, the group quickly boarded their plane—bound for Chicago, where they would play a single show at the International Amphitheatre that same evening. While they never returned to Milwaukee again, they did leave the city $30,000 richer.

Bob Barry, who became known as "Beatle Bob" after the concert, had these final thoughts: "It was the biggest emotional high of my life. Nothing else compares. It was just incredible. You couldn't believe the madness unless you were there. It changed my career. I became a local celebrity because I had emceed the Beatles concert and it honestly opened up doors for me. I'll never forget September 4, 1964!"

Like memorabilia from most stops on the tour, Milwaukee concert collectibles are incredibly hard to find. Only a few unused tickets have survived over the years, and even stubs are scarce. This was also the first instance on the tour when a program other than the generic U.S. tour program was offered. Triangle Theatrical Productions gave a specially printed program to concertgoers, and this piece has become quite collectible. It's interesting to note that, inside the program, John's and George's names are reversed under their respective pictures. No posters were printed to advertise the show.

The Beatles play in front of a sold-out Milwaukee Arena crowd of 12,000. Arena officials pushed the limit of the venue's capacity by adding 2,000 additional seats.

CHICAGO

September 5, 1964
International Ampitheatre
8:30 p.m.

The Beatles wave to the press and fans as they arrive in Chicago from Milwaukee. Two members of the Bill Black Combo can be seen in the plane windows on the left.

DURING VIRTUALLY ALL OF THE CONCERTS THEY'D PLAYED SO FAR on their North American tour, the Beatles had been pelted by just about every imaginable object, most notably jelly beans. But nothing could have prepared the group for the type of projectile they would face in Chicago. In this city known for its stockyards, at least one fan took aim at the group with … raw meat! As the band went through their onstage gyrations, Paul was hit in the breast pocket by a piece of steak hurled at close range, and his jacket was stained by the beef juice (though in some accounts, the purloined sirloin landed harmlessly near Ringo's drum kit). George, in disbelief, quickly kicked the meat to one side as Ringo leaned over his kit to get a better look. Other reports told of Paul getting hit squarely in the face by a spent flashbulb while never missing a beat. Just another typical evening at a Beatles concert.

Chicago, the thirteenth stop on the tour, was home to Vee-Jay Records, one of the Beatles' American labels. According to Beatles author and historian Bruce Spizer, the city's WLS was the first American

radio station to play a Beatles record ("Please Please Me"), reportedly as early as February 1963. The debut was inauspicious, however. Deejay Clark Weber recalled that he'd been supplied two singles by the Vee-Jay label and that the station played the recording for at least five weeks straight. The WLS deejays had been told by Vee-Jay reps that the group was hot in England. But, according to Weber, "the records just rolled over and died." The great state of Illinois had one additional Beatles tie: George's sister Louise lived in Benton, so, with the musician's visit to her there in September 1963, the state can lay claim to hosting the first-ever Beatle visit to America.

After a wild concert in Milwaukee, Wisconsin, the night before, the Beatles' chartered Electra arrived in the Windy City late in the afternoon of September 5. The group's grueling schedule was beginning to take its toll. Having played fifteen concerts in twelve cities in a span of only seventeen days—with

Approximately 5,000 fans met the Beatles at Midway Airport to welcome the Fab Four to the Windy City. Two homemade banners are on display.

The Beatles pose for photographers during a press conference at the city's famed Stockyard Inn, which was adjacent to the International Amphitheatre. Note Ringo's button showing his support for a local Chicago area fan club.

CHICAGO SUN-TIMES

During the press conference at the Stockyard Inn's Saddle and Sirloin restaurant, Paul said he missed seeing "gangsters with their broad hats and ties," an obvious reference to the city's history. Ringo was presented with a special gold snare drum from Ludwig company president, William Ludwig Jr. A bus pass (right) that brought fans to the concert from the surrounding Chicago suburbs.

just four days of rest since the tour began—they were exhausted. Indeed, one Chicago journalist commented on their gaunt appearance.

The flight from Milwaukee would be the shortest on the summer '64 tour, but instead of landing at O'Hare International as scheduled, city officials diverted the plane to nearby Midway Airport. By keeping the switch a secret, they'd hoped for a quiet arrival. Instead, word leaked to the media through local P.R. man Alan Edelson, sending thousands of fans to the Butler Aviation terminal to welcome the group. Mayor Richard Daley's director of special events, Jack Reilly, was furious at Edelson and called the media leak one of the "cheapest publicity stunts in the history of the United States." The beleaguered Reilly admonished the P.R. man, saying that he was going to remove police protection and that the Beatles would likely "get torn apart." Reilly further threatened Edelson with jail for attempting to incite a riot.

At the time of the Beatles' arrival, Chicago was still reeling from the Dixmoor race riot of August 16–17. As the band's plane touched down, Reilly grabbed a bullhorn and tried to quell the crowd of 5,000 as countless girls tried to scale the four-foot-high cyclone fence that bordered the runway.

BEATLES EXCURSION

Good for one transfer
by Chicago Transit Authority
Chartered Bus
from Sherman Hotel
to International Amphitheatre

7:00 PM CDT — Saturday, Sepbember

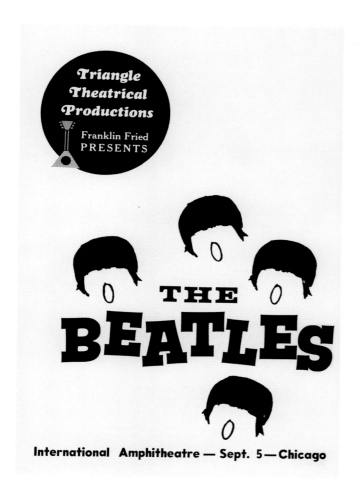

Triangle Theatrical Productions

Franklin Fried PRESENTS

THE BEATLES

International Amphitheatre — Sept. 5 — Chicago

See "THE BEATLES"
International Amphitheatre
September 5, 1964

CHICAGO SUN-TIMES
BEATLE BATTLE SALES CONTEST

This is to introduce

ScottSatten
(write your own name here)

who is selling subscriptions to the Chicago Sun-Times in order to win free tickets to the Beatles' performance at the International Amphitheatre on September 5 . . . and to earn extra summer cash. Thank you for helping, and we hope you'll enjoy Chicago's Bright One—The Sun-Times—every day.

Circulation Department
Chicago Sun-Times

Chicago cop Anthony Dizonne commented, "This is like Frank Sinatra multiplied by fifty or a hundred. These Beatles make about 50 million bucks a year and they don't even have to buy a haircut in this country."

Chicago would be another drop-in date, as the Beatles were whisked by motorcade from Midway Airport to Chicago's famed Stockyard Inn restaurant. Here they would eat dinner and conduct a press conference at the inn's Saddle and Sirloin Club. They would perform their concert at the venue next door and then leave the city in a driving summer thunderstorm late that same evening, bound for Detroit, Michigan,

CHICAGO SUN-TIMES
BEATLE BATTLE SALES CONTEST
401 N. WABASH AVE.
CHICAGO, ILL. 60611

See "THE BEATLES"
International Amphitheatre
September 5, 1964

Scott Satten
8853 Lowell Terrace
Skokie, Ill.

and another two-performance night. They would never get to see "gangsters with their broad hats and ties"—a common association with Chicago that Paul mentioned at the press conference.

Other highlights of the press conference included a girl with handcuffs, who apparently had designs on Paul and wanted to cuff herself to him to forge a lasting bond; fortunately for him, her clever ploy failed. Meanwhile, Ringo was presented with a special one-of-a-kind gold snare drum by Ludwig Drum Company president William Ludwig Jr., who said, "I have never known a drummer more widely acclaimed and publicized than you…. Your millions of fans have honored you and the other members of the Beatles by their overwhelming acceptance of your recordings and concert appearances. On behalf of the employees and management of the Ludwig Drum Company, I would like to thank you for choosing our instruments and for the major role you are playing in the music world today." A "Super-Sensitive" model, the drum bore a plaque reading "Ringo Starr, The Beatles."

The Chicago venue was the International Amphitheatre, the same indoor arena where the group would play two years later, as they kicked off their 1966 North American tour. Located on the city's

A special program was produced for the show (top left), something rarely done. The International Amphitheatre (top right) site of the 1964 and 1966 concerts. The *Chicago Sun-Times* (above) held ticket giveaway contests.

CHICAGO HISTORY MUSEUM/PHOTOGRAPHER: ROBERT ARVIDSON

south side at 42nd and Halsted Streets, it was built in 1934 by the Union Stockyard Company for the purpose of hosting the International Livestock Exhibition. Through the years, the arena witnessed many memorable music and sporting events. Elvis Presley debuted his famous gold lamé suit at a 1957 concert. The English group UFO recorded the album Strangers in the Night there, and the Chicago Bulls played their inaugural season there in 1966–67. But perhaps the most famous event at the arena was the tumultuous 1968 Democratic National Convention that erupted in riots and violence.

The promoters for the Beatles show were Franklin Fried and Dick Gassen of Triangle Theatrical Productions. Fried had teamed with Nick Topping to present the Milwaukee, Wisconsin, appearance the previous day. As he had for the Milwaukee show, Fried arranged a contract with General Artists Corporation (GAC) for a guarantee of $20,000 plus 60 percent of the gross.

Perhaps the most famous usher in history was also involved in this concert—Jack Gallagher of Andy Frain Services, Inc. The Frain Company specialized in ushering and security in the Chicago area. Its employees were easily recognized for their distinctive blue and gold uniforms and captain hats. Gallagher provided security for heads of state, sports personalities, politicians, and entertainers and was closely associated with the Beatles during all three of their Chicago appearances. He remembers the 1964 visit as chaotic but organized. He held the group in the general manager's office for several hours before the concert and was instructed to turn away anyone lacking credentials. Not even *Playboy* publicist Benny Dunn was allowed inside to interview the group. Beatles manager Brian Epstein requested that Gallagher's assistant, Lester Modesti, find a hair dryer for one of the Beatles—which Dunn, lurking around backstage, thought odd because at that time no man would use such a device.

At 9:20 p.m., the Beatles ascended the gold cloth–draped stairway leading to the stage and played their usual half-hour concert. On the plane after the show, journalist Larry Kane summed up the Beatles' performance in the notes he jotted down: "Ringo beating the drums so hard. Wonder how he can hear what's going on with the crowd noise. Looks around. Smiling. George kicks the slab of meat off the stage. McCartney and Lennon face-to-face, cheek-to-cheek, almost in perfect

One of the few images of the boys on stage at the International Amphitheatre. The group played to a sold-out, enthusiastic crowd as Andy Frain Company ushers and other officials tried to maintain order.

Officials at the International Amphitheatre wrote letters like the one pictured to the right, that the concert was indeed sold out and no second show had been added. Some promoters balked at hosting a second show, when offered by GAC, fearing the Beatles popularity was a just a passing fad.

INTERNATIONAL AMPHITHEATRE

43rd & HALSTED STREETS • CHICAGO • PHONE YArds 7-5580

July 9, 1964

Dear *Miss Uriche*

We regret that all tickets for the "Beatles" Concert at the International Amphitheatre, Saturday Evening, September 5th, 1964, have been sold and we cannot fill your order.

It was erroneously reported in a Chicago newspaper that the management of this building had reserved $5,000.00 worth of tickets. The facts are that regular patrons of the International Amphitheatre ordered many tickets. We purchased no tickets because we believe our patrons, Beatle fans, and especially teenagers should have had first call on admission tickets.

There is a false report that a second performance will be given. There will be one performance only at the International Amphitheatre, Saturday Evening, September 5th, 1964.

Should the "Beatles" return to the International Amphitheatre at a later date, we will notify you well in advance so that you may have a better opportunity to secure tickets. Your name is on file.

Unfortunately, there have been ten applications for each available seat. We regret that you and your friends were not among the one-in-ten lucky ones.

Very truly yours,

M. E. Thayer
Manager

MET/s

harmony on 'I Want to Hold Your Hand.' Girl behind me puts arms over my shoulders, reaching out to try and grab Paul's shoes. Her face is pressed against the strap of the tape recorder. Cop has arms spread out to prevent movement toward stage. Breathing difficult. Sweating loads. Girl in rear crying...."

Aside from the customary jelly beans tossed onstage—and that slab of beef—it was reported that a yellow stuffed animal, a jump rope, and a red rubber ball also landed at the Beatles' feet. (The ball might have been more appropriate for the group's 1966 performances, when supporting act the Cyrkle opened with their hit "Red Rubber Ball.")

It took 170 Andy Frain ushers and usherettes, along with 320 police officers, firemen, and other protective agency personnel, to quell the crowd. The thirty-five usherettes who worked the show had to be carefully selected to make certain that none were prone to hysteria.

Leighton McLaughlin, a reporter for the *Chicago Sun-Times,* wrote, "If the energy expended by the fans were directed properly, the United States could have a man on the moon tomorrow." In breaking down the financial prowess of the band, McLaughlin further reported, "In a sense, however, the energy has been captured. The Beatles made roughly $250 a man per minute. That is $15,000 an hour, or $600,000 for a forty-hour week. With fifty-two weeks in a year and with paid vacation, that's $31,200,000 a year apiece. But, of course, they don't work full-time."

Despite these financial claims, one Beatle quipped to the press that he had come to the United States with $150 in his pocket to spend on incidentals, but to date hadn't spent a dime. Bill Diehl, who covered the show for the *Pioneer Press* in Minnesota, commented that the Beatles "came, saw, [and] conquered. They were cool, calm, and collected—cool despite the crush, calm despite the turmoil, and collected about $30,000 for twenty-five minutes of work! And it was worth every penny."

In the aftermath of the $1,000-per-minute show, Beatles publicist Derek Taylor commented, "I hope I never see this place again—too hot and sticky." His wish would come true. By the time the Beatles returned to the venue for two shows in 1966, Taylor was long gone from their organization.

The Beatles had conquered New York, Los Angeles, and now Chicago. With another successful performance under their belt, they left the stage at the International Amphitheatre and were immediately driven to the airport for their short flight east to Detroit, where they'd play two shows. The amphitheatre survived for another thirty-five years, but with the addition of the sprawling McCormick Place on the city's lakefront and the construction of suburban sporting arenas, the sixty-five-year-old venue fell to the wrecking ball in August 1999.

Collectibles from the Chicago concert consist of the generic U.S. tour program as well as a specially produced program from Triangle Theatrical Productions. No posters or handbills were generated, and tickets are rare.

The Beatles earned $1,000 per minute for their short appearance on the International Amphitheatre's stage. The group would leave the stage and immediately fly to Detroit.

DETROIT

September 6, 1964
Olympia Stadium
Two Shows, 2 p.m. and 6 p.m.

Olympia Stadium, an indoor venue, played host to the Beatles in 1964 and 1966. Locals referred to the venue as the "Old Red Barn."

THE BEATLES' PLANE FROM CHICAGO ARRIVED AT DETROIT'S METROPOLITAN AIRPORT at 12:30 a.m. on Sunday, September 6. Three thousand fans waited patiently for their arrival. The group waved a quick hello before climbing into their limousines for the twenty-five-mile ride into the city. Everything seemed to be going according to plan when the police flanking the motorcade suddenly pulled away, leaving the group and their entourage completely exposed. Suddenly the fans who'd been following the motorcade were swerving dangerously close, trying to get the boys' attention. The wild ride into the city finally ended when the caravan entered the heavily fortified Whittier Hotel parking garage. Press releases had led many to believe that the group was booked at the downtown Sheraton Cadillac. That hotel's switchboard had been deluged with thousands of calls and its premises besieged with fans. Once the truth came out, the hordes made a mad dash to the Whittier Hotel.

The Whittier opened for business in 1927 as a combination hotel and apartment building. It was particularly popular during the Prohibition era, attracting the criminal element because of its location on the Detroit River and its proximity to Canada. Located at 415 Burns Drive, the hotel is listed on the National Register of Historic Places. The group was escorted to executive suite 1566, where they were still too wired to sleep. Instead, they stayed up most of the night eating dinner, playing cards, and listening to the radio. Ringo indulged in some television, watching a succession of old westerns and sci-fi flicks.

The formidable Olympia Stadium, better known to locals as the Detroit Olympia or, more fondly, as the Old Red Barn, was located on Grand River Avenue and played host to two Beatles shows on September 6—one each in the afternoon and evening—and then again for two shows on August 13, 1966. Home to the NHL's Red Wings hockey team, it was built in 1927 and stood for sixty years before falling to the wrecking ball in 1987. A National Guard Armory now stands on the site.

The promoter for the 1964 Detroit show was Art Schurgin, working in conjunction with Olympia Stadium. Schurgin brought in management from

Beauty queens from Detroit and surrounding states get up close and personal with the Fab Four. This was a common occurrence in cities throughout North America. Top picture (from left): Paul, Ann Marston (1960 Miss Michigan), George, Judy Callison (Miss Vermont), John, Diane Cenate (Miss Armed Forces), and Ringo.

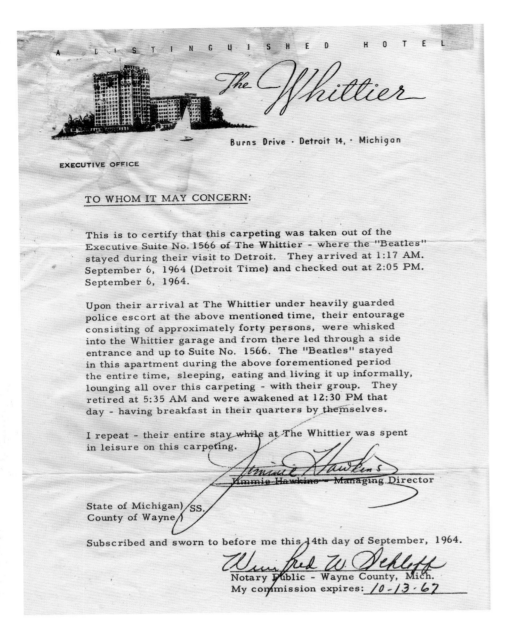

A DISTINGUISHED HOTEL

The *Whittier*

Burns Drive · Detroit 14, · Michigan

EXECUTIVE OFFICE

TO WHOM IT MAY CONCERN:

This is to certify that this carpeting was taken out of the Executive Suite No. 1566 of The Whittier - where the "Beatles" stayed during their visit to Detroit. They arrived at 1:17 AM. September 6, 1964 (Detroit Time) and checked out at 2:05 PM. September 6, 1964.

Upon their arrival at The Whittier under heavily guarded police escort at the above mentioned time, their entourage consisting of approximately forty persons, were whisked into the Whittier garage and from there led through a side entrance and up to Suite No. 1566. The "Beatles" stayed in this apartment during the above forementioned period the entire time, sleeping, eating and living it up informally, lounging all over this carpeting - with their group. They retired at 5:35 AM and were awakened at 12:30 PM that day - having breakfast in their quarters by themselves.

I repeat - their entire stay while at The Whittier was spent in leisure on this carpeting.

Jimmie Hawkins - Managing Director

State of Michigan) SS.
County of Wayne)

Subscribed and sworn to before me this 14th day of September, 1964.

Notary Public - Wayne County, Mich.
My commission expires: 10-13-67

A letter (above) from the Hotel Whittier, where the Beatles stayed, attests to the fact that the group "lounged all over the carpeting." A swatch (right) of the prized carpet.

the Olympia because of the large appearance fee—$30,000—required by the Beatles and General Artists Corporation (GAC). Nick Londes, general manager of the Olympia, recalled it as the highest fee ever paid for an entertainment act in Detroit, surpassing even Elvis Presley (whom they had brought several years earlier).

Schurgin booked all the big acts that came through Detroit, and because he and Norm Weiss of GAC were good friends, he was able to strike a deal to present the Beatles. Believing that the demand for tickets would be huge, Schurgin gambled on two performances. His instinct paid off. When tickets went on sale near the end of April, there were huge lines at the Olympia— so much so that he convinced a local beverage company to donate thirty to forty cases of soda to offer to waiting fans.

Schurgin did do no promotion for the concerts, instead relying on local radio to talk them up. WKNR not only had the largest share of the four stations in Detroit but also enjoyed a great relationship with Capitol Records. As a result, it was only logical that the station would be the official radio sponsor of the Beatles' appearance. (Interestingly, it was also WKNR that originated the "Paul Is Dead" rumor in the fall of 1969. Legendary deejay Russ Gibb's "Turn Me On Dead Man" was the standard when it came to fans searching for clues to Paul's purported death in a car crash.)

Deejay Bob Green was chosen to emcee the 2 p.m. show. He and a few fellow WKNR deejays went onstage bearing all the gifts that had been sent to the station by fans. He thought this might be a good way to fill time and quiet the crowd. When the time came for Green to introduce the Beatles, he'd gotten only as far as "And now..." when Paul McCartney popped his head out from backstage, sending the crowd into a frenzy. Promoter Schurgin (who died in 2003) vividly recalled the show: "The thing I remember the most was the flashbulbs. I've never seen so many go off in my life. It totally lit up the concert the whole time. It was as though someone had turned on the house lights and left them on during the entire performance. The screams were deafening. I don't know how the Beatles could have heard themselves play." Indeed, the police lining the perimeter of the stage were seen putting bullets in their ears in an attempt to block the nonstop roar of the crowd.

After a rousing performance, the Beatles were ushered backstage for their press conference. Fans were already queuing up for the 6 p.m. second performance as the beleaguered boys began to field questions from the Detroit press, including "Which artist or musical group do you think has most influenced

BOB BENYAS

your music?" Paul immediately answered "American colored groups," to which George added, "In fact, the Detroit sound. Tamla Motown artists are our favorites—the Miracles, the Impressions, Marvin Gaye, Mary Wells, the Exciters." John quipped, "Major Lance, to name but eighty."

John had obviously mixed up his black artists, as Major Lance was a leading force in the Chicago soul movement of the early 1960s. Still, the Beatle had nothing but high praise for Berry Gordy Jr.'s stable of talent at Motown. Detroit was the heart and soul of the Beatles' musical roots, but with only twenty-three hours in town, the group simply had no time to explore the city.

Once again, the subject of segregation was broached: "We've heard that you won't play in Jacksonville if they don't allow Negroes into the show," said one reporter. "Is that right?" Paul replied, "We understand that they let them sit in the balcony but not on the main floor and that is part of our contract—that we will not appear unless they're allowed to sit anywhere." John explained further, "We never play to segregated audiences and we're not going to start now. I would rather lose our appearance money."

Gerry Barker of the *Toronto Daily Star* asked George if the tour had started to wear on them. "To us this is a job," George replied. "We're getting used to living in hotel rooms, you know. If we didn't like it, we would bag it right now and go home."

The city of Detroit spawned both a "Stamp Out the Beatles" campaign (in 1964) and a "Paul Is Dead" rumor (in 1969). One can still purchase "Stamp Out the Beatles" sweatshirts in the style worn by manager Brian Epstein and George Harrison, and from time to time late-night radio rebroadcasts deejay Russ Gibbs's morbid clues pointing to Paul's rumored death in a 1966 car crash.

The Beatles pose for the press before taking their questions, which were becoming redundant.

The Sunliners (above), a local Detroit band was pegged to record a parody of Beatles hits. Recording under the name the Hi-Riders, they were at the forefront of the "Stamp Out the Beatles" campaign. Brian Epstein's personal sweat shirt (right) that went to auction. He and George were later photographed wearing these sweatshirts, tongue in cheek, of course.

KEENER LPs

1. More of Roy Orbison's Greatest Hits..................Monument
2. Make Way for Dionne Warwick.........................Scepter
3. All Summer Long—Beach Boys.........................Capitol

KEY LP OF THE WEEK

WHERE DID OUR LOVE GO—SUPREMES.....................MOTOWN

Your First Exclusive Photo!
Keener and The Beatles Backstage at Olympia!

1st of a series

WKNR newsman George Hunter interviews Ringo Starr. In the background are Keener's Gary Stevens and Bob Green, and to the right is Robin Seymour.

WKNR's weekly record survey, detailing the most popular hits, was printed for their listeners and often included photographs. Local radio stations would go to battle for the right to promote a Beatles' show. WKNR had the largest audience share in the area and a great relationship with Capitol Records. Note the look of exhaustion on Ringo's face.

The former campaign had already been addressed seven months earlier at JFK Airport, during the Beatles' first American press conference. As the group faced reporters just moments after arriving in America, one journalist said, "In Detroit, Michigan, they're handing out car stickers saying 'Stamp Out the Beatles.'" Paul snapped back, "Yeah well, first of all we're bringing out a Stamp Out Detroit campaign."

The "Stamp Out the Beatles" campaign began in early 1964, perhaps more as a promotional stunt than as a serious attempt to rid America of the Beatles. According to a member of the Sunliners, a local Detroit band, a law firm approached them after one of their gigs and asked if they were interested in

The Beatles in performance at the "Old Red Barn." The group played two shows, one at 2 p. m. and another at 6 p.m.

TONY SPINA/WALTER P. REUTHER LIBRARY

recording a parody single titled "Stamp Out the Beatles." The band saw it as nothing more than cashing in on a trend, but nonetheless agreed. To guard their reputation, though, they changed their name to the Hi-Riders and signed a one-record deal with Scepter Records of New York.

The record was released but experienced limited exposure and success due to legal injunctions initiated by Epstein himself to block its airplay. (An interesting side note: The Sunliners eventually morphed into Rare Earth, whose twenty-one-minute version of Smokey Robinson's "Get Ready" filled the entire second side of their first Motown album in 1970.)

After the press conference and customary opening acts, the Beatles took the stage for their evening performance. WKNR'S Bob Green also had the pleasure of emceeing the second show and remembers having to "ad-lib for about eight minutes while the Beatles got ready to come on stage." He recalls that "the second show became a blur, as my head was still spinning from the noise at the afternoon show." He was prepared for what he called a "sonic boom" as the Beatles ran onstage, though, and simply yelled, "The Beatles!" Of course "the place exploded as they came on. It was wild!" Green recounts: "Knowing I was one of only like seventy people that ever introduced the Beatles in North America, I would say it was something special." Still, he regrets not having saved anything from the concert or asked for their autographs. "What can I say?" he laments. "I was more into the audio stuff."

Tony Spina of the *Detroit Free Press* shot this classic image of the group (left) on stage. The strain of the fast paced tour is clear to see on all four of their faces. Paul and George (below) share the mic. Paul looks considerably more energized than does George!

BOB BENYAS

During the performance, journalist Larry Kane, who had seen jelly beans, pins, stuffed animals, raw meat, and shoes thrown onstage, witnessed a new one as "a young lady from up in the balcony took a beautiful gold watch and threw it on the floor of the stage." Kane noticed a policeman pick it up and take it to lost and found. The timepiece was, in Kane's words, "inscribed to a certain name and a beautiful keepsake." He was dumbfounded that anyone would intentionally toss away such a valued and sentimental piece.

The Beatles made far more money than what promoter Schurgin promised for the two performances, doubling the $30,000 guarantee with a payout of $60,000.

After the Beatles checked out of their hotel suite and left for Olympia Stadium the next day, it took nearly 200 policemen to clear the hotel of fans, some still hiding out hours after the entourage had

Flowers thrown onto Ringo's drum platform (far left) as the boys rock the crowd at the Olympia. George (left), enjoying a moment onstage with Paul.

departed. Subsequently, almost everything the band had touched, slept on, or bathed with was pillaged for commercial purposes and sold. An offer of $50 for the doorknob to their suite was politely declined, but the nine-year-old carpeting was purchased by the Alan Lori Carpet Company for $1,500 and cut up into squares that sold for $1 each. The Chicago office of ABC-TV got into the act as well, purchasing all the group's bedding for $400, then cutting up the linens and giving them away to *American Bandstand* contestants.

Jimmy Hawkins, ABC-TV's general manager, even had Whittier management toss in a Ringo-used washcloth and towel. As reported by the *Detroit Daily Press,* Hawkins needed to use a phone while with the Beatles, but all the noise in the band's living room forced him to use the one in the bathroom. Pushing open the lavatory door, he nearly knocked Ringo off his feet while he was shaving, "hitting his arm and almost cutting his throat."

Mementos from the Detroit concerts are sparse, with only tickets and the generic U.S. tour program available to collectors. Schurgin had no need to print posters, handbills, or special programs, as the concert sold out almost immediately. He later recalled selling $6,000 to $7,000 worth of tickets himself. Despite the Beatles' take of nearly $60,000, the promoter remembered that "the money never evened out for me." Full tickets and stubs from either performance are seldom offered for sale.

After the Motown shows, the boys were rushed to Metropolitan Airport, where they boarded their plane for the short hop north to Toronto and their second official performance on Canadian soil.

TORONTO

September 7, 1964
Maple Leaf Gardens
Two Shows, 2:30 p.m. and 8:30 p.m.

Storied Maple Leaf Gardens. The Beatles played six shows at the Gardens, the most of any venue during the three years they toured North America.

DURING THE BEATLES' PRESS CONFERENCE BETWEEN SHOWS at Toronto's famed Maple Leaf Gardens, an aging newsman posed one of the more frequently asked questions: "How long do you think you'll last?" John wasted no time with his somewhat caustic comeback: "Longer than you anyway."

The Beatles found themselves on Canadian soil once again a mere twelve days after performing in Vancouver. The Beatles Canadian Fan Club, an ardent and dedicated group led by Trudy Medcalf, boasted the largest membership of any Beatles club—54,000 die-hards. There was no question that Toronto was ready for its "B-Day," when the group would perform two shows to a packed Labor Day audience.

Before that could take place, however, there would be weeks of heated negotiations between General Artists Corporation (GAC), Beatles manager Brian Epstein, and two of the Maple Leaf Gardens' top executives—president Stafford Smythe and owner Harold Ballard (known as one of the "most loved and hated men in Canada"). GAC's original planning schedule for the tour gave Epstein two options: one show at the Gardens for a $15,000 guarantee or one show at Toronto's famed CNE Exposition Grounds for a bigger crowd and an even larger guarantee of $40,000. Epstein had told Norman Weiss of GAC that he wanted the Gardens.

Ballard and Smythe initially booked only one show, even though GAC and Epstein tried to convince them to book two. A contract was signed on April 16 for a larger-than-estimated $20,000 guarantee plus 60 percent of the gross. After seeing the high demand for tickets, Ballard and Smythe contacted Epstein to request a second performance; in the manager's mind, however, they'd missed their opportunity. Too much time had lapsed, and the tour was set.

Ballard and Smythe remained resolute and pursued Epstein and GAC regarding a second show. The tour organizers eventually relented, but it would come at a high price to the Gardens' top brass. On May 6, another contract was signed that added an afternoon show at an increased rate of $25,000 plus 70 percent of the gross. Both contracts were signed by Gardens executive Henry F. Bolton, with full approval from Smythe and Ballard. Marvin Kane, the promoter for the Montreal shows scheduled for the next day, had also been successful in securing two shows. Now the already-harried group would be playing six shows in just three days.

John and Ringo, flanked by security, above) make a mad dash to the elevator of the King Edward Hotel. The Beatles in between shows (left) giving a press conference to a large gathering of journalists.

Immediately before the press conference, the boys posed for photographers (above and right) behind Ringo's black oyster pearl Ludwig drum kit and then met with lucky fans (below) who were able to get up close and personal with the Fab Four.

Things would have worked out differently for Smythe and Ballard had Epstein gone with Norm Weiss's suggestion to play New York City's Freedomland. Those gigs would have taken place over a three-day period (September 5, 6, and 7), leaving the Toronto promoters to scurry for another date.

On a cold, rainy day in late spring, fans began queuing up in front of Maple Leaf Gardens to secure tickets for the September 7 concerts. At the head of the line was eighteen-year-old Robin Timmerman, who had staked out her spot a full seventy-three hours before the windows opened. For many of the fans, maintaining a place in line meant skipping school. Because of the rampant class-cutting, the Toronto Board of Education actually considered sending a truant officer down to the Gardens, but ultimately decided that each principal could discipline the Beatles-crazed students under his or her watch. Smythe and Ballard, sensing a photo opportunity, donned Beatles wigs and ventured into the cold to serve coffee to the crowd. Rival radio stations CHUM and CKEY were parked on each side of the Garden and sending news crews to secure on-the-spot interviews with fans. In the midst of all this, the Gardens was playing host to the fifth game of the Stanley Cup Finals and had to issue numbered cards so Beatles fans could come back the next morning and claim their rightful position in line. Tickets sold out quickly, which spelled disappointment for the thousands of fans still lined up for blocks in all directions.

YORK UNIVERSITY LIBRARY, CLARA THOMAS ARCHIVES & SPECIAL COLLECTIONS, TORONTO TELEGRAM FONDS (3)

The Beatles arrive in Toronto, the second of three Canadian cities they visited on the summer tour.

The King Edward Hotel or "King Eddy" (right) as the locals called it. The group stayed at the hotel all three times they visited Toronto. Schick placed ads (below) on the back of the evening performance ticket.

At 12:30 a.m. on Monday, September 7, the Beatles' chartered aircraft descended into Toronto's Malton Airport fresh from two concert performances in Detroit, Michigan. An estimated 7,000 to 10,000 fans had been waiting patiently in the darkness for their idols to arrive. Police dubbed the fence that separated the fans from the runway "the little Berlin Wall." Pressed against the fence, the fans sang "O Canada" (the Canadian national anthem), changing the lyrics from "O Canada! Our home and native land!" to "O Beatles! Our idols true and dear!" Journalist Larry Kane remembers that "the crowd was so loud that we could hear the people screaming over the sound of the turboprop engines."

Upon landing, custom officials rapidly boarded the plane more on a mission to meet the four pop stars and obtain their autographs than to check them through customs. George commented to a reporter that he despised signing his name for officials, journalists, police, and friends of the promoters. The Beatles' serious fans, he felt, were those who waited for hours in the cold hoping to catch a glimpse of the group, and they were rarely rewarded.

In Toronto, the Beatles barely had time to wave to fans before being herded into limousines and spirited away. A few eyewitnesses said it took all of twenty-six seconds from the time they left the plane until they were gone, and that only about five hundred of the thousands of fans present saw them at all. Fans were further disappointed when the limousines escaped along a restricted service road and onto the main highway, well ahead of those trying to pursue them. To add insult to injury, the police had falsely informed early arrivals that the Beatles' convoy would definitely leave from the main airport entrance, further frustrating fans who had lined both sides of the highway for quite some distance.

The Beatles' entourage was booked to stay at the Sheraton King Edward Hotel at 37 King Street East. Opened in 1903 and now designated by the Ontario Heritage Trust as a historic landmark, the hotel has welcomed such guests as Mark Twain, Margaret Thatcher, and Britney Spears. Known by locals as the "King Eddy," the hotel had never witnessed pure bedlam until the Beatles arrived. With over 5,000 crazed fans swarming the area, the 100 police officers assigned to control the crowd (including mounted horsemen) proved woefully inadequate. When the Beatles' caravan reached the hotel well after 1 a.m., the police line virtually collapsed, spilling fans onto the cars transporting the boys. The hysterical teenagers pounded on the car windows and latches in a desperate attempt to get to their idols. Luckily, the police were able to momentarily regroup and form a human shield to safely escort the band into the lobby. Even so, Paul's shirt was torn. John later commented that "the best view of the country is over the blue shoulder of a policeman."

When it came to seeing the Beatles up close and personal, most fans were kept at bay. But a pair of enterprising twin sisters had a scheme that seemed foolproof. Edith and Herta Manea had cased the King Edward Hotel in the months prior to the Beatles' arrival, taking note of every nook and cranny—back staircases, elevators, and service doors—until they stumbled on an idea they hoped would prove successful. The sisters noticed a key-drop box next to the front lobby doors that afforded guests the luxury of a quick checkout in lieu of leaving their key at the front desk. Noting several discarded keys inside, the girls used a thin stick covered with chewing gum on one end to fish through the opening and retrieve a key. Now, with a key in hand, the sisters had full run of the hotel.

On the night of the Beatles' arrival, the Manea girls sneaked out of their bedroom at 11 p.m., dressed in clothes that made them appear a bit older. With room key in hand, they casually strolled past security, flashing the key, and then made their way into the lobby, stationing themselves next to the elevator. What happened next was sheer chaos. As the group hastily entered the hotel and made their way to the elevators, followed by the press and police officials, both Edith and Herta were knocked down by police. In the ensuing melee, George's boot heel cut Edith's hand. Undeterred, and on all fours, the sisters managed a brief encounter. Edith grabbed Paul with both of her hands. "Paul, hi!," she blurted. "Hello there, luv," Paul replied. As the elevator doors closed, the sisters felt total satisfaction at what they'd pulled off, despite the punishment they faced at home. It seemed their father had watched the local news, which reported his daughters' antics. Still, this didn't stop the sisters from making a beeline to the King Eddy the next morning to use their key trick again. Beatle-Manea, indeed.

It was now after one o'clock in the morning on Monday. Safely ensconced in their rooms, the boys could hear the chants of "We want the Beatles!" emanating from the streets below as they snacked on cheese sandwiches, stacks of crisp bacon, and endless pots of tea. Police officials finally calmed the crowd after announcing that the group had gone to sleep—but the peace was fleeting. In a few hours, the streets in front of the King Edward would once again fill with fans. Police chief James Mackey would later report that 1,300 officers spent an estimated 9,600 hours of overtime over a three-day period protecting the Beatles and their entourage.

Paul McCartney greets Toronto with his camera at International Airport.

Paul McCartney talks to CHUM'S J. J. Richards & Dave Johnson.

Jungle Jay introduces the BEATLES to Toronto.

BEATLES pose with their fan club President Trudy Medcalf.

MAPLE LEAF GARDENS
Press Conference
FOR THE
BEATLES
SEPTEMBER 7th, 1964
TIME - 6.30 p.m.

IMPORTANT—After the first show, 4.00 to 6.00, proceed immediately to Press Room, Centre East Side, while house is cleared.

— ADMIT ONE —

CHUM Radio (top) was the official sponsor of the show, a press conference pass (above) and a copy of the "After Four" section (left) of the *Toronto Telegram* about the upcoming 1964 tour.

640 Fifth Avenue
NEW YORK 19, N.Y.
Circle 7-7543

8 South Michigan Avenue
CHICAGO 3, ILLINOIS
STate 2-6288

9025 Wilshire Blvd.
BEVERLY HILLS, CALIF.
CRestview 3-2400

M

GAC
GENERAL ARTISTS CORPORATION

RIDER ATTACHED HERETO IS HEREBY MADE PART OF THIS CONTRACT AND MUST BE SIGNED

AGREEMENT made this ___16th___ day of ___April___, 19__64__,

between ___NEMS ENTERPRISES LIMITED___ (hereinafter

referred to as "PRODUCER") and ___Henry F. Bolton, Maple Leaf Gardens___
(hereinafter referred to as "PURCHASER").

It is mutually agreed between the parties as follows:

The PURCHASER hereby engages the PRODUCER and the PRODUCER hereby agrees to furnish the entertainment presentation hereinafter described, upon all the terms and conditions herein set forth, including those on the reverse side hereof entitled "Additional Terms and Conditions."

1. PRODUCER agrees to furnish the following entertainment presentation to PURCHASER:

A show of approximately two hours in duration starring the BEATLES, plus

additional supporting attractions to be selected at the sole discretion of

PRODUCER.

for presentation thereof by PURCHASER:

(a) at ___Maple Leaf Gardens, Toronto, Ontario, Canada___;
(Place of Engagement)

(b) on ___Mon. September 7, 1964___;
(Date(s) of Engagement)

DEP. REC'D.
Amt $10,000.
4-14-64

(c) at the following time(s) __Concert perform. commencing at approx. 8 PM__;

(d) rehearsals: ___As required by PRODUCER.___

CANADIAN

2. FULL PRICE AGREED UPON: **Twenty Thousand Dollars ($20,000.00) guaranteed against 60% of gross box-office receipts after applicable admission taxes have been deducted therefrom, whichever amount is greater.**
All payments shall be paid by certified check, money order, bank draft or cash as follows:

(a) $ __10,000.00__ shall be paid by PURCHASER to and in the name of PRODUCER'S agent, GENERAL ARTISTS CORPORATION, not later than **Immediately upon signing hereof.**

(b) $ __10,000.00__ shall be paid by PURCHASER to the ER not later than XXXXX XXXXXXXXXXX General Artists Corp. by cert. check, money order or bank draft no later than 8/7/64.
(c) All earned percentage to be paid to representative of NEMS ENTERPRISES, XXXXXXXXXXXXXXX XXXXXXXXXXXXXXXXXXXXXXXXXXXXXXXXXX
LTD., in cash, certified check, money order or bank draft not later than 9PM.
PURCHASER shall first apply any and all receipts derived from the entertainment presentation to the payments required hereunder: All payments shall be made in full without any deductions whatsoever.

3. SCALE OF ADMISSION **Cap. 13,000 -- tickets max price $5.50 incl. tax.**

NEMS ENTERPRISES, LTD. (PRODUCER)

By _[signature: Brian Epstein]_

(PURCHASER)
Henry F. Bolton, Maple Leaf Gardens.

By X _[signature]_

Return all signed copies to agent:
General Artists Corporation
640 Fifth Avenue
New York, New York
Att: Irv Dinkin

Address: __60 Carlton Street__

__Toronto, Ont. Canada__

Phone: _____

Musicians' Union
27 JUL 1964

ALL COPIES OF CONTRACT MUST BE SIGNED ON REVERSE AS WELL AS FACE SIDE.

Form AA-1

On Monday afternoon, Dr. Edward Foreman was dispatched to check on the boys' colds, which they couldn't seem to shake as they traveled around North America. The good doctor administered some much-needed medication. "They've got bad colds," he said. "But they're like race horses rarin' to go." The same could be said for the fans outside the hotel, as they made several attempts to break through the secured lines of Toronto's finest. Rumors even spread that the group would be visiting nearby Niagara

640 Fifth Avenue
NEW YORK 19, N.Y.
Circle 7-7543

8 South Michigan Avenue
CHICAGO 3, ILLINOIS
STate 2-6288

9025 Wilshire Blvd.
BEVERLY HILLS, CALIF.
CRestview 3-2400

N

GAC GENERAL ARTISTS CORPORATION

Attached Rider is part of this contract and must be signed.

AGREEMENT made this _____ 6th day of _____ May , 19 64 ,

between ___ NEMS ENTERPRISES, LTD. _____ (hereinafter

referred to as "PRODUCER") and Henry F. Bolton - Maple Leaf Gardens _____
(hereinafter referred to as "PURCHASER").

It is mutually agreed between the parties as follows:

The PURCHASER hereby engages the PRODUCER and the PRODUCER hereby agrees to furnish the entertainment presentation hereinafter described, upon all the terms and conditions herein set forth, including those on the reverse side hereof entitled "Additional Terms and Conditions."

1. PRODUCER agrees to furnish the following entertainment presentation to PURCHASER:

A show of approximately two hours in duration starring THE BEATLES, plus additional

supporting attractions to be selected at the sole discretion of the producer.

for presentation thereof by PURCHASER:

(a) at Maple Leaf Gardens - Toronto, Ontario, Canada
   (Place of Engagement)

(b) on Monday, September 7, 1964
   (Date(s) of Engagement)

(c) at the following time(s): concert performance at 4:00 P.M.

(d) rehearsals: As required by Producer

DEP. REC'D.
Amt $12,500
By ___ 7/3/64

2. FULL PRICE AGREED UPON: TWENTY FIVE THOUSAND CANADIAN DOLLARS ($25,000.00) guarantee against 70% of the gross box office receipts after applicable admission taxes have been deducted therefrom, whichever is greater.

All payments shall be paid by certified check, money order, bank draft or cash as follows:

(a) $12,500.00 Canad. shall be paid by PURCHASER to and in the name of PRODUCER'S agent, GENERAL ARTISTS CORPORATION, not later than immediately upon signing of contract ;

(b) $12,500.00 Canad. shall be paid by PURCHASER to PRODUCER not later than By Certified Check not later than 8/7/64.   General Artists Corp.

(c) Additional payments, if any, shall be paid by PURCHASER to PRODUCER no later than all earned percentage to be paid to representatives of NEMS ENTERPRISES Ltd., in cash, Certified Check, money order or bank draft not later than 5 p.m. on day of engagement.

PURCHASER shall first apply any and all receipts derived from the entertainment presentation to the payments required hereunder: All payments shall be made in full without any deductions whatsoever.

3. SCALE OF ADMISSION _____

NEMS ENTERPRISES, LTD.   (PRODUCER)

By _Brian Epstein_

Return all signed copies to agent:
General Artists Corporation
640 Fifth Avenue
New York, New York

Att: Irv Dinkin

Henry F. Bolton, Maple Leaf Gardens (PURCHASER)

By _____ MAPLE LEAF GARDENS LIMITED

Address: 60 Carlton St.

Toronto, Ontario, Canada

Phone: _____

Musicians' Union
27 JUL 1964

ALL COPIES OF CONTRACT MUST BE SIGNED ON REVERSE AS WELL AS FACE SIDE.

Form AA-1

Ballard and Smythe got their wish as a second performance contract was signed. It took several weeks of back and forth negotiation between Epstein, GAC and Maple Leaf Gardens executives to place another show on the bill.

Falls, sending several fans scrambling to the tourist attraction on a futile journey to meet them. In reality, the Beatles spent their leisure time holed up in their suite. They caught up on some fan mail and relaxed while they could. Soon enough, they'd be onstage performing two sold-out shows at Maple Leaf Gardens.

Late that afternoon, at the request of Chief Mackey, decoy limousines were sent to the front of the hotel while officers rushed the group through the hotel's kitchen, out a rear service door, and into a

Lost in the moment. John seems unaware of the 17,000-plus fans surrounding him.

©BORIS SPREMO (2)

waiting police paddy wagon. The fans who broke police lines in a mad rush to the limos soon discovered that it was all a ruse: the Beatles were already on their way to the venue.

The famed and historic Maple Leaf Gardens opened in 1931 on Carlton Street in Toronto's Garden District. Elvis Presley performed there in 1957 at one of his few concerts outside the United States, and the Toronto Maple Leafs hockey team hoisted eleven Stanley Cup championship banners in its rafters. And by 1966, it would also have the distinction of being the only venue to host the Beatles during each of their three North American tours.

The first of the two Labor Day shows began with emcee Jungle Jay Nelson of CHUM, the station that had beat out rival CKEY as the sponsor of the show, taking the stage. Nelson described his hosting duties as "unreal ... the proudest moment of my life."

Two Toronto newspaper reporters gave contradictory accounts of the show. Bob Pennington of the *Toronto Telegram* was nauseated by what he saw, writing, "These pitiful kids ... had been conditioned by

months of high-powered pressure, until these four Pied Pipers of our sick society would have stampeded them like demented sheep. If Niagara Falls had been outside, they would have followed John and George over in a barrel without question." Nathan Cohen, however, considered Canada's most respected critic, gave a far more positive review: "They are energetic, good-natured, and robustly masculine. They have a sense of independence about them, of enjoying life to the fullest, which makes their appeal to the teenage generation easy to understand. On stage, they are strictly for the young teenager and the chances are they are going to remain popular for quite awhile."

The press conference was held on the Gardens floor between shows. In attendance was fourteen-year-old Michele Finney, co-host of the CBC-TV show Razzle Dazzle. She was also given unprecedented access to the Beatles in their dressing room. Finney had been assigned by the *Toronto Daily Star* to pose questions to the group and then report back as "a voice of the youth." Trying to maintain her composure despite being a huge fan, Finney asked the band what they thought their strongest appeal might be—their music or themselves. John replied, "Definitely the music." She then asked if they had any idea why millions of teenagers the world over had gone so completely crazy about them. With a slight pause to reflect, George countered, "People are always looking for idols. In this age, it just happens to be us."

Promoters were asked not to seat people behind the stage, but it was always disregarded as demand for tickets soared, and promoters smelled the money. The Beatles performing one of two shows at Maple Leaf Gardens. Paul and George share the mic.

In between songs, Paul seems to give a nod to Ringo and the fans seated behind them, as George prepares for the next song in the set. Opposite page: Ringo, an unidentified woman, John and Paul prepare to leave Toronto.

With the Jacksonville, Florida, appearance looming, the Beatles were once again asked about segregation and the impact it would have at the Deep South venue. Paul responded, "We've all talked about this and we all agree that we would refuse to play. We all feel strongly about civil rights and the segregation issue." John threw support to his bandmate: "We will not appear unless Negroes are allowed to sit anywhere they like!" These were courageous comments about a country that, at the time, was embroiled in debate and turmoil over civil rights. On the lighter side, the Beatles also had time to meet and pose for pictures with Mary Lou Farrell, the reigning Miss Canada.

At the end of the second show, the Beatles were loaded into a police van and driven back to the King Edward Hotel. By 11 p.m. they were once again relaxing and entertaining company in their suite. Toronto mayor Phil Givens was attending another function at the hotel and assumed he could have instant access to the boys. When the mayor and his wife knocked on the door of the Beatles' suite at 1:30 a.m., however, press secretary Bess Coleman rudely and abruptly turned away His Honor despite his pleas. On the other hand, Miss Canada, whom the band had met earlier at the press conference, had no problem in gaining entrance to the inner sanctum to enjoy the festivities.

During the two shows in Toronto, staff nurses at the Gardens treated approximately 200 fans who had fainted. The story was much the same in every North American tour city: wherever the boys went, fans were under their spell. Replying to a newsman who asked how the staff had handled the situation, one nurse said, "We wipe their faces with a cold cloth, be firm with them, give them no sympathy whatsoever, and they work themselves out of it in ten or fifteen minutes."

Songwriters of the century—John and Paul (above) survey the crowd before boarding the plane. Bound for Montreal, John, Ringo and Paul say goodbye (right) to Toronto. The group and management were concerned about threats made by the French-Canadians, particularly to Ringo, calling him an "English Jew."

The Beatles spent the night at the King Edward and were presented with a check for $93,000 for the two shows. On the morning of Tuesday, September 8, they caught the short flight to Montreal as approximately 300 fans positioned along the runway fence said their good-byes. George immediately entered the plane and didn't re-emerge. The rest of the group took time waving to the crowd and snapping pictures. Paul took special note of seven young ladies who each wore a dress emblazoned with a letter. Standing side by side, they spelled out "B-E-A-T-L-E-S." Fortunately for Toronto fans, this would not be the group's final farewell. They would return to the city for a show on August 17, 1965, and again on the same date in 1966.

The only collectibles from the September 7, 1964, appearance are admission tickets and the generic program. No posters or handbills were used to promote the show. A Schick razor ad was placed on the back of the 8:30 p.m. ticket, but not on the ticket for the first performance. Many afternoon tickets also have a notch on one of the corners, probably to aid ushers in quickly distinguishing attendees of the first and second shows. A Toronto ticket is considered unused only when the bottom audit stub is securely attached. Very few unused tickets have survived, and they are considered extremely rare. Oversized press passes were also issued, designed to resemble a movie ticket for A Hard Day's Night, complete with die-cut Beatles heads.

MONTREAL

September 8, 1964
The Forum
Two Shows, 4 p.m. and 8:30 p.m.

Under heavy guard, the Beatles arrive in Montreal to perform two shows.

"IT WAS THE WORST GIG OF MY LIFE," said Ringo of the two performances at Montreal's storied hockey arena, the Forum. Indeed, as the 1964 tour soldiered on, the Beatles had more and more reasons for concern. First came a threat of an assassination attempt during their visit to the French-Canadian city. Then Mother Nature started to wreak havoc on Jacksonville, Florida, the city where they were scheduled to play three days later.

The Beatles had just played two shows in Toronto and spent the night at the King Edward Hotel there, allowing them some much-needed rest before their morning flight to Montreal on September 8. Unfortunately, their visit came at a time of tensions and factional fighting between French and English Canadians, which peaked over the summer. The Quebec Liberation Front (FLQ), a militant separatist wing, had been making headlines with a series of bombings and death threats against the Queen Mother despite the recent visit she'd made to quell tensions. The Beatles, of course, were seen as an English import by the French separatist movement, and Paul even wondered aloud if the group would be welcome in the city. More disconcerting—at least for the group—was a death threat phoned in to police authorities calling Ringo an "English Jew" who would be assassinated. The Beatles, manager Brian Epstein, and local police authorities took the threat seriously and immediately implemented stricter security measures, which included two plainclothes detectives assigned to the drummer. John defiantly declared, "We'll not be anybody's pawns. We're here to play music."

The other problem facing the group was a massive hurricane named Dora, which had been brewing in the Caribbean and appeared poised to hit Jacksonville, the next tour stop. The Beatles had been scheduled for two days off in the warm Florida sun prior to the Gator Bowl show. Since journalist Larry Kane was from the area and knew about hurricanes, Epstein asked for his advice as they flew from Detroit to Toronto. Kane suggested that the entourage fly into Key West, Florida, for their scheduled days of rest, judging that it would be safer. Epstein agreed.

AP IMAGES (2)

Tour officials had originally booked the group at Montreal's Queen Elizabeth Hotel, but with Hurricane Dora headed for Jacksonville, it was decided they would remain in the city for only around eight hours before flying to Key West. This game plan proved to be a relief for the boys, who were happy to be removed from the threats to their safety and the political unrest that gripped Montreal.

The Beatles' chartered aircraft arrived at Montreal's Dorval airport in the early afternoon. Unlike other airports, Dorval had an observation deck that afforded fans an unobstructed view of the group's arrival. An estimated 5,000 cheered and waved as the aircraft door opened and Paul popped his head outside. The "Cute Beatle" feigned a heart attack in response to the large number of fans present. According to newspaper accounts, Ringo received the biggest ovation of the four. As the group walked down the air stairs, they actually had a few seconds to wave to fans before being ushered to their cars. The two plainclothes detectives flanked Ringo before entering the transport with the band members.

There has been much speculation regarding the mode of transportation the Beatles took from the airport. Most newspaper accounts report that they left in limousines. Unfounded tales abound that one of the drivers raced to downtown Montreal, outrunning the motorcycle escort that flanked the limo; after the driver ran two red lights, George demanded that he slow down before they were all killed. One airport witness, however, popular CFCF deejay Dave Boxer, begged to differ. Boxer, who had a prime viewing spot for the band's arrival, claims they were driven to the Forum in a King's Transfer Van Lines truck.

Thirty-year-old Marvin Kane was the promoter for the Montreal shows. During the tour's planning stages, Epstein was given a choice of either the Forum or Percival Molson Stadium. (Norman Weiss mistakenly listed Vancouver's Empire Stadium on Epstein's planning sheet for Montreal rather than the 25,000-seat Molson Stadium.) While the Beatles' manager chose the smaller Forum, he boosted the

Montreal fans line the observation deck to welcome the group at Dorval Airport. Beatles' management decided against staying the night—instead flying directly to Key West, Florida immediately after the show.

THE BEATLES
APPEARING AT THE
MONTREAL FORUM
TUESDAY, SEPT. 8th
AFTERNOON TICKETS STILL
AVAILABLE FOR 4 P.M. PERFORMANCE
ADMISSION $4.50 and $5.50
TICKETS NOW ON SALE AT THE FORUM BOX OFFICE
MONDAY TO FRIDAY FROM 10 A.M. TO 5 P.M.
MAIL ORDERS WILL BE ACCEPTED
SORRY! Evening Performance
Sold Out

l'ouragan
BEATLES

The venerable
Montreal Forum
(top left). Promoter
Marvin Kane placed
ads in French and
English (top right).
The evening show
sold out in hours.
The caption with
Paul (above) reads,
"Beatles Hurricane."

gross by adding a second show. Kane's Bevmar Enterprises secured the group on April 16 for a guarantee of $40,000 plus 60 percent of the gross receipts. General Artists Corporation's Frank Barsalona, a future entertainment heavyweight, negotiated the contract with Kane.

Opened in 1924, the Montreal Forum has been dubbed the "most storied building in hockey history" by the *Sporting News*. The building, which stands at the northeast corner of Atwater Avenue and Saint Catherine Street, was home to twenty-four Stanley Cup championships. In 1997 it was declared a National Historic Site of Canada, but it no longer hosts the Canadiens hockey team. Today it's a multi-use development boasting theaters, shops, and restaurants.

Tickets went on sale May 15 for the September shows, and promotional ads were printed in both French and English. Around 9,500 fans were on hand for the afternoon show and 11,500 for the evening one. Had it not been both the first day of school and a Jewish High Holiday, more fans would likely have attended. Kane called his promotion of the concert a "huge success" and commended "the behavior of the youngsters."

Dave Boxer recalled: "I was the only disc jockey playing the Beatles in early 1964. All the other stations didn't want to have anything to do with them." Boxer received a call from promoter Kane, offering him the emcee job for both shows. Kane needed someone to make the introductions in French, however. To that end, he told Boxer he would be joined onstage by Michael Desrochers of CJMS radio. Desrochers, who eagerly accepted Kane's invitation, had been on the air for two years and had acquired a loyal following of French-speaking teens. Kane then told Boxer of his plans to invite George Morris (aka "Buddy G") of rival station CKGM to share the emceeing duties for the evening performance. Morris, who was not a

Beatles fan at the time and was more into doo-wop, recalled that Kane offered him $50 for the gig.

By cleverly involving these three deejays, Kane snared promotional help from the three top radio stations in Montreal (both French and English). This was no easy feat, as they were all rival stations. Most promoters in the other tour cities relied on just one station for their promotional efforts.

As in other tour stops, a decoy tactic was used in Montreal to deliver the Beatles to the venue—in this case, from the airport to the Forum. Police dispatched a black airport taxi carrying four rookie police officers, each wearing a Beatles wig—and delivered them to front of the Forum. The scheme worked and the fans, thinking this was a genuine encounter, were thrilled. Even those who had stationed themselves at the back door of the Forum were fooled into running around to the front. With the back entrance now cleared of fans, police sealed off the area, allowing the real Beatles to arrive without incident. Promoter Marvin Kane didn't want a repeat of the Vancouver concert,

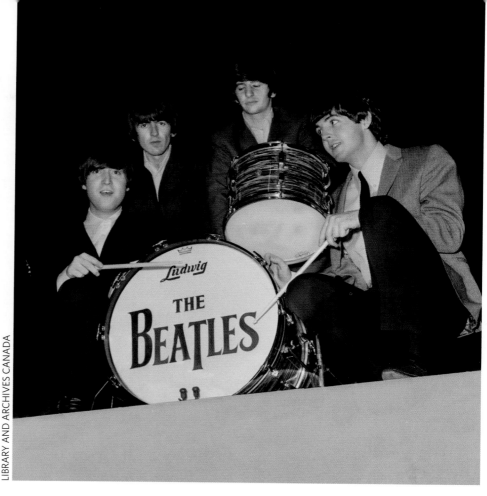

The Fab Four pose for photographers (above) during the press conference between shows. The Beatles (left) pose with the Four Frenchmen, who opened the show ahead of the tour's usual support acts. Ringo looks unnerved in the face of death threats.

Despite the threats, the boys have a good time as they belt out one of their hits.

where unruly fans broke through police barriers and wreaked havoc, so he employed extra security.

With the group safely inside the arena, emcee Michael Desrochers received a welcoming tap on his back from Paul. "I turn around to hear 'I got ya' … and it was Paul," he said. "He took my breath away and my heart started pounding a mile a minute." The deejay noted, "Paul smiled at me and says, *'Bonjour, comment ca va?,'* which means 'How are you?'" Desrochers, after seeing the other three Beatles walk by, thought to himself, "What a great day this is going to be."

The Fab Four, however, were in a much different mood, their nerves rattled. Epstein, in speaking to journalist Larry Kane, was visibly upset and fired off expletives about the French Canadians and their anti-British sentiments. Ringo was dreading the thought of performing in such a hostile environment, feeling that he was a marked man. But cancelling the two Montreal shows wasn't an option. It would have spelled disaster—not only because the fans would have been disappointed, but because the revenue loss would have been staggering. The (Beatles, along with Epstein and GAC) team was comforted, though, by their plan to leave the city as soon as the second performance ended.

A brief moment of panic took place as the Beatles were backstage preparing for their first show. Ready to change into their stage suits, they quickly realized there were no stage suits to wear. Officials raced back to the airport after it was learned that the garments had been left behind. Meanwhile, there was a slight change to the supporting act program. Instead of Clarence "Frogman" Henry, a group called Les 4 Français (the Four Frenchmen) opened the show, followed by the Bill Black Combo, the Exciters, and Jackie DeShannon. The Four Frenchmen opened the second show as well.

In the meantime, Boxer was nervously sweating his introduction of the group. He recalled, "The Beatles told me to introduce them and then get off the stage. No one was allowed to be on the stage with the Beatles." Now facing an audience of 9,500 avid Beatles fans, Boxer and Desrochers bantered back and forth as the energy level inside the Forum grew to a fever pitch. Boxer recalled that, at the moment he made the introduction, "the roof almost came off the Forum and the noise level was unbelievable. Flashbulbs burst onto the stage like a spotlight and continued for the next thirty minutes." He remembers looking out into the audience and seeing girls "with expressions of overwhelming worship on their faces. It was astonishing!" Boxer watched the concert from backstage with Epstein, but found it impossible to converse with him over the noise. Still, many who attended the show claim it was much more tame than Toronto or Vancouver and that the fans could actually hear the music.

The detectives who had flanked the Beatles since their airport arrival were also at the concert. Ringo, crouching low behind his drums during the first performance, recalled, "I was really worried. We were

playing the gig and, as always, I was on the high riser. I had the cymbals up towards the audience to give me a bit of protection; usually I had them flat on. I also had a plainclothes policeman sitting there with me. But I started to get hysterical, because I thought, 'If someone in the audience has a pop at me, what is this guy going to do? Is he going to catch the bullet?'" (This is a direct quote from Ringo) The Beatles raced through their usual repertoire, delighting the crowd just the same. Despite frayed nerves, they survived the first show.

Between shows, a press conference was held on the stage of the Forum. The group was asked, "What do the Beatles do when they're cooped up in a hotel room between shows?" George shot back, "We ice-skate!" Serious questions about their music were few and far between as the group endured the

Fans in Montreal having a fabulous time listening to the Beatles perform hit after hit.

On stage in Montreal. According to Ringo, a plainclothes police officer was assigned to sit below him in case of any trouble from French separatists. "What was he going to do, catch the bullet?" quipped the drummer.

typical barrage of inane queries about what they ate for breakfast or whether they were wearing wigs. Their impatience with such absurd questions was reflected in their trite replies. Promoter Kane recalled the scene in the Canadiens' locker room as a blue truck from the Queen Elizabeth Hotel delivered a huge catered meal complete with white-gloved hotel waiters. Bottles of Cutty Sark were passed around while the group played poker with fistfuls of American dollars.

The second show included 2,000 more fans than the afternoon show. George "Buddy G" Morris and Dave Boxer took to the stage to introduce the group. Boxer recalled, "George and I had a contest going over the air during the weeks leading up to the concert. I told all my kids not to scream and shout and listen to the music. George told his kids to do the opposite. Once it was time to bring the Beatles out, I asked the kids, 'Where are all the people who are not going to shout?' and a small faction cheered. George then asked, 'Where are all the kids who are going to cause pandemonium?' and the place went bananas. Unlike the matinee show, where I watched from backstage, this time I decided to get a different perspective. I made my way around the entire Forum and, no matter where I stopped, it was all the same: I couldn't hear a thing!" With the second show finished, the group raced offstage into waiting cars for the trip back to the airport.

Three hundred fans had staked out the airport to say their good-byes, but the Beatles, eagerly anticipating a few days of rest in Key West, bounded onto the plane with renewed energy. Their Electra turboprop flew out of Dorval at 11:46 p.m., a mere eight hours after the group had arrived. Now they faced a new obstacle in the form of Hurricane Dora. On a collision course with their next stop, Jacksonville, the tropical storm threatened to cancel or postpone the Gator Bowl appearance. But it was still September 8, and the Gator Bowl show wasn't until September 11. A lot could change in those three days. In the meantime, the flight would bypass Jacksonville for the relative safety of Key West.

Collectibles from the Montreal show are among the rarest. Only a few unused tickets have surfaced from either performance, and stubs are just as difficult to find. The generic mass-produced North American tour program was sold at the event, and no posters or handbills were created. Ads in various publications, both English and French, were purchased by the promoter.

ANTOINE DESILETS

JACKSONVILLE

September 11, 1964
Gator Bowl
8:30 p.m.

"We've never played to a segregated audience before and it just seems mad to me. It just seems a bit daft. It's the way we all feel."
—Paul McCartney, Las Vegas, 1964

"I would rather lose our appearance money."
—John Lennon, Detroit, 1964

The Key Wester Motel served as a refuge for the touring company while Jacksonville was being ravaged by Hurricane Dora. Opposite page: The Beatles arrive in Jacksonville, looking refreshed from their unscheduled visit to Key West.

THESE WERE COURAGEOUS COMMENTS FOR BRITISH ROCK 'N' ROLLERS TO MAKE, especially when their tour included a stop in the segregated South.

When the Beatles began their North American conquest in San Francisco on August 19, the United States was only a year removed from Dr. Martin Luther King Jr.'s famous "I Have a Dream" speech. The Civil Rights Act had been signed into law on July 2, only a few weeks prior to the group's arrival. So despite these advances in the area of racial equality, the question of playing before a segregated audience dogged the Beatles from the beginning of the tour. The boys never wavered or backed down: they would refuse to play before an audience separated by the color of their skin. But they were scheduled to perform in a city that still embraced segregation.

For their appearance in Jacksonville, Florida, the Beatles required absolute assurances from the city—as well as promoter W. J. (Bill) Brennan—that the concert would not have segregated seating. These negotiations in the early spring of 1964 may have resulted in General Artists Corporation (GAC) adding a clause to every performance contract rider for all three North American tours that read, "ARTISTS WILL NOT BE REQUIRED TO PERFORM BEFORE A SEGREGATED AUDIENCE." The American Guild of Variety Artists also got into the act and were threatening to picket the Gator Bowl unless the Beatles agreed to join the Guild. Given little choice, the band reluctantly agreed to pay the $1,200 membership fee and the annual dues.

In early April 1964, when Beatles manager Brian Epstein and GAC's Norm Weiss were planning the tour, a proposal was made for the band to appear in Jacksonville on Friday, September 11, followed the next evening by a show at the 25,000-seat Cramton Bowl in Montgomery, Alabama. The concert was to be sponsored by the Brennan Broadcasting Group's WVOK radio. Unfortunately for Alabama Beatles fans, the Montgomery appearance was cancelled because there was no

assurance of integrated seating at the venue. As a result, the Jacksonville show was booked for September 11, and Brennan's powerful station WAPE (The Ape) would handle the promotion.

As radio regimes went, the Brennan brothers (W. J. "Bill," Cyril, and Dan "The Music Man") practically owned the southeastern part of the United States, with a network of stations that included WVOK in Birmingham, Alabama; WBAM ("The Big Bam") in Montgomery; WFLI in Chattanooga, Tennessee; and WAPE in Jacksonville. WAPE was *the* station and carried a 50,000-watt signal up and down the coast. The station featured the notorious "Ape Call," and its well-appointed broadcast facility boasted a pool and modern furnishings. When President Kennedy was assassinated in November 1963, WAPE eliminated commercials and rock music for three straight days and nights and played only elevator-type music. Because Bill and Cyril promoted their "Shower of Stars" concert series—big-name, multi-act presentations that rivaled those of Dick Clark—the Brennans were the logical choice to present the Beatles in Jacksonville. They received one of the better deals

PRIVATE COLLECTION

The Gator Bowl (above) was the largest stadium —62,000 seats—in which the group performed during the 1964 tour. Radio station WAPE sent out tickets for the concert in these envelopes (below right).

from GAC—a flat $50,000 appearance fee, with no requirement to pay a gross percentage on gate receipts—the only promoters to accomplish that feat on the 1964 tour.

Through the years, the three brothers have been blamed for threatening to segregate the concert, but the fingers should have been pointed at the Jacksonville-owned Gator Bowl, whose lease stipulated segregated seating for events such as concerts. When the tour was being planned in early April, the clause to segregate was still in the Gator Bowl lease, but after the Civil Rights Act became law in July, that clause was rendered moot and the concert allowed to be performed before integrated audiences. Alabama wasn't as quick to adapt, so Beatles management scrubbed the Montgomery show early on, in deference to the boys' beliefs.

Gator Bowl Stadium, originally named Fairfield Stadium, was built in 1927 as the home field for Jacksonville's three high school football teams. In 1946 the first annual Gator Bowl game was held, with Wake Forest trouncing South Carolina 26-14. Initially accommodating only 7,600, in 1948 the stadium

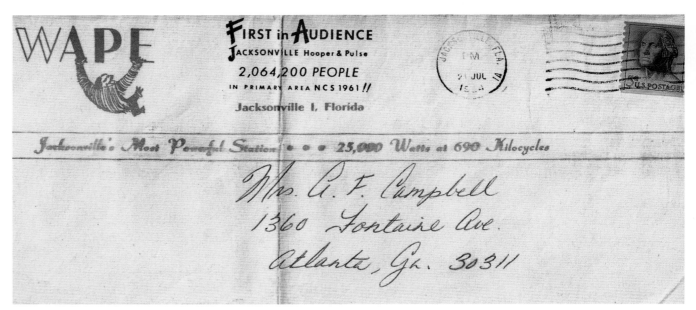

was expanded to 16,000 seats and renamed the Gator Bowl. A year later, its seating capacity more than doubled to just over 36,000 seats.

On July 20, 1964, Norm Weiss sent Epstein a letter offering the Beatles and their inner circle the services of a chartered yacht for September 10 and 11. The *Fostoria,* Weiss promised, would offer the group complete privacy and rest prior to their Gator Bowl concert. Epstein turned down Weiss' offer fearing a scene would erupt, endangering everyone involved. He would also reject a similar offer when the band visited San Diego in 1965.

Even before the Beatles arrived in Jacksonville, their schedule had to be altered. Hurricane Dora was threatening destruction in the area, so on the flight between their concerts in Detroit and Toronto, a decision was made to spend the group's two days off in Key West rather than in Jacksonville.

The Beatles' chartered plane landed in Key West in the early-morning hours of September 9. All flights in and out of northern Florida had been either diverted or scrubbed, so the boys were fortunate to reach their destination. Accommodations were arranged at the Key Wester Hotel, a quiet retreat not far from the airport. Featuring spacious cottages, tennis courts, a huge pool, and a restaurant, the hotel provided welcome relief to the exhausted quartet, supporting acts, and road crew. Key Wester employees were shocked to learn that the Beatles were staying in their quaint hotel. Word quickly spread that the island was hosting these very famous guests, so it was no surprise when the press and local fans made a beeline to the property.

Navy corpsman John Trusty was stationed at the adjacent naval hospital and frequented the Key Wester's bar. On the night the Beatles were there, he arrived with a friend. Though recognized as a regular, he and his buddy were subjected to a quick pat-down by security. Once inside, Trusty witnessed a spirited soiree that included live music, cold drinks, hot girls, and,

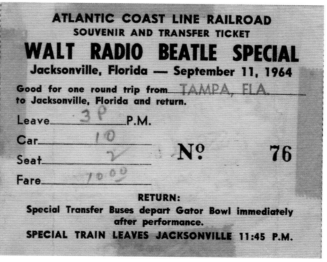

ATLANTIC COAST LINE RAILROAD
SOUVENIR AND TRANSFER TICKET
WALT RADIO BEATLE SPECIAL
Jacksonville, Florida — September 11, 1964
Good for one round trip from TAMPA, FLA.
to Jacksonville, Florida and return.

Leave 3P P.M.
Car 10
Seat 2   No. 76
Fare 10 00

RETURN:
Special Transfer Buses depart Gator Bowl immediately after performance.
SPECIAL TRAIN LEAVES JACKSONVILLE 11:45 P.M.

No room in the inn: The Beatles had their reservations cancelled at the Hotel George Washington (left) but still held the press conference there. A railroad ticket (below left) for a special train trip. Fans came across the state to see the Fab Four live in concert.

in the middle of it all, the lads from Liverpool. Hoping to meet Jackie DeShannon, he looked by the pool, where he encountered Ringo cavorting with members of the Exciters. Interviewed years later, he recalled what a strange sight it was in 1964 to see black women in bathing suits, especially swimming with a white man. He bellied up to the bar with John and later snapped a picture of him posing with Paul, but the camera was instantly destroyed by security; Trusty had crossed the line, and he and his friend were shown the door.

The group had plenty of entertainment during their stay in the Keys. Tony Martinez, a local millionaire, offered the Beatles and their entourage the use of his pool. Members of the Exciters cooked up a full-scale Southern dinner. Bob Tucker, bass player for the Bill Black

The Jacksonville performance contract. Brennan Broadcasting Group received perhaps the best deal of the tour, paying a $50,000 flat fee for the Beatles to come to Jacksonville.

640 Fifth Avenue
NEW YORK 19, N.Y.
Circle 7-7543

8 South Michigan Avenue
CHICAGO 3, ILLINOIS
STate 2-6288

9025 Wilshire Blvd.
BEVERLY HILLS, CALIF.
CRestview 3-2400

GENERAL ARTISTS CORPORATION

RIDER ATTACHED HERETO IS HEREBY MADE PART OF THIS CONTRACT AND MUST BE SIGNED

AGREEMENT made this ___16th___ day of _____April_____ , 19 64 ,

between ___NEMS ENTERPRISES LIMITED_____ (hereinafter

referred to as "PRODUCER") and ___W. J. Brennan, WBAM Radio Station_____
(hereinafter referred to as "PURCHASER").

It is mutually agreed between the parties as follows:

The PURCHASER hereby engages the PRODUCER and the PRODUCER hereby agrees to furnish the entertainment presentation hereinafter described, upon all the terms and conditions herein set forth, including those on the reverse side hereof entitled "Additional Terms and Conditions."

1. PRODUCER agrees to furnish the following entertainment presentation to PURCHASER:

___A show of approximately two hours in duration starring the BEATLES, plus___

___additional supporting attractions to be selected at the sole discretion of___

___PRODUCER.___

for presentation thereof by PURCHASER:

(a) at ___Gator Bowl (in event of inclement weather purchaser has right to present package in 2 shows at the Coliseum) Jacksonville, Fla.___ ;
(Place of Engagement)

(b) on ___Friday, September 11, 1964___ ;
(Date(s) of Engagement)

(c) at the following time(s): ___Concert performance commencing at approx. 8 PM___ ;

(d) rehearsals: ___As required by PRODUCER___

2. FULL PRICE AGREED UPON: ___Fifty thousand Dollars ($50,000) flat guarantee.___

All payments shall be paid by certified check, money order, bank draft or cash as follows:

(a) $ ___25,000.00___ shall be paid by PURCHASER to and in the name of PRODUCER'S agent, GENERAL ARTISTS CORPORATION, not later than ___immediately upon signing hereof.___ ;

(b) $ ___25,000.00___ shall be paid by PURCHASER to PRODUCER not later than General Artists Corp. by certified check, money order or bank draft no later than 8/11/64. ;

(c) Additional payments, if any, shall be paid by PURCHASER to PRODUCER no later than _____ .

PURCHASER shall first apply any and all receipts derived from the entertainment presentation to the payments required hereunder: All payments shall be made in full without any deductions whatsoever.

3. SCALE OF ADMISSION _____

NEMS ENTERPRISES, LTD. (PRODUCER)

By_____

W. J. Brennan, WBAM Radio Station (PURCHASER)

By X_____

Address: Radio Station WBAM

Return all signed copies to agent:
General Artists Corporation
640 Fifth Avenue
New York, New York

Frank Barcelona

Montgomery, Alabama

Phone: _____

ALL COPIES OF CONTRACT MUST BE SIGNED ON REVERSE AS WELL AS FACE SIDE.

Form AA-1

Combo, recalled that Paul and Ringo wanted some new rock and country albums and handed him some money to go record shopping for them. The musician retrieved all sorts of new music, with plenty of money left over. Tucker further remembered that the Beatles really perked up to numbers by Jerry Lee Lewis and Carl Perkins. Clarence "Frogman" Henry recalled urging the group to play a few songs beyond their regular set, suggesting tunes by Jimmy Reed and Bill

ADDITIONAL TERMS AND CONDITIONS

The parties hereto hereby acknowledge that the following additional terms and conditions are incorporated in and made a part of the Agreement between the parties hereto:

1. PURCHASER agrees to furnish at its own expense all that is necessary for the proper presentation of the entertainment presentation at performances, and if required by PRODUCER, at rehearsals therefor, including a suitable theatre, hall or auditorium, well-heated, lighted, clean and in good order, stage curtains, properly tuned grand piano(s) and public address system in perfect working condition including microphone(s) in number and quality required by PRODUCER and comfortable, lighted dressing rooms; all stagehands, stage carpenters, electricians, electrical operators and any other labor as shall be necessary and/or required by any national or local union(s) to take in, hang, work and take out the entertainment presentation (including scenery, properties and baggage); all lights, tickets, house programs, all licenses (including musical performing rights licenses); special police, ushers, ticket sellers for advance or single sales (wherever sales take place), ticket takers; appropriate and sufficient advertising and publicity including but not limited to bill-posting, mailing and distributing of circulars, display newspaper advertising in the principal newspapers and PURCHASER shall pay all other necessary expense in connection therewith. PURCHASER agrees to pay all amusement taxes. PURCHASER agrees to comply with all regulations and requirements of any national or local union(s) that may have jurisdiction over any of the materials, facilities, services and personnel to be furnished by PURCHASER and by PRODUCER. PURCHASER agrees to furnish all necessary material and equipment and to promptly comply with PRODUCER's directions to arrange the stage decor and settings for the performances hereunder. In addition to those musicians, if any, to be furnished by either PRODUCER or PURCHASER pursuant to any other provision hereof, PURCHASER agrees to furnish at its sole expense such musicians, including musical contractor, as may be required by any national or local union(s) for and in connection with this engagement and rehearsals therefor; PRODUCER shall have the right to name the local music contractor and to approve the choice of musicians hired locally. The following Special Props and Lighting required by PRODUCER shall be furnished by PURCHASER at PURCHASER'S sole expense:

See Rider "A" attached hereto

2. PRODUCER shall have the sole and exclusive control over the production, presentation and performance of the engagement hereunder, including, but not limited to, the details, means and methods of the performances of the performing artists hereunder, and PRODUCER shall have the sole right, as PRODUCER may see fit, to designate and change at any time the performing personnel. PRODUCER's obligations hereunder are subject to detention or prevention by sickness, inability to perform, accident, means of transportation, Acts of God, riots, strikes, labor difficulties, epidemics, any act or order of any public authority or any other cause, similar or dissimilar, beyond PRODUCER'S control.

3. PURCHASER shall not have the right to broadcast or televise, photograph or otherwise reproduce the performances hereunder, or any part thereof. PURCHASER agrees that no performers other than those to be furnished by PRODUCER hereunder will appear on or in connection with the engagement hereunder. PURCHASER shall not have the right to assign this agreement, or any provision hereof. Nothing herein contained shall ever be construed as to constitute the parties hereto as a partnership, or joint venture, or that PRODUCER shall be liable in whole or in part for any obligation that may be incurred by PURCHASER in PURCHASER's carrying out any of the provisions hereof, or otherwise. The person executing this agreement on PURCHASER's behalf warrants his authority to do so, and such person hereby personally assumes liability for the payment of said price in full.

4. The entertainment presentation to be furnished by PRODUCER hereunder shall receive billing in such order, form, size and prominence as directed by PRODUCER in all advertising and publicity issued by or under the control of the PURCHASER.

5. PURCHASER agrees that the entertainment presentation will not be included in a subscription or other type of series without the written consent of PRODUCER. Free admissions, if any, (except to local press) shall be subject to PRODUCER's prior written approval. In the event that payment to PRODUCER shall be based in whole or in part on receipts of the performance(s) hereunder: (a) the scale of ticket prices must be submitted to and approved by PRODUCER in writing before tickets are ordered or placed on sale; (b) PURCHASER agrees to deliver to PRODUCER a certified statement of the gross receipts of each such performance within two hours following such performance; and (c) PRODUCER shall have the right to have a representative present in the box office at all times and such representative shall have the right to examine and make extracts from box office records of PURCHASER relating to gross receipts of this engagement only.

6. If before the date of any scheduled performance it is found that PURCHASER has not performed fully its obligations under any other agreement with any party for another engagement or that the financial credit of the PURCHASER has been impaired, PRODUCER may cancel this agreement. In the event that PURCHASER does not perform fully all of its obligations herein, PRODUCER shall have the option to perform or refuse to perform hereunder and in either event PURCHASER shall be liable to PRODUCER for damages in addition to the compensation provided herein.

7. This constitutes the sole, complete and binding agreement between the parties hereto. GENERAL ARTISTS CORPORATION acts only as agent and manager for PRODUCER and assumes no liability hereunder.

8. PRODUCER shall have the sole and exclusive right, but not the obligation, to sell souvenir programs and other souvenir items including phonograph records in connection with, and at, the performance(s) hereunder and the receipts thereof shall belong exclusively to PRODUCER.

9. This Agreement may not be changed, modified or altered except by an instrument in writing signed by the parties. This Agreement shall be construed in accordance with the laws of the State of New York. Nothing in this Agreement shall require the commission of any act contrary to law or to any rule or regulation of any union, guild or similar body having jurisdiction over the performances hereunder or any element thereof and wherever or whenever there is any conflict between any provision of this Agreement and any such law, rule or regulation, such law, rule or regulation shall prevail and this Agreement shall be curtailed, modified, or limited only to the extent necessary to eliminate such conflict.

The foregoing additional terms and conditions are approved:

X _____ _____
PURCHASER   PRODUCER

Doggett—but the boys, while familiar with the blues, stuck to the tunes they were comfortable with.

Even though they were on break, the group managed an impromptu press conference and posed for pictures outside their cottage before leaving the Keys for Jacksonville on September 11. They'd no sooner left the hotel when employees began scooping up vials of water from the pool and cutting their bedsheets into strips to be sold to charity.

The back of the Jacksonville contract, with its terms and conditions.

RIDER "A" TO CONTRACT DATED ___April 16, 1964___ BETWEEN NEMS ENTERPRISES

LIMITED (HEREINAFTER REFERRED TO AS "PRODUCER") AND ___W. J. Brennan,___

___WBAM Radio Station___ (HEREINAFTER REFERRED TO AS "PURCHASER").

1. The PURCHASER agrees, at his sole expense, to supply police protection to the BEATLES of not less than one hundred uniformed officers, for the engagement covered herein, and said policemen will be present at least one hour prior to performance and thirty minutes following completion of performance.

   If, in PRODUCER's opinion, additional police protection is required, PURCHASER agrees to hire such additional police at PURCHASER's sole expense.

2. PURCHASER will furnish at his sole expense the following:

   a. A hi-fidelity sound system with adequate number of speakers, four floor-stand Hi-Fi mikes with detachable heads and forty feet of cord for each microphone. If sound system and microphones do not meet with PRODUCER's satisfaction, PRODUCER has the right to change or augment the system in order to meet PRODUCER's sound requirements. Any costs in relation to such changes shall be borne solely by the PURCHASER.

   b. Not less than two Super Trouper follow spotlights with normal complement of gelatins and necessary operators.

   c. A first-class sound engineer who will be present for technical rehearsals, is required by PRODUCER and this same engineer will work the entire performance.

3. PURCHASER will submit to PRODUCER for PRODUCER's approval, a list of people PURCHASER wishes to include on his complimentary ticket list; in no case will the number of complimentary tickets exceed one hundred.

4. No interviews of the BEATLES or any other artists to appear on the show will be scheduled by the PURCHASER without the express written consent of the PRODUCER.

5. The PURCHASER will arrange for one general Press Conference the day of the engagement. The exact time of that Press Conference to be approved by the PRODUCER.

6. Artists will not be required to perform before a segregated audience.

7. PURCHASER will comply with exact billing requirements as furnished to PURCHASER by PRODUCER not later than 90 days prior to engagement.

8. PURCHASER will make available, at his sole expense, the place of performance, fully staffed for necessary music and technical rehearsals on the day of engagement. PURCHASER to be notified of exact rehearsal time by PRODUCER, not later than 30 days prior to date of engagement.

9. PURCHASER warrants that no seating of audience will be permitted behind stage.

10. In event of outdoor appearance, PURCHASER warrants that stage will be covered.

11. Attached contract together with this rider must be signed by PURCHASER and returned to GENERAL ARTISTS CORPORATION accompanied by deposit as outlined in contract no later than May 1, 1964.

12. PURCHASER will be required to furnish the Master of Ceremony for this engagement

ACCEPTED AND AGREED TO:

_____   _____
PURCHASER   PRODUCER

Musicians' Union
23 JUL 1964

Rider A, an attachment to all the 1964 contracts. Clause 6 states, "Artists will not be required to perform before a segregated audience." It was perhaps the City of Jacksonville, not the promoters, who required a segregated audience.

As the Beatles flew into Jacksonville that afternoon, the city resembled a war zone. George recalled that "it was windy as hell, and it was dark with heavy black clouds everywhere. As we were approaching, we could see the devastation—palm trees fallen over and a mess laying everywhere." To further complicate matters, the Beatles' arrival was delayed in order to accommodate the departure of Lyndon Johnson and Air Force One after the president had surveyed the damage from Dora. The boys' chartered Electra had to circle Jacksonville until they were authorized to land. Several members of President Johnson's security detail remained behind to help control a crowd of hundreds of Beatles fans who had made the trek to Imeson Airport to welcome the group.

When the 1964 tour was in its planning stages, GAC had booked the Beatles and their entourage at the Hotel George Washington in Jacksonville. At the press conference in Denver on August 26, however, George was asked about potential segregation issues awaiting them in the South and, in particular, at their Jacksonville hotel. "[The Beatles] don't appear anywhere where there is segregation," he replied, referring to not only concert venues but also lodgings. At the time the Hotel George Washington was segregated and, because the Exciters and Frogman Henry were black, the hotel had cancelled the reservations of the entire Beatles touring party. Still, perhaps seeking the publicity the Beatles would bring them, the George Washington, nicknamed "the Wonder Hotel of the South," agreed to host their press conference.

Had this been a year or two later, the Beatles would likely have taken their business elsewhere. But the 1964 tour was without precedent, and each stop was a learning experience. Not wanting to make waves the first time around, the Beatles followed protocol and gave their customary press conference at the hotel while enjoying turkey sandwiches, potato chips, and tea. Ringo replied to a question about their room situation: "We usually eat in the room, but seeing the hotel's got no room for us, we have to eat here." Paul was asked if the group ever went unnoticed. "Only when we take off our wigs," he replied. When asked what he thought about Dora, he responded, "Never met her."

At 7 p.m., the press conference ended and the Beatles were ushered to the hotel's back elevator and down to the garage, where limousines were waiting to take them to the Gator Bowl. Any chances of a quiet escape were foiled as 500 Beatles fans took on fifty police officers inside the parking garage. The place was so packed that it took fifteen minutes for the limos to travel about twenty-five feet. Using a flying wedge formation, police were finally able to disperse the crowd enough to assist the Beatles' passage. Shortly after, they arrived at their destination: a temporary house trailer parked underneath the east stands at the Gator Bowl. As they awaited their appearance onstage, they dined on roast beef and mashed potatoes prepared by a local cook.

So far, the Jacksonville stop had proved daunting. There had been an unscheduled stop in Key West, cancelled hotel reservations, and a near-riot in the parking garage. Now the Beatles had another challenge to face: winds gusting across the stage at an estimated forty miles an hour, in one final reminder of Hurricane Dora's sweep through the area. Cyril Brennan, one of the promoters, recalled that Ringo refused to go onstage until some kind of barrier was built so he wouldn't blow offstage. Brennan promptly ordered that a wooden fence be placed behind Ringo's riser to keep the drums from overturning.

WQAM's 560 Charlie Murdock interviews Ringo.

On stage in Jacksonville. Note Hurricane Dora's winds ripping off the "W" in "Welcome Beatles."

FLORIDA TIMES-UNION

More friction arose involving a crew of Los Angeles–based newsreel and movie cameramen who were following the band on their tour in an attempt to film them live in concert. Even though they'd been ejected from every previous venue where they attempted filming, they had stubbornly persevered and were now in Jacksonville. Later, George recalled the filmmakers' insistence on shooting at the Gator Bowl despite the Beatles' warning them to "bugger off" and appealing to the promoters to put an end to the harassment. He said the promoters "were getting stroppy with us" instead of taking a stand and ejecting the film crew from the venue. Beatles management knew that any unauthorized footage would be distributed to theaters and television networks, with no royalties paid to the group. One of the clandestine cameramen insisted that they had been invited with other members of the press and had every right to be there.

With the Beatles' patience running thin, press officer Derek Taylor went onstage and used the public address system to implore the police to physically remove the eight cameramen, cover their lenses, and escort them from the area. Taylor then addressed the fans: "The Beatles are 100 feet away; they came thousands of miles to be here. The only thing preventing their appearance is eight cameramen." George later recalled, "Derek Taylor went onstage and was like Adolf Hitler up there, shouting to the crowd, 'These camera people are not wanted, they must be removed.' He was yelling, 'Do you want the Beatles on this stage? Yeah? Well then, do you want to get rid of the cameras? Yeah?' It was like a big Nuremberg rally." The inner circle later called it "the Jacksonville Address."

Finally, Dan Brennan was ready to introduce the Beatles, but not without some drama of his own. He and his brother Cyril both lived in Alabama; he had flown to Jacksonville while Cyril had driven. With Hurricane Dora in full force and the airports a mess, Dan's luggage was lost and, with it, his clothes for the evening. He appealed to Cyril, who had bought an expensive sharkskin suit to wear at the show, to let him borrow it for the evening, since he would be the one bringing the Beatles onstage. (Cyril would be working strictly backstage on the sound.) Under the steely gaze of his wife, Louise, Cyril reluctantly agreed to lend his suit to Dan. Louise recalled that it was the only time the suit was ever worn.

Dora had a significant impact on concert attendance. While 30,000 to 32,000 seats had been sold, some 7,000 to 9,000 fans were no-shows due to the hurricane. During the show, the Gator Bowl was fed electricity from underground lines while most of Jacksonville was still without power. The Beatles' thirty-minute set was marked by heavy winds and, as elsewhere, out-of-control fans who frantically rushed the stage. Luckily, the police and a specially constructed six-foot fence kept the band safe. Tour manager Bob Bonis crouched down beside Ringo, who was concerned he'd blow away in the heavy winds. Ringo recalled that his "hair was blowing, and I thought it was weird, but the drums were tied down, so we made it, you know." At the show's end, the fans were told that the boys were taking a break when, in fact, they were leaving for Imeson Airport. On the way, their convoy had to dodge trees that had been felled by Dora. They boarded their plane shortly after midnight for their flight to Boston, the next stop on their whirlwind tour.

In 1994, the original Gator Bowl structure was almost completely razed and rebuilt. Now called Everbank Field, it can seat 80,126 football fanatics. The Key Wester was torn down in 1999 and replaced by a Hyatt hotel, the Windward Pointe. Today the Abbey Road Snack Shack sits poolside and pays homage to the hotel's famous visitors.

The song "Here Today," Paul's poignant 1982 tribute to his fallen bandmate John, makes reference to their stay at the Key Wester in its line "What about the night we cried because there wasn't any reason left to keep it all inside." According to Paul, "we stayed up all night, and we got drunk and we talked a lot, and we got way too deep, and got into each other's characters. We never had much time to do that with the Beatles, so this was probably a good thing, and we ended up crying."

Because so many fans were unable to attend the concert, it would seem that untold numbers of unused Gator Bowl tickets would be available to collectors. Surprisingly, few have surfaced, making them among the rarest of Beatles concert tickets. Stubs, though scarce, turn up from time to time, and many still bear the scars of Dora in the form of water stains. The mass-produced tour program was sold, and no poster or handbills were produced for this show.

The band endured 40 mph wind gusts on stage—the after effects of Dora.

BOSTON

**September 12, 1964
Boston Garden
8 p.m.**

The group sits for their nineteenth press conference of the tour at the Hotel Madison, clearly glad that they made it out of Jacksonville and the path of Hurricane Dora.

THE FIRST BRITISH INVASION BEGAN when the first shots of the American Revolution were fired in Lexington, Massachusetts, on April 19, 1775. Just 189 years later and a mere thirteen miles southeast, the British once again lay siege to the area with the September 12, 1964, appearance of the Beatles at the Boston Garden.

After death threats in Montreal and a hurricane in Jacksonville, Florida, Boston provided some welcome relief to the Beatles, who were both mentally and physically exhausted. Leaving Jacksonville immediately after the Gator Bowl show, the boys flew into Beantown, arriving at Hanscom Air Force Base at 3:22 a.m. About 200 fans, some of whom had waited over ten hours to welcome the group, were kept about a mile from the runway. Even so, Boston officials took no chances with security, protecting the Beatles with a guard that rivaled any in the city's history. As they exited the plane, they were swiftly

KEVIN COLE/BOSTON HERALD (2)

Fans (above) hold fast to their tickets admitting them to see their idols in person, while several girls (left) can't believe they are in the same concert hall as the Fab Four.

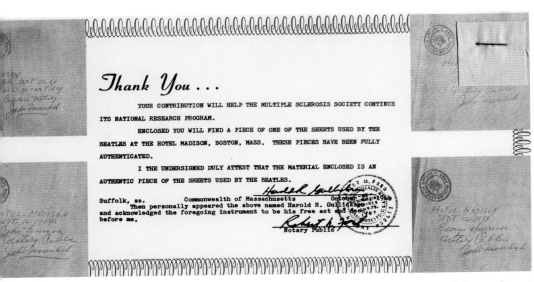

Thank You . . .

YOUR CONTRIBUTION WILL HELP THE MULTIPLE SCLEROSIS SOCIETY CONTINUE ITS NATIONAL RESEARCH PROGRAM.

ENCLOSED YOU WILL FIND A PIECE OF ONE OF THE SHEETS USED BY THE BEATLES AT THE HOTEL MADISON, BOSTON, MASS. THESE PIECES HAVE BEEN FULLY AUTHENTICATED.

I THE UNDERSIGNED DULY ATTEST THAT THE MATERIAL ENCLOSED IS AN AUTHENTIC PIECE OF THE SHEETS USED BY THE BEATLES.

Suffolk, ss.   Commonwealth of Massachusetts   October 21, 1964
Then personally appeared the above named Harold R. Gullickson
and acknowledged the foregoing instrument to be his free act and deed
before me.

Notary Public

This is a Genuine Piece of Bedsheet slept on by one of the BEATLES on their N. American tour—Aug.-Sept., 1964. Beatles Historical Society 1246 Folsom S. F.

PERSONAL

BEATLE Bed Sheet

A group billing themselves as "The Beatles Historical Society" sold off bed sheets (above and right) to benefit the Multiple Sclerosis Society. The venerable Boston Garden (below), and an official press pass (lower right) in the form of a ribbon that journalists wore instead of carried.

whisked away in limousines, escorted by at least two dozen police vehicles. In this hasty retreat, however, both Ringo and press officer Derek Taylor were left behind. Taylor vehemently complained about the rough treatment they had received.

After the fifteen-mile trip into Boston, the caravan arrived at the Hotel Madison, which was connected to the Boston Garden by a series of underground walkways. Using a ramp and a freight elevator, the entourage safely entered the hotel, making its way to the eleventh floor, which had been reserved in its entirety for the Beatles party. Only a few fans were waiting at the hotel to welcome the Beatles when they arrived in the pre-dawn hours, but by midafternoon some 3,000 fans crowded the streets below the group's window. Hotel Madison

PRESS

BEATLES

BOSTON

GARDEN

SEPT. 12

HOTEL *Madison*

BOSTON 14, *Mass.*

BOSTON GARDEN·ARENA
CORPORATION

WESTON W. ADAMS
CHAIRMAN

WALTER A. BROWN
PRESIDENT

NORTH STATION
BOSTON 14, MASSACHUSETTS
(AREA CODE 617) 227-3206

EDWARD J. POWERS
VICE PRESIDENT AND TREASURER

LES STOUT
DIRECTOR OF PUBLIC RELATIONS

Q4

May 14, 1964

General Artists Corporation
640 Fifth Avenue
New York City, New York

Att: Mr. Irv Dinkin

Gentlemen:

Enclosed herewith are four copies of signed contracts between this
Corporation and NEMS Enterprises, Ltd. for the personal appearance of the
Beatles plus additional supporting attractions at Boston Garden on Saturday
evening, September 12, 1964.

It is our understanding that in the event of cancellation of this
performance by the Beatles due to circumstances beyond our control, that
all monies advanced as a guarantee under terms of this contract, will be
returned to this corporation within twenty-four hours after such cancellation
by General Artists Corporation.

Also under paragraph 1 of Additional Terms and Conditions "Stage
Curtains", we would like to advise that our arena stage setup does not have
stage curtains.

I am enclosing four copies of this letter to be considered as part of
the enclosed contracts. Will you kindly arrange to have these copies
executed by the properly designated person.

Very truly yours,

BOSTON GARDEN-ARENA CORPORATION

By _____
President

Accepted and Agreed:

By _____
(Authorized Signature)

WAB:am

proved to be the perfect lodging because there was no need to transport the group to the concert venue. Originally opened in 1930 as the Hotel Manger, it had hosted dozens of celebrities, sports teams, and politicians in its heyday.

As the tour was being planned, General Artists Corporation (GAC)'s Norm Weiss had recommended to Beatles manager Brian Epstein that the group play Boston's historic Fenway Park on September 3. Fenway had a seating capacity of 30,000, and an offer was on the table for a $25,000 guarantee plus 60 percent of the gross. Epstein quickly nixed the idea, however, and later chose the Indiana State Fair for September 3. Meanwhile, September 12, originally slotted for a concert in Montgomery, Alabama, had been become available because of the group's opposition to the state's

WMEX'S BEATLEMANIAC
Fan Club

THIS CERTIFIES THAT THE HOLDER IS A MEMBER IN
GOOD STANDING AND LOVES THE BEATLES TO PIECES.

TWO GOOD RULES TO FOLLOW

1. Listen to the WMEX Good Guys to hear all the latest Beatle Records.

2. Be a Credit to your Community.

A postcard from the Hotel Madison (above left). The hotel was connected to the arena and made it convenient for the Beatles during their stay in Boston. Walter Brown (above), president of Boston Garden, signed this letter addressed to GAC. A WMEX fan club card (left). The station was locked in a ratings battle with WBZ to lure Beatles listeners.

stance on segregation. Consequently, the legendary Walter A. Brown, president of the Boston Garden-Arena Corporation, stepped in and worked with GAC's Irv Dinkin to book the Beatles for that date.

Walter Brown was born in the Boston area and is credited with the development and expansion of ice hockey in America. He also cofounded the Ice Capades and was the original owner of the NBA champion Boston Celtics. The Walter A. Brown Trophy was awarded to the NBA champs until it was renamed the Larry O'Brien Trophy in 1977. Sadly, Brown passed away just five days before the Beatles played in his beloved arena. The Garden, which opened in 1928 as the Boston Madison Square Garden, was initially built for boxing matches and had some notable flaws, such as a shortened hockey rink and a

Fans line up in front of the Garden box office (right) and the Fab Four on stage (far right) with Ringo's drum riser draped in colorful bunting.

lack of air conditioning. Nevertheless, the arena's history is unparalleled in terms of sporting events, political rallies, and concerts.

The Boston Garden contract, signed on May 11, 1964, matched the Fenway deal—a guaranteed fee of $25,000 plus 60 percent of the gross receipts. The savvy Brown included his own rider stating that "in the event of cancellation of this performance by the Beatles due to circumstances beyond our control that all monies advanced will be returned in 24 hours." He was the only promoter on the 1964 tour to make this request. Brown also made it clear to GAC and Epstein that the Boston Garden stage setup "does not have curtains," a provision GAC required of promoters.

Tickets to the September 12 show were sold out three months in advance. Scalpers asked as much as $50 a ticket—an almost unheard-of sum in 1964. Prior to the Boston performance, the city's number-one radio station, WBZ, and Cleveland's KYW held a contest whose first prize was a trip to London to see the Beatles. The contest rules were simple: "In twenty-five words or less, tell us why you want to see the Beatles." Of course, thousands of entries poured in. WBZ's Bruce Bradley announced the winner on the air: sixteen-year-old Rosemary Hanagen, who sadly admitted that she looked like Ringo. As Bradley later stated, "How could we turn that down?" The deejay made good on his promise and, with Rosemary and her chaperone in tow, traveled to London to see the Beatles perform at the Prince of Wales Theatre, site of their historic Royal Command Performance the previous November. Bradley fondly recalled the concert and how fans were poised to rush the stage as Paul belted out "Long Tall Sally," the last song of the evening. As the group gave their

Paul and John belt out one of their hits to the 13,909 fans that attended. Promoters tried to cash in by presenting a U.K. based band called the Minets in an arena a mile away, but only 500 people showed up to hear the "Purveyors of the Surrey Sound."

customary bow, Bradley sensed a riot coming on. But just then, "God Save the Queen" began playing on the venue's PA system. To his amazement, the audience stopped in its tracks and stood silent as the anthem was played. It was, as he recalls, "one of the most unbelievable things I've ever seen"—at least until the Boston show.

On the evening of Saturday, September 12, some 5,000 teenagers waited in line outside the Boston Garden, eager to enter the venue. The police on duty were ordered to remove their badges for fear of having them ripped from their vests. Traffic was stopped in all directions around the arena, and WBZ newsman Gary LaPierre, microphone in hand, gave this report: "I've never seen so many kids around a building in my life. There were thousands just standing and trying to get into the Garden. If the kids saw a microphone or a camera, they would come up to you and ask about the Beatles. If you mentioned you saw them or talked to them they would rip buttons off your jacket or beg for cigarette butts from the Beatles. It was really crazy."

In the meantime, the Beatles were subjected to yet another press conference. Bruce Bradley recalls a tender moment between Paul and a girl of seven or eight in the hotel's Madison Room. The entire news staff had brought their kids to the conference—a real no-no, as there were strict rules regulating attendees. The little girl told Paul that she had all of his bubble gum cards and asked, "Is all the stuff on the cards true?" Without missing a beat, Paul reassured her, saying, "Yup, it's all true, of course it's true!" Fourteen-year-old Kathie Logue also infiltrated security, brazenly entering the press conference with a *Datebook* press pass she had sent away for in the mail.

Three college buddies—Steve Small, Rich Hershenson and Charlie Kimball—crashed the press conference and managed to sneak in a few questions to the group. Steve worked at Yale University's radio station, WYBC, and simply called Beatles press secretary Bess Coleman for permission to attend the conference. Her reply? "Sure. Come up to the second floor. If you have any trouble, ask for me." He was astonished that his ploy had worked. Steve invited Rich and Charlie to join him, but at their own risk. When the trio showed up at the Madison Room, Steve simply flashed his Yale press card. Rich and Charlie, who had not been invited, carried Steve's camera equipment so it would appear that they were with him. Unfortunately, the security guard allowed only Steve to enter.

Undeterred, Rich and Charlie devised a new plan. The pair returned to the same door and passed off their Harvard and Dartmouth freshman ID cards as press cards. Incredibly, they were admitted. But another hurdle lay in their path as they approached another ring of guards close to the entrance of the Madison Room. The two young men quickly slipped into the restroom until things quieted down. When they felt it was safe to peek out, they encountered a bedraggled Coleman. After some quick thinking, Rich told her that he was Steve Small from Yale Radio and that she had promised him entry into the press conference. Coleman readily agreed, instructing the guards to allow both Rich and Charlie inside.

Steve, sitting in the front row, was dumbfounded when he felt a tap on his shoulder and looked up to see his two good friends sitting behind him. Three ordinary teenagers had cracked the Beatles' tight security and were now front and center as the Beatles entered the room. They were able to ask questions, take photographs, and shake hands with their idols. Steve remembered calling out to Ringo just before snapping his photo. The drummer turned toward him and

WMEX's Arnie Ginsberg, a widely popular DJ, seems to be enjoying the chaos unfolding around him. Ginsberg would also emcee the 1966 Boston Suffolk Downs show.

In perhaps one of the more unusual images of the 1964 tour, four somber Beatles clutch their instruments in the back seat of a limo. They were often transported to various venues around the country in this fashion. This image is from Atlantic City.

quipped, "Now, what newspaper could you be from ... with a Polaroid!?" Upon leaving, the teenagers snapped up used chewing gum and cigarette butts from the press table. They also got several autographs, including John's inside his book, *In His Own Write*. Rich remembered discarding the cigarette butts after his mother informed him she would not tolerate them in her house.

Because they were so preoccupied with getting into the press conference, the three friends never bothered to get tickets to the show. A Boston official heard of their plight and offered them the one ticket he had with him. Since it wouldn't have been fair for only one of them to go, they chose a girl standing outside the Garden whose mother had been pleading for a ticket. They sold it at face value and split the proceeds three ways.

Perhaps one of the more unusual questions of the night was from a reporter who asked, "Do you ever get the melancholy thought that your days of song and money may be numbered, and that you may suddenly awake one day to discover you've gone by the way of other fads, particularly miniature golf?" Paul replied, "We'll get out before we fade, and anyway, we've made more money than anyone in miniature golf."

After the press conference, the Beatles changed into their stage clothes and readied themselves to play a single show at the Garden. The boys, with instruments in hand, were transported by limousine to the adjacent venue to prepare for their single show.

As 13,909 fans filled the Garden for the concert, Bruce Bradley of WBZ and Arnie Ginsberg of WMEX (WBZ's crosstown rival) strode to the microphone to introduce the Beatles. Each of the emcees would have preferred to host the show on his own, but Capitol Records requested the pairing in an effort to maximize airplay. As George repaired a broken guitar string backstage, the deejays stalled for time by performing their own rendition of "Love Me Do," complete with harmonica.

Ginsberg had just rushed back from Detroit, where he'd been on a promotional visit to Ford Motors. While there, he test-drove their newest creation, the Mustang. Exhausted from the trip and running purely on adrenaline, he made the introduction before taking his assigned seat right in front of the stage. He'd never seen anything like what he witnessed that night, recalling "girls screaming, crying, fainting, going into convulsions and jumping up and down." Through all the commotion, he managed to keep his own emotions in check, as evidenced the next day in the *Boston Globe*. The paper ran a photograph of the Beatles onstage with the caption "Fans enjoying the Beatles while an unidentified man seems unimpressed by the whole thing." The unidentified man was Ginsberg.

A mile from the Garden, another concert was in progress. Promoters looking to cash in on the Beatles craze hoped to fill a 7,200-seat arena for an appearance by an obscure British group called the Minets, whose members had "the same type of haircuts and dress as the Beatles and have often been mistaken for them around Boston." But only 500 showed to watch these purveyors of the "Surrey Sound," leaving thousands of seats empty—proof positive that these imitators had nothing on the real deal. The Minets would become little more than a footnote in British Invasion lore.

At the conclusion of yet another spirited performance, the Beatles left the stage, boarded a freight elevator, jumped into limousines, and raced toward Hanscom Field. Arriving at 10:15 p.m., they would have to wait another hour for the rest of the touring party to arrive before departing for their next stop, Baltimore, Maryland, where they would play two shows the following day. With only seven cities remaining, the tour was finally starting to wind down.

As the Beatles' Hotel Madison suite was being cleaned, approximately 150 teenage girls happily followed the maids around, snapping up used toothpaste tubes and tissues while removing every metal room number on the eleventh floor. Several wouldn't leave without first kissing the doorknob to room 1123, the group's private quarters.

The Hotel Madison closed its doors forever in 1978 and was imploded in 1986 to make room for the Tip O'Neill Federal Building. The Boston Garden, which had long served as the home of two legendary sports teams (the NBA's Celtics and the NHL's Bruins), met the same fate in 1997. After holding its final event in 1995, it sat vacant for two years before it was demolished. The original site is now a parking lot adjacent to the Garden's successor, an arena currently named TD Garden.

Memorabilia from the Boston Gardens concert are among the most sought-after of any on the '64 tour. Very few tickets, used or unused, have survived of the 13,909 that were sold. Because the show was sold out months in advance, neither handbills nor posters were needed to advertise it.

The boys wave goodbye at Boston's Hanscom Field for a short flight to the next tour stop in Baltimore, Maryland.

BALTIMORE

September 13, 1964
Civic Center
Two Shows, 2:30 p.m. and 7:30 p.m.

The Baltimore Civic Center. Two Beatles concerts rocked the venue 150 years to the day, after the British Army bombed the city's harbor.

THE BEATLES ARRIVED IN BALTIMORE, MARYLAND, on September 13, 1964, 150 years to the day after another encounter with the British took place in the city's famous harbor. Francis Scott Key, a thirty-five-year-old Washington lawyer and budding poet, was an eyewitness to his country's survival from bombardment by the British Royal Navy on September 13, 1814. The brave defenders of Fort McHenry made a heroic stand against the enemy that night. The tattered American flag that survived the assault inspired Key to pen the words to "The Star Spangled Banner"—America's national anthem. While Key witnessed the "rockets' red glare and the bombs bursting in air" during the twenty-five-hour battle, Baltimoreans endured a thirty-seven-hour British assault in 1964, this time in the form of Beatlemania.

Baltimore began preparing for the Beatles' arrival well in advance. At Friendship Airport, manager John Scott had heard reports of how fans, especially females, would tear up the premises wherever the group was seen. Anticipating the worst, he wisely moved newly purchased airport furniture into a nearby hangar. Meanwhile, at the downtown Holiday Inn where the group would stay, mounted police stood by to protect the hotel.

The Beatles were set to play two shows at the Civic Center—an afternoon performance at 2:30 and an evening show at 7:30 p.m. When their chartered American Flyers Constellation appeared in the early-morning sky over Baltimore, it brought delight to the assembled fans—reports of crowd size ranged from 500 to 2,000—and perhaps dismay to the 200 police officers called in to maintain order. For their part, after their raucous performance in Boston, the Beatles were relieved to see the limousines that would take them into downtown Baltimore.

From the airport terminal, the entourage sped along the Baltimore-Washington Parkway flanked by twenty-two patrol cars and pursued by carloads of fans. Once they reached the city limits, the limos were allowed to travel the wrong way down one-way streets in order to ditch the fans on their way to the Holiday Inn parking garage. Reaching the hotel, the Beatles were led to the service elevator. Within minutes, they entered suite 1013, their tenth-floor, four-room digs located just off the elevator. Still pumped from their sold-out Boston show and unable to sleep, they stayed up for a while.

The Holiday Inn chain is an American icon. Founder Kemmons Wilson opened the first of his hotels in 1952 and, through a franchising program, built the brand into one of the largest hotel chains in the

world. First dubbed the "Nation's Innkeeper" and later the "World's Innkeeper," the hotel, with its instantly recognizable roadside sign, provided travelers with quality and consistency. The Baltimore location featured an eatery atop the hotel called Circle One—one of the nation's first revolving restaurants. Although Circle One closed in 1974, visitors can still stay at the hotel, which is remarkably unchanged since the Beatles' visit.

Joel Krisch, whose company American Motor Inns Inc. was one of the largest Holiday Inn franchisers, was the builder and owner of the Baltimore property. He offered General Artists Corporation (GAC) and Beatles management an entire floor of free rooms if they would agree to meet his children. Krisch's daughter Linda, who was ten at the time, waited in the basement with her father at 2 a.m., clutching his hand in antici-pation of the limos that would enter the parking garage. After the group's arrival, Krisch marched her and her thirteen-year-old sister to suite 1013 to meet the Beatles. Linda (now Vinson) recalled that Paul, the unofficial ambassador of the group,

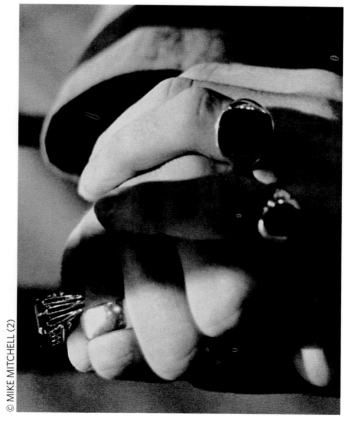

© MIKE MITCHELL (2)

Three weeks into the tour and the Fab Four (above) are all smiles, except for Ringo. A close up (left) showing off the many rings of the talented drummer.

WCAO Radio was the official sponsor of the show, DJ Kerby Scott introduced the band to the fans in Baltimore. "Official sponsoring" stations made up after-concert fliers to one-up their competitors.

WCAO PRESENTS "The Beatles" IN BALTIMORE

WINNERS OF THE WCAO "Youth Creed" CONTEST

Judy Dalgreen
Kathy Petschin

Do You Want To Know A Secret

And I Love Her

Paul

All My Loving

GEORGE

P. S. I Love You

Kerby Scott

Twist and Shout

JOHN

George

Can't Buy Me Love

Johnny Dark

If I Fell

STARR

Hard Days Night

John   RINGO

LENNON

McCARTNEY

I Wanna Hold Your Hand

Civic Center
Sept. 13, '64

Love Me Do

PAUL

Boys

HARRISON

Frank Luber

Please Please Me

I'll Be Back

"stands up, bends down and shakes my hand and said, 'It's a pleasure to meet you, Miss Krisch." Krisch-Vinson vividly remembered other girls riding the elevators up and down, trying to get to the tenth floor. One even dressed as a maid to try to get to the Beatles.

Hotel manager Carl Hurd recalled how frightened the Beatles were after they'd come so close to getting ripped apart by fans in other cities. He also observed how perfectly content they were in their rooms, away from the public eye. Frank Luber, the news director from WCAO, was allowed into the group's inner sanctum to interview them and just hang out. The newsman recalled that the Beatles, while "in their rooms, could play music, write songs, make jokes, and simply relax."

The promoters of the Baltimore concert were Irvin and Israel Feld and their company, Super Attractions, Inc. The brothers not only produced rock 'n' roll shows but also promoted ballets and Broadway shows and represented such headliners as Dean Martin and Jerry Lewis. The Felds partnered with GAC in promoting the ill-fated Winter Dance Party tour that ended with the plane crash claiming the lives of Buddy Holly, Ritchie Valens, and J. P. "The Big Bopper" Richardson. The brothers also co-promoted the Beatles' first American concert, at the Washington Coliseum on February 11, 1964 (with Coliseum owner Harry Lynn); assisted Stan Irwin in Las Vegas; and promoted the band's appearances in Dallas on September 18, 1964, and at the D.C. Stadium on August 15, 1966.

Despite their Beatles connection, the Feld brothers are probably best known for buying the Ringling Bros. and Barnum & Bailey Circus in 1967. Irvin's only son, Kenneth, joined the company in 1970 as co-producer. The Felds sold the circus to Mattel in 1971 but bought it back in 1982. Kenneth continues to run the company (now named Feld Entertainment). Along with the circus, Feld also produces large-scale Broadway, Las Vegas, and sports-related shows. For the Beatles' only Baltimore appearance, the brothers negotiated with GAC to book two shows at the Civic Center for a $25,000 guarantee plus 60 percent of the gross.

The downtown Holiday Inn (left) with its novel rooftop revolving restaurant. The Beatles threw a party here after the show. Souvenir promoters cut up bed sheets (below) and sold them to fans desperate to own a piece of anything a Beatle had touched.

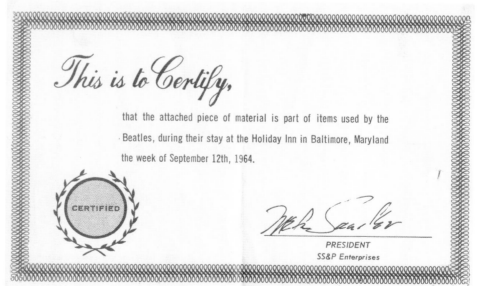

This is to Certify,

that the attached piece of material is part of items used by the Beatles, during their stay at the Holiday Inn in Baltimore, Maryland the week of September 12th, 1964.

CERTIFIED

PRESIDENT
SS&P Enterprises

When the Beatles awoke to a light, chilly drizzle on the morning of September 13, they found the Holiday Inn utterly besieged with fans under the watch of over 100 police officers. The morning paper reported that "the steady rain had little effect on the teen-age libido but it did bog things down a bit for the older set. The annual Defender's Day parade was cancelled. More than 25,000 persons were to have participated and another half million were expected to watch."

As the time drew closer for the short trek to the Civic Center, an elaborate transportation plan was hatched to fool the unsuspecting fans. Limousines, police cars, and ambulances were parked adjacent

CARROLL JAMES AND THE BEATLES IN BALTIMORE

Mitch Litm

Carroll James of WWDC in Washington D.C. (above), was among the first DJ's to play Beatles records in the States. He was the master of ceremonies at their first American concert. The Feld Brothers promoted the show (right) evidenced by this news ad.

The Feld Brothers • Super Attractions Inc. PRESENTS

THE BEATLES IN PERSON

BALTIMORE CIVIC CENTER

201 W. BALTIMORE ST.—BALTIMORE, MD.

SUNDAY, SEPT. 13 2 BIG SHOWS 4 P.M. and 8:30 P.M.

Remaining Tickets For These 2 IN PERSON Performances
Go On Sale Tomorrow Morning at 10:00 A.M. At The
Civic Center Box Office and Central Ticket Agency, 206 N. Liberty St.
PRICES: $2.50, $3.00 and $3.75, ALL SEATS RESERVED
BALTIMORE IS ONE OF THE FEW FORTUNATE CITIES THAT WILL
HAVE THE OPPORTUNITY OF SEEING THE BEATLES IN PERSON.
This may be your only chance to see these World Famous Artists
BEFORE YOUR VERY EYES. Your favorite D.J.s from local stations
will be on stage.

IMPORTANT NOTICE! Originally the Beatles In Person Show was scheduled
for 2:30 P.M. and 7:30 P.M. THE NEW CORRECT TIMES FOR BOTH SHOWS
ARE: The Afternoon Show 4:00 P.M. and The Evening Show at 8:30 P.M. PLEASE
REMEMBER THESE CORRECT TIMES AS BOTH SHOWS WILL START PROMPTLY.

GOOD SEATS ARE STILL AVAILABLE FOR THE BEATLES SHOW
GET YOUR TICKETS IMMEDIATELY • AVOID DISAPPOINTMENT
ON SALE TOMORROW MORNING, STARTING AT 10 A. M.
AT THE CIVIC CENTER BOX OFFICE & CENTRAL TICKET AGENCY, 206 N. LIBERTY ST.

to the hotel, leading fans to believe that the group was leaving in one of these conveyances. Instead, they were lured into a trap. As the vehicles left in different directions, fans took off running after each while the Beatles calmly entered an unassuming laundry truck. They crouched down for the thirty-second drive to the Civic Center before dashing into the back entrance under heavy guard.

Around 5 p.m., as Jackie DeShannon finished her set for the afternoon show, seventy-one police officers and security guards took their places next to the stage. The audience of 13,000 knew what was coming next. The Beatles hit the stage after being introduced by WCAO's Kerby Scott. Linda Sherwood, a fan sitting far back in the audience, recalled, "We could see them, but only in between the bouncing heads and flailing arms in the crowd. Even my mother got up on one of the chairs, which really surprised me." Frank Luber, the newsman from WCAO, was sitting right next to the stage and remembered that he "couldn't hear a thing and I don't even know if they could hear themselves." The *Baltimore Sun* reported that more people showed up for the previous year's Peter, Paul and Mary concert, an obvious swipe at the Beatles' drawing power and decidedly non-folk style.

As the first show drew to a finish, the boys had to patiently wait backstage, clean up, change, and attend another press conference. Some adventurous young girls thought they had an ingenious plan to meet the Beatles—by literally delivering themselves to the band as the press conference was about to begin. In Trojan horse fashion, the girls placed two of their own in a box and tied a large red ribbon around it, then stamped it "Beatle Fan Mail," hoping they could slip inside without being discovered. Unfortunately, a guard checked the box as it was being wheeled into the Civic Center, and the ruse was up.

During the press conference, the Beatles were asked how long they thought they would last and what they would do to occupy their time. All replied in unison, "Play basketball!" When asked what he thought of American television, Ringo mocked it: "You get eighteen stations, but you can't get a good picture on any of them."

Journalist Larry Kane interviewed John backstage between shows, asking an insightful question about ways to stop war. The young singer's response spoke of frustration: "I don't think there is one [way to stop war], you know. Not if everybody was all rich and happy, and each

On stage at the Civic
Center, 28,000 fans
attended the two
shows.

country had all they wanted. They'd still want the next bit." John would have much more to say on that subject during his activist years of the late '60s and early '70s, of course. Prompted by Kane, he reflected on America: "I think it's marvelous, you know. I like it, and especially places like New York and Hollywood, you know. I like the big places. And it's amazing to see a place like Las Vegas. Who ever thought of building a place in the middle of a desert, you know? Things like that are marvelous."

With the press conference finished, the Beatles were treated to dinner in the dressing room of the Civic Center before heading to the stage for the evening performance. The second show was essentially a repeat of the first show, as fans twisted and shouted to the hits they'd heard only on their radios. Someone had hung a banner in the rafters that read "Hail Britannia," an action that, in Francis Scott Key's day, would have been considered treason. It was reported that the smell of urine drifted through the crowd as the girls literally lost control. Seventy-five inconsolable adolescents were treated by Civic Center staff for various levels of hysteria.

After playing two shows for a total of 28,000 fans, the Beatles returned safely to the Holiday Inn. But instead of heading to bed, they hosted a party at the Circle One rooftop restaurant until 3:15 a.m. as members of the Exciters entertained. It remains unclear whether George was present at the party. Some sources claim that the lead guitarist, still fighting a bad cold, was taken from the downtown Holiday Inn to another Krisch-owned Holiday Inn in north Baltimore for some much-needed peace and quiet. The hotel, located just off the intersection of Joppa Road and Loch Raven Boulevard, still stands today as a Ramada Inn.

The story, bolstered by firsthand accounts, gets stranger at this point. Some accounts hold that George wanted to visit some American schools the next day, including Mercy High, a Catholic school for girls not far from the hotel. According to these reports, the principal, Sister Michelle Carroll, personally took the Beatle and two members of the group's entourage on a tour of the school, with stops at the cafeteria and gymnasium. To avoid pandemonium, she hid George away between classes. At the school today, a commemorative plaque has been placed over the drinking fountain where the Beatle is said to have taken a sip of water. Sister Michelle claimed she also accompanied George on a tour of Leith Walk Elementary School, a public school a few blocks away. If this story is true, it must be considered one of the craziest stunts to take place on the 1964 American tour.

Another event that some say took place in Baltimore is equally questionable: the signing of the only guitar known to be autographed by all four Beatles. According to press officer Derek Taylor in his 1984 book *Fifty Years Adrift*, guitar teacher Tony Saks had asked if Taylor could get Saks's Rickenbacker guitar

signed by the group. After much prodding by Saks, Taylor reluctantly agreed. The morning after the Baltimore concert, as the Beatles awoke, Taylor handed them the guitar along with explicit instructions from Saks on how the signatures should be made (written with a hard pen through strips of gold leaf). The Beatles dutifully agreed.

This account, of course, conflicts with the claim that George awoke at a different Holiday Inn and later toured two schools. Whether or not Saks received genuine signatures is open to conjecture. A recent assessment of the signed guitar by a prominent Beatles autograph expert ruled that it was actually signed by road manager Neil Aspinall. It's interesting to note that Taylor's book was edited by none other than George himself—the one person who knew what actually occurred on the morning of September 14.

What history does tell us is that the Beatles showered, ate lunch, and hopped into their limousines for the ride back to Friendship Airport, where they departed for their twentieth stop on the tour: Pittsburgh, Pennsylvania. As Baltimore faded from the Beatles' sight, Holiday Inn workers were busy tearing out the shaggy DayGlo carpet in suite 1013. The carpet was sold by Krisch for $1,000 to hucksters who cut it up into one-inch squares that sold for a dollar apiece.

Collectibles from the Baltimore concerts consist of tickets from the show and the generic mass-produced North American tour program. The Felds didn't need to produce handbills or posters; only newspaper advertisements were placed to announce the shows. Unused tickets for either concert are extremely rare; because stubs list only the date, venue, price, section, and seat number, most were likely thrown away.

Framed in the spotlight, the Fab Four sing one of their hits to the enthusiastic crowd in Baltimore.

PITTSBURGH

September 14, 1964
Civic Arena
8 p.m.

ON SEPTEMBER 14, THE BEATLES HEADED TO PITTSBURGH, Pennsylvania, for the twentieth stop on the tour—one made possible by a generous gesture from a factory worker to his son. An employee of the Westinghouse plant in East Pittsburgh lent $5,000 to help his son bring the Beatles to Steel City. The father had never heard of the Beatles, but upon learning of their incredible popularity from one of his nine children, he decided to borrow money from his credit union by putting a lien on his house.

The story began when twenty-five-year-old Pat DiCesare, who managed a local record distribution outlet named Regal Records, noticed a huge demand from local record shops for anything Beatles. DiCesare knew instinctively that the group was going to be special, so he recommended to Tim Tormey, the most successful concert promoter in town, that he book the group. But things wouldn't be that simple; the Beatles booking would be very expensive.

Tormey called the William Morris Agency in New York for guidance, and they referred him to their competition: Norman Weiss, the Beatles' American booking agent at General Artists Corporation (GAC). Tormey had never worked with Weiss, so he continued working with Roz Ross, his contact at William Morris. Meanwhile, other Pittsburgh promoters, such as Lenny Litman and the powerful Westinghouse-owned KDKA radio station, began announcing around town that they'd secured a date for the Beatles. Undeterred, Tormey quietly continued his contact with Ross, hoping he'd get the nod from GAC.

In early spring, Tormey received a call from Ross informing him that if he could raise $5,000, he'd stand a good chance of landing the Beatles. As in a scene from a Hollywood gangster film, Ross told Tormey he would need to deliver the cash to the bartender at Brooklyn's Club Elegant as soon as possible. Neither Tormey nor his new partner, DiCesare, had such a sum readily available—and trying to lure potential investors based on a clandestine meeting with a bartender in Brooklyn seemed likely to be tough. Meanwhile, Ross was putting pressure on Tormey to have the money to her the next day or risk losing the date.

TIM TORMEY PRESENTS

★ IN PERSON ★

THE Beatles

Plus . . . AN ALL-STAR SHOW

CIVIC ARENA • MON., SEPT. 14 • 8 P.M.

GOOD SEATS STILL AVAILABLE

Tickets are $5.90 each and may be purchased BY MAIL ONLY!! Send check or money order to "BEATLES", P. O. Box 431, Pittsburgh 30, Pa., enclosing a self-addressed stamped return envelope. Make check payable to Tim Tormey Associates. All Seats Are Reserved. *In answer to the numerous inquiries, Good Seats Are Still Available for those who act NOW!*

DO NOT CALL ARENA — BY MAIL ONLY!

Determined to round up the $5,000, DiCesare approached his partners at the Regal Records distribution plant, but they turned him down flat. He remained convinced that a Beatles concert would be a surefire success, however. After all, his record retailers would regularly try to bribe him to get Beatles records into their stores ahead of the competition. But securing the $5,000 fee was looking more and more unlikely—until he told his father about his predicament. DiCesare's dad listened intently to his frustrations and then, the next day, slid an envelope across the kitchen table containing a cashier's check for $5,000. It was more money than the factory worker would make in a year, but he trusted his son to get the deal done and book the hottest act in entertainment. Fortunately, DiCesare and Tormey were able to get the money into the proper hands on time—wiring it to an attorney, not handing it over to a bartender as originally planned. Then the wait began as they prayed they could secure a concert date with GAC and Beatles manager Brian Epstein.

The following week, booking agents from GAC called Tormey to set the date: September 14 at Pittsburgh's Civic Arena. He was shocked to learn there would be a guarantee of $35,000. The promoter had never paid more than $3,500 for a one-night headline act—but with some fast negotiating, Tormey and GAC settled on a $20,000 guarantee against 60 percent of the gate. The Beatles were secured.

DiCesare assured the promoter that the concert would be a sellout. Unfortunately, just after putting the deal together, he was faced with the draft and a likely stint in the army. He joined the National Guard and was ordered to report to Fort Knox in Kentucky at the end of May for six months of training, meaning he would miss the Beatles concert he had worked so hard to get. Before departing, he agonized with Tormey over the ticket price. The men had never charged over $3.50 a ticket, but because of the high-priced guarantee with a percentage on top, they figured they'd need to clear $5

As the boys make their way down the airline steps Ringo ducks an apple thrown from the crowd. Pittsburgh was the Beatles 20th stop on the tour.

Radio station KQV won a tight battle against rival KDKA for exclusive rights to promote the concert. This KQV flier from 1966 invited fans to travel to nearby Cleveland for the show at Municipal Stadium.

September 14, 1964

KQV's "FUN LOVIN' FIVE"

Welcomed

THE BEATLES

To Pittsburgh

NOW . . . KQV invites you

To help Welcome The Beatles

To Cleveland on Sunday, August 14th

DIAL KQV-AUDIO 14

For Details

on how you can WIN a Free Trip

To Cleveland to see The Beatles

per ticket. In the end, they settled on $5.90.

Tickets were sold by mail order only, and Tormey decided to use local nuns to handle all of the requests. Orders arrived as quickly as the nuns could process them. Within a couple of days, all 12,600 seats had been sold. The sellout allowed DiCesare to proudly repay his father the $5,000 loan while thanking him for his trust. Complimentary tickets were out of the question; even Mayor Joe Barr was turned down. On the original proposed tour schedule sent to Epstein that spring, Weiss had penned in Pittsburgh's Forbes Field for September 10, but Epstein preferred the smaller Civic Arena. Weiss had also suggested Allentown, Pennsylvania (300 miles from Pittsburgh), as a concert location.

After the Beatles performed in Baltimore, Maryland, they stayed the night at the Holiday Inn there, leaving the next day for the short flight into Pittsburgh. On board their plane were two disc jockeys from KQV, whose mere presence set off a firestorm given the ongoing war between that station and rival KDKA, which each wanted the Beatles concert to themselves.

KQV program director John Rook met with Tim Tormey, who promised him exclusive sponsorship of the Beatles concert in return for free promotion of several other acts he was bringing to Pittsburgh prior to the Beatles. Rook agreed and gave airtime to such acts as the Rolling Stones and the Dave Clark Five. The Stones played a venue called Danceland and attracted only about 400 people, although the next year, riding high on the success of "Satisfaction," Mick and the boys attracted over 9,000 fans to the Civic Arena, much to Tormey's delight.

Because of KQV's support of Tormey, the two went on to produce and sponsor shows together until the early 1970s. Rook, who was a good friend of rocker Eddie Cochran, couldn't understand the Beatles' popularity and was not receptive to their music—that is, until the Fab Four told him how much Cochran had influenced it.

As the concert drew nearer, the radio wars in Pittsburgh heated up. KQV, to which Tormey had given exclusive rights to promote the concert, was locked in a fierce battle with KDKA. (Interestingly, it was KDKA's parent company, Westinghouse, that employed Pat DiCesare's father.) While KDKA didn't get the sponsorship for the Beatles show, it did broadcast exclusive reports by Beatles entourage members Jim Stagg and Art Schreiber, reporters for its sister station KYW in Cleveland, Ohio. KDKA also planned to send four reporters to cover the show while dispatching its deejay Clark Race to Baltimore, where he would later join the Beatles on their plane to Pittsburgh.

KQV, badly needing a ratings boost and a way to jinx KDKA's plans, hatched a scheme of its own. The station sent deejays Dex Allen and Chuck Brinkman to Baltimore. When they arrived, they met their boss, John Rook, and promptly contacted Bess Coleman, who was assisting Beatles management with logistics. Allen and Brinkman requested seats on the Beatles' plane from Baltimore to Pittsburgh. While Coleman tried her best to get the two deejays a place on the flight, she was unsuccessful. Instead, the men flew to Pittsburgh ahead of the Beatles and awaited their arrival along with the thousands of fans assembled at the airport.

Rook had told Allen and Brinkman that no matter what happened, they were to keep Clark Race off the Beatles' plane. Rook would get his wish. Despite pleas from Stagg and Schreiber, who wanted one of their own to be on board, Race ultimately failed to get a seat on the flight. In all likelihood, he was bumped after Allen and Brinkman complained that he shouldn't get a seat if they couldn't get one. Assuming that this was the work of his rivals, a sheepish Race went on the air the next day to tell his listeners of the unfair tactics employed by KQV. Still not satisfied, KQV had another ratings maneuver up its sleeve that would upstage KDKA at the upcoming press conference and concert.

The plane carrying the Beatles landed at Greater Pittsburgh Airport at 4:36 p.m. amid the screams of 4,000 teenagers who had been gathering since 9 a.m. As expected, the group made a quick escape from the plane into the waiting limousines that would carry them down the Penn-Lincoln Parkway to the Civic Arena. The *Pittsburgh Post-Gazette* would later remark that the security seemed of a level that "no president had ever been afforded." Neal Holmes of Allied Detectives informed his men that "if we're stopped, we'll jump out and surround the Beatles' car. If the crowd breaks the line out here, we'll surround each Beatle." Fans at the airport gave the police notebooks filled with poems and drawings, hoping they might be passed along to the Fab Four. Alas, none were delivered.

The Civic Arena was one of the more interesting venues on the 1964 tour. Built in 1961 primarily for the Civic Light Opera, it was designed with a retractable roof, by architect Edgar Kaufman, so that performances could be staged under the stars. In fact, at the time it opened, the stainless steel venue sported the world's largest dome and retractable roof. Unfortunately, the roof could be opened only when there was less than a 60 percent chance of rain and the wind speed was no more than seven miles per hour. As fans began to queue up for the concert, many were pressing on the arena's tall plate-glass windows. Fearing a collapse, assistant superintendent of police Lawrence J. Maloney ordered barricades erected.

As the Beatles arrived at the venue, they were quickly shuffled to the press conference, where they faced a barrage of questions, including one about their success. Responding to a query about the

The Civic Arena (above) with its retractable roof, an engineering marvel of the day. John quipped in the press conference, "I hope they don't lift the roof while we are playing!" Tormey had National Record Mart handle ticket sales (left).

HERE'S WHAT YOU'VE BEEN WAITING FOR!!

THE **BEATLES**

WILL BE IN

Pittsburgh on September 14th

ONE PERFORMANCE ONLY
CIVIC ARENA—8:00 P. M.
ALL SEATS RESERVED

Tickets will be sold on first-come, first-served basis, only through the mail, not at the Civic Arena, and go on sale immediately. Tickets are priced at $5.90 each and may be obtained by writing: Beatles, P. O. Box 431, Pittsburgh 30, Pa., ENCLOSING A SELF-ADDRESSED STAMPED ENVELOPE. Checks should be made payable to National Record Mart.

PLEASE! Do not call the Arena or National Record Mart--By Mail ONLY

The Fab Four
take questions
from the press in
Pittsburgh. "When
will your fame
end?" they were
asked. Conferences
like these were
becoming mundane
as the group was
being asked the
same questions
repeatedly.

PRIVATE COLLECTION (2)

defining moment in their career, Paul answered, "The turning point was probably stepping up to Brian Epstein as our manager … [and] … the Royal Variety performance in England when we played for the Queen." They were also asked about the venue: "Gentlemen, I would like your reaction to the Civic Arena in which we're located. Did you see the outside?" George responded, "Is this the place that can be changed into an open air?" John added, "I hope they don't lift the roof while we are playing!"

After the press briefing, the boys were treated to a catered dinner inside the converted dressing room of the Penguins hockey team. Tormey wanted his special guests to be comfortable, so he had a local department store, Kaufmann's, furnish the sparse and cold locker room with couches, tables, lamps, and televisions. At first the store was reluctant, but then it realized the potential of selling furniture used by the Beatles. Naturally, they sold it all at a premium. The Beatles commented that it was the most lavishly appointed dressing room on the tour.

Upon entering the arena to prepare for the concert, Rook was pleased to see KQV banners ringing the stage and other areas of the venue; in return for all of the station's free promotional work, Tormey had been true to his word. Now it was time for KQV to get another leg up on its competition—this time by using wireless remote microphones. At the time, ABC owned KQV, and the network was always keen to use the latest technology. Rook had put in an urgent call to ABC and gotten the microphones he wanted. His plan entailed live broadcasts of both the press conference and the concert. When KDKA officials caught wind of Rook's plan, they protested. Tormey had to inform Rook that Beatles management wouldn't allow anything to be carried live. Ultimately, Rook circumvented the issue by recording everything but delaying it seven seconds. By doing so, KQV would still have the upper hand over KDKA.

Existing audio of the show captures all the excitement of the evening, particularly when KQV's Chuck Brinkman took the stage to introduce the group: "All right, make some noise!," he bellowed. "Make some noise! I know you're going to do it, and you're going to be a great audience. KQV welcomes the Beatles!" Brinkman recalled that after his introduction, "the Civic Arena just exploded. I mean pure pandemonium, and you couldn't hear a thing. I had just witnessed the

Promoter Tim Tormey's advertising paid off as 12,603 fans filled the Civic Center, affectionately called the "Igloo" by locals.

same thing twenty-four hours earlier in Baltimore but because it was our city and our stage, the roar seemed so much more intense."

Using his remote microphone, KQV production director Don Shaffer reported back to in-studio deejay Joel Rose, "I can't hear anything! The whole place just blew apart. I thought we were in an air raid! The lights were blinking on and off, and all the little Brownie cameras with their flashbulbs were going bing, bing, bing! And it was really dark in there except for the flashbulbs, which made it seem like the sun was up. I'm going to go home now and have nightmares!"

After the concert, the Beatles left the Civic Arena by ambulance, and then a line of cars, mobile news units, and the like started coming out. KQV newsman Keeve Berman interviewed station personalities as they made their way back to the studio. One had a harrowing experience when he and the engineers were trying to get out of the Civic Arena. The fans outside "were thoroughly convinced that the Beatles were still in the auditorium, and that we were smuggling them out." The hair of one reporter was a mess—so much so that he was mistaken for Ringo. As fans crushed against the car, the tousle-haired

reporter had to open his window and attempt to convince them that the Beatles were already gone. Suddenly a scream went up in the crowd: "He touched the Beatles!" Bedlam ensued, with fans grabbing at the car's interior until the police intervened and escorted the car to safety.

Berman concluded his segment with a question for the harried reporter: "In all of your years of news coverage, have you ever seen anything like this?" The KQV employee replied, "Not in my broadcasting background. I've covered Nikita [Khrushchev], I've covered Lyndon [Johnson], I've covered Barry [Goldwater], and a little bit of everything, but I've never in my life, as far as news value, seen anything like this."

In the aftermath of the Beatles concert, Tim Tormey and Pat DiCesare split the small fortune they made on their joint promotion. DiCesare had already repaid the $5,000 his father had lent him; years later, using proceeds from other shows he promoted, he paid off his parents' $3,500 home mortgage and gave them an additional $5,000, leaving them speechless. It was the least he could do, he said, to thank them "for giving me the chance of a lifetime."

The Beatles left that night for Cleveland and never returned to Pittsburgh. The Cleveland stop would prove to be the most dangerous of the tour, as unruly fans in the city where rock 'n' roll began nearly tore the group to pieces.

The Pittsburgh Civic Arena went on to host such legendary rock acts as the Doors (who recorded their seminal live album *Live in Pittsburgh 1970* at the venue) and the Penguins of the National Hockey League. Affectionately known by locals as the "Igloo," the arena met the wrecking ball on March 31, 2012.

Collectibles from the Pittsburgh show are few. Because the concert quickly sold out, Tormey had no need to print posters or handbills. Unused tickets are extremely rare, and even stubs are hard to locate. On the stub, "The Beatles Show" is printed so fans could keep them as souvenirs. The generic North American tour program was sold at the venue, and after the concert, KQV printed a now quite collectible poster that featured photos from the show and portraits of their on-air personalities.

KQV DJ Chuck Brinkman introduced the Fab Four on stage. The group rocked Pittsburgh for one show and then left the city that night, headed to Cleveland.

CLEVELAND

**September 15, 1964
Public Auditorium
8 p.m.**

"This has never happened to us before, anywhere."
—John Lennon, Cleveland Public Auditorium, September 15, 1964

Paul, George, John, and Ringo answer questions from Cleveland's press as manager Brian Epstein keeps careful watch.

AFTER LITERALLY HUNDREDS OF PERFORMANCES, including those at Liverpool's Casbah, Cavern, and other rough-and-tumble venues, it was in Cleveland, Ohio, that a Beatles gig was stopped cold in its tracks. As Paul McCartney was belting out "All My Loving," the crowd at the Public Auditorium (aka Public Hall) began to push forward toward the stage. Security officials tried desperately to control the onslaught, but to no avail. Teenagers began to fall down in the ensuing chaos, and, fearing they'd be crushed, Inspector Michael Blackwell and Deputy Inspector Carl Bare decided to take matters into their own hands. With the house lights up, Inspector Bare yelled into the stage microphone, declaring the concert over. The Beatles, none too happy to see police officials onstage, at first were intent on continuing to play. The police had other ideas, however, literally forcing the band offstage. After that, it took the pleas of local deejays and a newsman from a local radio station to persuade the group to return and finish their set.

Having been on the road in America for almost thirty days straight, the Beatles just wanted to leave Cleveland, for the next city. But being consummate professionals, they stepped back into the spotlight and completed the concert.

The Beatles' flight from Pittsburgh had landed at Cleveland's Hopkins Airport at 12:32 a.m. on September 15. Mindful of what had happened in other cities, officials were careful not to reveal any information about the arrival. Once the band had safely deplaned and departed for their hotel, an announcement to that effect was made to the 2,500 fans assembled on the other side of the airport. Having waited for hours, the fans were distraught at having missed their chance to see the group.

On the drive to downtown Cleveland, the Beatles' three limousines were guarded by seventeen patrol cars. Police Chief Richard Wagner had told the press before the group's arrival that "our planning for this was more along the lines of a natural disaster." Indeed, by the time the Beatles left town, the taxpayers had been saddled with $14,000 in expenses, including pay for 500 police officers, who racked up 5,000 hours of overtime. Mayor Ralph Locher's comment on the matter showed his disregard for the British musicians: "It does seem extremely costly," he said, "especially when the culture of the city has not been materially advanced."

COLLECTION OF WHK RADIO

© GEORGE SHUBA

Not only did the Cleveland visit get off on the wrong foot, but the mayor would later ban the group from the city, along with rock 'n' roll concerts in general, effectively eliminating Cleveland from the 1965 tour. It would take some fast talking by Norman Wain, owner of WIXY 1260 AM, to bring the boys back in 1966, for a concert that unfortunately resulted in another near-riot.

As in Pittsburgh, a very public sponsorship battle for the Beatles concert had raged between two radio stations—in this city, the Metromedia-owned WHK and the powerhouse 50,000-watt giant KYW. A little misrepresentation as well as some good timing and luck secured the concert for WHK, for which Norman Wain, Bob Weiss, and Joe Zingale all worked. (Wain would later start his own station, WIXY, which brought the group back to Cleveland in 1966.)

During the initial tour planning stage in April, Cleveland was bypassed. It took a daring and creative plan by WHK's Wain, Weiss, and Zingale to bring the Beatles to their city. Zingale was sent to New York to persuade General Artists Corporation (GAC) to grant WHK sponsorship of the Cleveland concert, but GAC and Beatles manager Brian Epstein were more impressed with the larger KYW. Zingale, a sales executive for WHK, met with Epstein at a New York hotel and pleaded his case. Epstein told him that KYW had the date locked up and had already booked Public Hall.

With little to lose, Zingale did what he had to do: he lied. He told Epstein it was impossible for KYW to claim Public Hall because WHK had beaten them to the punch and obtained a contract from the venue's manager. A somewhat skeptical Epstein informed Zingale that if he could produce proof that his station had booked Public Hall, then WHK could have the date.

The group poses with WHK DJ's. The station scored a coup by beating out rival 50,000-watt giant KYW in promoting the show.

The group stayed at the Downtown Cleveland Sheraton (below) both in 1964 and 1966. Officers (right) guard the first floor of the hotel. The Chief of Police secretly bumped the group's accommodations from the Presidential suite down to the first floor, out of concern for their safety.

Back in Cleveland, Wain and Weiss were trying to persuade the commissioner of Public Hall, Frank Duman, to allow WHK to have the venue on September 15. Unsure whether WHK could match KYW's popularity, Duman refused to agree without evidence that the station could indeed get the Beatles. The two sales executives hurried to the station and sent a not entirely truthful telegram to Zingale in New York claiming that they'd successfully booked Public Hall. Zingale presented the telegram to Epstein, who, being a man of his word, gave Zingale the nod in return: WHK would be the sponsor. With Epstein's approval secured, Wain and Weiss hurried back to Public Hall to relay the news to Duman, pay for the lease, and officially book the Beatles. Thus it took WHK two outright lies to beat its rival, KYW.

A contract was signed on May 7 by George Etkin, assistant secretary for Metromedia in New York, and GAC, with Epstein countersigning. Terms called for WHK to pay a guaranteed fee of $30,000 plus an astonishing 70 percent of the gross. When the GAC's Weiss sent the final

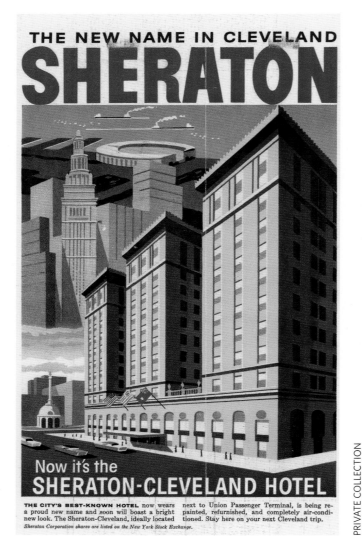

THE NEW NAME IN CLEVELAND
SHERATON

Now it's the
SHERATON-CLEVELAND HOTEL

THE CITY'S BEST-KNOWN HOTEL now wears a proud new name and soon will boast a bright new look. The Sheraton-Cleveland, ideally located next to Union Passenger Terminal, is being re-painted, refurnished, and completely air-conditioned. Stay here on your next Cleveland trip.
Sheraton Corporation shares are listed on the New York Stock Exchange.

A swatch of carpet (right) and a letter from the Sheraton Cleveland's General Manager, Allen Lowe (above). The carpet came from the Beatles' suites.

tour schedule to Epstein on May 9, Cleveland was listed among the other cities. In addition, for the first time in any tour city, a special rider was attached stating that the Beatles would not make any live personal appearances in Cleveland or within a fifty-mile radius. Perhaps this was a special request by WHK to prevent KYW from scheduling a promotional function outside of Public Hall, which would have threatened WHK's exclusive arrangement for promotion.

Once the booking was secured, WHK was inundated with requests for tickets. Some reports indicate there were 100,000 requests for 10,000 seats. When tickets finally became available (priced at $4.50, $5.50, and $6.50), they sold out quickly. WHK also had an on-air promotion in the form of a ticket giveaway. In what was thought to be the first automated audience selection, ticket winners were chosen by an IBM computer. Fans were encouraged to send in an entry—one postcard per person—with a deadline of May 22. The station informed them that the computer could detect if anyone sent in more than one entry and that rule violators would be automatically disqualified. In early June, Jack Thayer, vice president and general manager of WHK, sent notification letters to the winners, instructing them to come down to the Public Hall box office, where they could select two seats.

Disappointed at losing the Beatles show, KYW wouldn't bow to its rivals, still striving to remain atop the ratings. At a sales meeting, news correspondent Art Schreiber appealed to his boss by citing the station's prowess. KYW was owned by Westinghouse, Schreiber reasoned, so it must have New York connections that could pull some strings. He asked management to place him on the tour—and got his wish, at least in part: KYW, along with Miami's WFUN (which sent journalist Larry Kane for the entire tour), was invited by Epstein to cover the tour. KYW's Jim Stagg covered the concerts through August 28 at Forest Hills, and Schreiber took over from there. It was a major coup for KYW, which was still reeling from WHK's exclusive promotion at Public Hall. First through Stagg and later through Schreiber, KYW garnered live feeds and exclusive interviews for its own use and the use of several subscribed stations. The station would also manage to steal a bit of thunder from WHK on the night of the concert.

The Beatles were booked to stay at what was considered Cleveland's finest hotel: the downtown Sheraton. Built in 1918, the 1,000-room hotel was once one of the largest in the world, playing host over the decades to such dignitaries as Harry Truman, Charles Lindbergh, and Dr. Martin Luther King Jr. In advance of the Beatles' arrival, Cleveland Police Chief Richard Wagner contacted hotel management and suggested that the band's reservations be changed from the Presidential Suite to a bank of rooms

on the ground floor, in order to outsmart any fans plotting to crash the group's digs. With the press conference also taking place on the hotel's ground floor, police would have greater control of a potentially explosive situation if fans began to swarm the building.

When it came to employing creative and diverse methods to meet the Beatles, the fans didn't disappoint. Several girls tried the Trojan horse method, packing themselves inside mailing boxes set to be delivered to the group's suite. One girl fainted at the hotel entrance, claiming she thought there was a first aid station inside. In their efforts to throw the fans off the trail, police ran riot buses to and from Public Hall continually, hoping that fans would eventually pay them no attention, at which point authorities would slip the group into one of the buses and drive them to Public Hall. It was a brilliant diversionary tactic—and it worked beautifully.

Throughout the Cleveland visit, KYW worked relentlessly to sabotage WHK's exclusive promotion. When the group arrived at the airport, which was plastered with WHK banners and signs, John spotted KYW's Art Schreiber coming off the plane. Schreiber and the Beatles had been together for the previous thirteen cities and had gotten to know each other. John called the journalist

CONGRATULATIONS!

You have been selected by the automatic IBM Computor to be a part of the Cleveland audience as WHK Radio presents, "The Beatles" in person at the Public Auditorium, September 15th.

Upon presentation of this letter at the Music Hall Box Office, East Sixth and St. Clair, Saturday morning, June 13th beginning at 10 A.M., you may purchase two (2) tickets of your choice. The tickets are priced at $6.50, $5.50 and $4.50 each, and are available on a first come, first serve basis.

This letter is your key to a wonderful evening of fun and excitement with WHK Radio and "The Beatles".

Remember, bring this letter with you to the Music Hall Box Office on Saturday, June 13th.

Best wishes,

Jack Thayer
Vice President and
General Manager

June 5th of WHK's
Forty-Second Year
1922-1964

JThayer:njs

A rudimentary IBM computer selected fans in a WHK promotion to receive tickets (above). Cleveland's Public Hall (left), which hosted the riotous concert.

over to talk, which infuriated the WHK deejays.

At the press conference, WHK protested KYW's presence and tried to bar the station from entry. KYW made a plea to Epstein, but the overwhelmed manager washed his hands of the flap and ordered press officer Derek Taylor to handle it. In the end, because Stagg and Schreiber had established a relationship with the Beatles organization, KYW was allowed entry. In order to keep WHK happy, Taylor organized a five-minute mini-conference for WHK contest winners.

In an ironic twist, it was KYW personnel who convinced the Beatles to finish the concert after a near-riot forced them offstage. As the opening riff of "Twist and Shout" echoed throughout Public Hall, the crowd went wild. Ron Sweed, known for his work with Ernie Anderson, a popular star of Cleveland late-night television, attended the show as a teen and remembers it well. In an interview with Dave Schwensen, author of *The Beatles in Cleveland*, Sweed recalled the thousands of Kodak flashbulbs all over the floor and said the constant flashing was like a "sheet of lightning," while the fans' shrieking, coupled with the loud music, sounded like an incessant siren.

As Paul gave his all to "All My Loving," the third song in the set, all hell broke loose. Fans from one end of the venue to the other proceeded to storm the stage. This was the breaking point for police officials, who immediately stopped the concert and pushed the group offstage. Expletives flew at the police from the mouths of the bewildered Beatles, who objected to the interference. In the ensuing chaos, with no deejays from sponsor station WHK in sight, KYW deejays Harry Martin and Specs Howard took to the stage and asked police officials to give them a chance to calm the crowd. Having gained permission, they also used the opportunity to shamelessly plug KYW. Hearing the two jocks promise that the Beatles would return, the crowd began to settle down.

Meanwhile, backstage, the deejays' KYW cohort, Art Schreiber, was scoring a scoop—an exclusive interview with a furious John Lennon—while Derek Taylor pleaded with the boys, who had already partially peeled out of their stage clothes, to give him a chance to resolve the problem. He told them he would go onstage and address the crowd as he'd done in Jacksonville. After the group reluctantly agreed, Taylor joined the KYW deejays onstage and cooled the audience enough to placate the police. The Beatles were summoned back to the stage, continuing the show with "She Loves You."

Years later, when asked in an interview about the incident in Cleveland, Paul said he had thought the concert was over and had no idea why police officials brought them back on. Epstein agreed with the action of police officials. "The police were absolutely right," he said. "This has never happened before, but it was clear to me from the start that there was something terribly wrong. The enthusiasm of the crowd was building much too early." After the show, the Beatles sped away from Public Hall along back streets to Hopkins Airport, where their plane was waiting to take them into Bayou Country. Next stop: New Orleans, Louisiana.

In the aftermath, two writers for Cleveland's Plain Dealer newspaper had quite different opinions. Music critic Robert Finn was disparaging: "In the twenty-plus years of concert going, this music critic has often been moved, amused, charmed, and exalted by what he heard. But this is the first time he was ever terrified. It sounded more like air raid sirens, cherry bombs, and starving orangutans ... the effect on this listener was overwhelming—fractured eardrums and

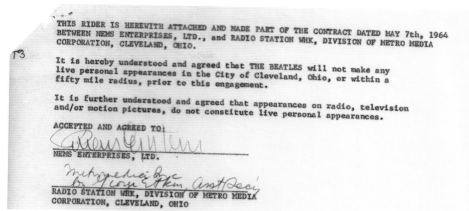

THIS RIDER IS HEREWITH ATTACHED AND MADE PART OF THE CONTRACT DATED MAY 7th, 1964 BETWEEN NEMS ENTERPRISES, LTD., and RADIO STATION WHK, DIVISION OF METRO MEDIA CORPORATION, CLEVELAND, OHIO.

It is hereby understood and agreed that THE BEATLES will not make any live personal appearances in the City of Cleveland, Ohio, or within a fifty mile radius, prior to this engagement.

It is further understood and agreed that appearances on radio, television and/or motion pictures, do not constitute live personal appearances.

ACCEPTED AND AGREED TO:

NEMS ENTERPRISES, LTD.

RADIO STATION WHK, DIVISION OF METRO MEDIA CORPORATION, CLEVELAND, OHIO

Opposite page: Ringo drums below the group's name. Brian Epstein was required to sign a special rider (above) by WHK, the only one on the 1964 tour, which guaranteed the Beatles would not appear anywhere else within a fifty mile radius. A rare WHK ticket flier giveaway (below).

THE WHK GOOD GUYS
Invite you to take a chance to see and hear . . .
"THE BEATLES"
AT THE
WHK BEATLE CONCERT
Cleveland Public Auditorium, September 15, 1964
2 TICKETS AWARDED DAILY AT THE WHK BOOTH . . . 8:00 P.M.
40 TICKETS AWARDED ON WHK DAY AT THE PARADE OF PROGRESS, SEPTEMBER 5, 1964. DRAWING WILL TAKE PLACE AT THE BIG WHK STAGE SHOW . . .
2:00 P.M. AND 8:00 P.M. (You must be present to win.)

PRIVATE COLLECTION

© GEORGE SHUBA

a headache." Meanwhile, columnist George E. Condon offered an opposing view: "I fully expect that the music will sound strange to most of us at first," he wrote. "But we should strive to be as patient and appreciative as we can until the harmonics begin to make sense or take on an attractive form."

WHK fought hard for the right to promote the show, but its dishonest tactics may have proven to be its downfall in the ratings war with KYW. Three years later, the station's rock-pop format changed to easy listening.

As the Sheraton (now a Marriott Renaissance property) recovered from its famous guests, general manager Alan Lowe decided it would be in bad taste to sell the Beatles' bed linens. A few days later in Kansas City, the owner of the Muehlebach Hotel would make a different choice—selling the group's linens to two enterprising young businessmen whose dreams of a lucrative payoff, alas, were to turn a bit sour.

Collectibles from the Cleveland show are among the scarcest from the first tour. Only tickets and the generic mass-produced program were needed. To date, no unused Cleveland tickets have surfaced; as a result, the 1964 Cleveland concert holds the distinction of being the only show from all three American tours without a known surviving unused ticket. Stubs from this show are also limited because, unlike many tickets from the tour, they featured the Beatles' faces. Fans found them attractive keepsakes and tucked them away for posterity.

NEW ORLEANS

September 16, 1964
City Park Stadium
8 p.m.

AFTER A NARROW ESCAPE FROM A NEAR-RIOT AT CLEVELAND'S PUBLIC HALL, the Beatles would face madness of unforeseen proportions at their next stop: New Orleans, Louisiana. First, the promoters and organizers sent transportation to the wrong airport. Later, when the Beatles were finally on their way to the motel, their limo took a wrong turn, leaving them at the mercy of fans pursuing them in the dark Louisiana night. Arriving at their destination, manager Brian Epstein was horrified to see that their motel was nothing more than a one-story building in a swamplike setting surrounded by trees and tall weeds. It had been booked at the last minute after the group's original hotel cancelled their reservations, fearing that its property would be destroyed. To make matters worse, the outdoor concert the next day at City Park Stadium erupted into a free-for-all, with fans spilling onto the field in all directions as police desperately tried to maintain order.

After weeks on the road in America, perhaps the only person breathing a sigh of relief was supporting act Clarence "Frogman" Henry—a native of Algiers, a community within New Orleans—who was able to go home for a bit of peace and quiet. For their part, the Beatles were limping to the end of a whirlwind tour and looking forward to some welcome rest at the Missouri ranch of Reed Pigman, owner of American Flyers, their chartered airline. Later, in the aftermath of their New Orleans visit, John would comment to Larry Kane, "I was beginning to have hysterics ... it was just a scream!"

In the original schedule for the 1964 tour, the date of September 16 was left open, with several cities, including New Orleans, vying for that slot. As in other cities, local radio stations battled each other for the sponsorship rights to the Beatles

City Park Stadium was an outdoor venue that is currently named Tad Gormley Stadium.

concert—in this case, WNOE with its Good Guys and WTIX with its Boss Jocks. In bayou country, people were fiercely loyal to these two stations, sometimes coming to blows over which was better. Because WNOE deejay Herb Holiday was a friend of Bob Astor of General Artists Corporation (GAC), he was able to not only book the Beatles but secure them for a mere $20,000 plus 60 percent of the gross. Of course, it didn't hurt that Astor also happened to be Frogman Henry's manager.

The original plan called for the Beatles' plane to land at Lakefront Airport, where they would be taken by helicopter to the Congress Inn. But as the aircraft descended into New Orleans in the early-morning hours of September 16, plans changed rapidly. As Captain Pres Cooper radioed ahead for landing instructions at Lakefront, he learned that the waiting helicopter was experiencing mechanical difficulties. The Beatles

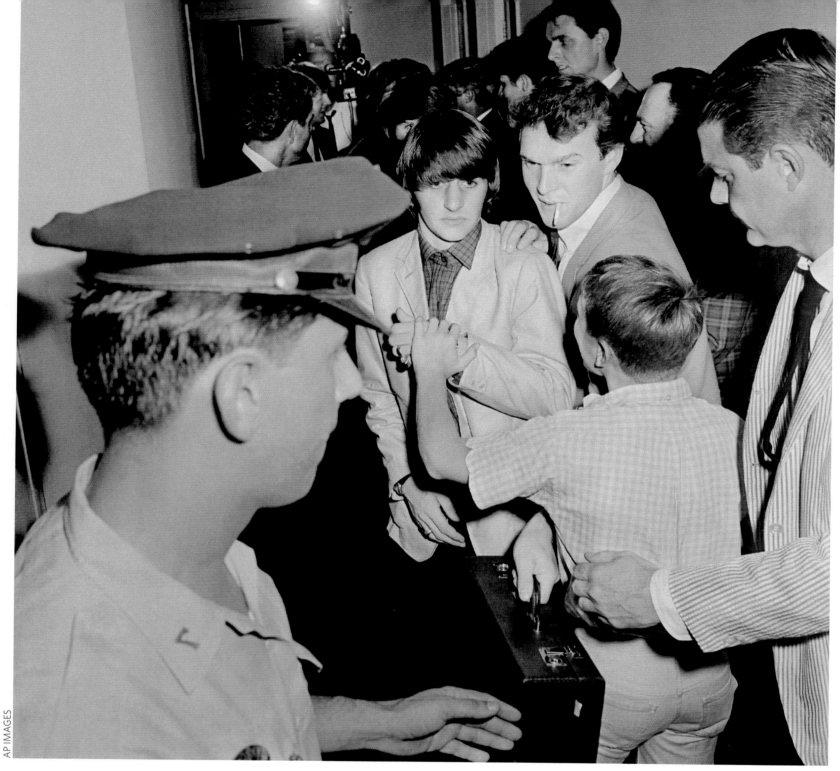

would have to travel to their accommodations by limousine. Fans and city officials had been queuing up at Lakefront for hours. As the Electra was preparing to land, Captain Cooper received another dispatch informing him that the limos had been mistakenly sent to Moisant Field (now known as Louis Armstrong New Orleans International) in the New Orleans suburb of Kenner. The pilot had to quickly ditch the landing at Lakefront and change course.

Moisant ramp agents Noel LeBlanc and Albert Jacob were about to clock off their shift, figuring that all planes had landed for the night. As they were changing clothes to go home, they received word that they needed to assist a diverting Electra. They were thrilled to make a little extra money that night, but shocked beyond belief to find themselves face to face with the Beatles. The ramp agents assisted the group with their luggage, emptied the aircraft's cargo bins, and transferred the contents to the limousines.

As in a scene from a slapstick comedy, the Beatles' car had just begun the forty-five-minute trip to the Congress Inn when the driver took a wrong turn. The few fans lucky enough to see the group at Moisant (as most were at Lakefront) tailed the lone Beatles car until the driver realized his mistake. Facing the

Ringo is accosted at the Congress Inn by a young fan trying to get noticed.

danger of being overtaken by the pursuit cars, the limousine made a quick U-turn. While backing up, it slammed into a Kenner police escort cruiser, then sped off in the right direction. With no major freeways yet in existence, the entourage traveled narrow surface roads lined with hundreds of fans welcoming their heroes to town.

Meanwhile, the Congress Inn was besieged with fans. As the group reached the motel, Beatles management was aghast to see plywood installed over the windows of the boys' rooms in a move to prevent damage and discourage intruders. The Beatles had no choice but to make a mad dash through the lobby to their rooms. Originally the Roosevelt Hotel, near the city's famed French Quarter, had been booked, but the Roosevelt's manager, hearing of the chaos in other cities, asked tour organizers to find different accommodations.

City councilman Daniel L. Kelly had been appointed by Mayor Victor Schiro to greet the group at Lakefront Airport and present them with an official proclamation declaring September 16, 1964, "Beatles Day in New Orleans." Learning of their arrival at Moisant Field, the councilman dashed to the other airport, but missed them. Undeterred but exasperated, Kelly next arrived at the Congress Inn. When he approached one of the rooms occupied by the Beatles party, however, he was quickly rebuffed and told the Beatles were already asleep. Not content to let his famous guests go without some kind of official recognition, Mayor Schiro would organize an elaborate ceremony to take place before the press conference later that day.

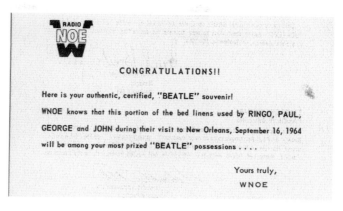

CONGRATULATIONS!!

Here is your authentic, certified, "BEATLE" souvenir!

WNOE knows that this portion of the bed linens used by RINGO, PAUL, GEORGE and JOHN during their visit to New Orleans, September 16, 1964 will be among your most prized "BEATLE" possessions . . . .

Yours truly,

WNOE

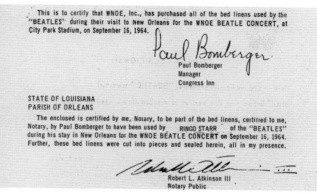

This is to certify that WNOE, Inc., has purchased all of the bed linens used by the "BEATLES" during their visit to New Orleans for the WNOE BEATLE CONCERT, at City Park Stadium, on September 16, 1964.

Paul Bomberger
Manager
Congress Inn

STATE OF LOUISIANA
PARISH OF ORLEANS

The enclosed is certified by me, Notary, to be part of the bed linens, certified to me, Notary, by Paul Bomberger to have been used by RINGO STARR of the "BEATLES" during his stay in New Orleans for the WNOE BEATLE CONCERT on September 16, 1964. Further, these bed linens were cut into pieces and sealed herein, all in my presence.

Robert L. Atkinson III
Notary Public

Radio station WNOE made a deal with the Congress Inn to purchase and resell the Beatles' linens. The station also sliced up the microphone chords from the concert and sold them.

The Beatles awoke in early afternoon and readied themselves for the twenty-second official press conference of the tour. Before it began, Mayor Schiro got his moment in the sun. For the first time on the tour, Epstein allowed newsreel crews to film the press conference. With cameras rolling, Schiro first presented the group with keys to the city, along with certificates of honorary citizenship. John, both honored and amused by the mayor's gesture, remarked that he wanted to put his arm around the "nice fellow." Schiro then read the proclamation aloud, citing the group's "cousinship with jazz" and his city. He also noted the arrival of the Beatles in September, the hurricane month, calling them an "English storm." The good mayor then produced a duplicate copy of the proclamation and asked that each Beatle sign it. John, returning the mayor's pen, remarked, "Your pen, your Lordship."

The signed proclamation was later copied and thousands made available at City Hall. The original proclamation was held in the files at City Hall until Mayor Schiro, upon leaving office, gave it to a trusted employee. The employee took the document home for safekeeping. Miraculously, it was saved from destruction during Hurricane Katrina in 2005 as flooding lapped the bottom of the desk at the city employee's home where it was stored. The only such signed proclamation from any city on the three North American tours, it now safely resides with a private collector in New Orleans and stands as a valuable piece of city history. Copies of the proclamation were made available to anyone who visited City Hall, with one catch: teenagers had to make a sworn pledge to pick up trash along city roadways in order to get one. Proclamations were also given out to school groups visiting City Hall.

As the press conference began, the Beatles remarked that their New Orleans arrival had been the roughest so far on the tour. Asked if they intended to visit the city again, they replied, "Yes, when we're older." When one reporter asked their opinion of topless swimsuits, George replied, "We've been wearing them for years." Of course, they also faced the customary questions about their haircuts, their impressions of America, and the hysteria that followed them wherever they went. They were clearly growing weary of the repetition. With the press conference finished, the group was transported to the 12,000-seat City Park Stadium for their sold-out performance. The stadium, which resembled a high school field, had opened in 1937 and was about to host the most chaotic event in its twenty-seven-year history.

As the Beatles waited in a small trailer, they received a surprise visit from one of their greatest musical influences: Fats Domino. Bob Astor of GAC, a good friend of the singer, had arranged the meeting. Afterward, Fats told Astor, "Man, them cats talk funny!" The Beatles were obviously impressed with Domino, not only for his musical prowess but also for his flashy diamond-encrusted, star-shaped

The Honorable Mayor Victor Schiro with the Fab Three—George's image was pasted in later. Mayor Schiro made New Orleans' teenagers take a pledge (right) to pick up trash in order to receive a copy of the signed proclamation (see opposite page).

CITY OF NEW ORLEANS

OFFICE OF THE MAYOR

VICTOR H. SCHIRO
MAYOR

PROCLAMATION

WHEREAS, the Beatles are coming!

which WHEREAS, this event will be acknowledged, assented to and even acclaimed by presumably a large segment of our people; and

WHEREAS, what the Beatles do and sing is based on a cousinship with jazz, the jumping, danceable historic art form which New Orleans has contributed to world culture; and

WHEREAS, in order to be hospitable to our English cousins, the Beatles, who will serenade New Orleans in the hurricane month of September, it devolves upon myself to officially welcome this English storm:

NOW, THEREFORE, I, Victor H. Schiro, Mayor of the City of New Orleans, do hereby proclaim the day, Wednesday, September 16, 1964, to be

BEATLES DAY IN NEW ORLEANS

Given under my hand and the Seal of the City of New Orleans on this the 9th day of September, 1964

Victor H. Schiro
Mayor.

The original signed "Beatles Day in New Orleans" proclamation. This is the only known official city document that the Beatles signed on any of their three tours. It barely survived Hurricane Katrina, when floodwater lapped up to the bottom of the desk drawer where it was stored. Now, the proclamation is safe with a private collector.

The boys meet one of their idols, Fats Domino. Note Fats' diamond-studded, star-shaped watch and "Fats" embroidered on his shirt cuff. The meeting took place just before the Beatles took the stage.

wristwatch. Domino, in later interviews, would be asked if he had been impressed with the Beatles. He would always reply, "The Beatles really came to meet me."

Epstein and press officer Derek Taylor were dining at New Orleans' famed Antoine's restaurant that night and so missed the legendary singer. George later remarked to Taylor, "You can't have dinner with Brian Epstein *and* meet Fats Domino."

On concert day, the battle between WNOE and WTIX reached its boiling point. Not to be outdone by their rival station, the WTIX jocks came out in full force, distributing flyers to concertgoers stating, "WTIX welcomes you to this Beatles concert. Have fun and listen to WTIX after the show." Unlike at the Vancouver concert, there was no field seating, except for select fans who had won tickets in local radio contests and those in wheelchairs.

At approximately 9:30 p.m., the Beatles hit the stage. Promoter Herb Holiday later said, "It was pandemonium; it was nuts. We had kids dropping out of the trees [which were hanging over the fence of the stadium] like apples." As the Beatles broke stride onstage, waves of kids left their seats and started pouring onto the field, rushing toward the front. Holiday's attention soon turned from gate-crashers to the melee unfolding in front of him. He shouted to police, "Let 'em go. I don't care. We're sold out. Get your guys in front of the stage now!"

The New Orleans Police Department, accustomed to crowd control at events such as Mardi Gras, employed mounted officers to quell the disturbance. John, enjoying the riot unfolding in front of him, had plenty to say between songs. "We'd like to continue with our next number," he joked, "if you would stop playing football in the middle of the field." Minutes later, he introduced the next song as one "for those of you who are still alive!" Police were seen making open field tackles as girls charged the barricades positioned near the stage. Introducing the evening's last number, "Long Tall Sally," Paul added, "We'd like to thank everybody for coming, including the football players." Police superintendent Joseph Giarrusso called the scene both "amusing and tragic at the same time" and couldn't recall any other incident of that magnitude involving teenagers in the city's history.

Once again, the Beatles narrowly escaped another near-riot. The following day—September 17—had originally been slated as a rest day, and the band clearly could have used the time off after New Orleans. But they sacrificed it when an extraordinary offer in Los Angeles led to the addition of a Kansas City concert on that day. Beatlemania would have to march on.

The Beatles show was a coup for WNOE and promoter Holiday. Not only had he secured the group for a smaller-than-usual fee, but he'd saved an additional $8,000 when he gambled and declined a Lloyd's of London rainout insurance policy. For the policy to pay, it would have had to rain at least a quarter inch. He researched the city weather history for September 16 and discovered that it had rarely rained on that date over the previous thirty years. Rolling the dice, he passed on the insurance. On the night of the show, storm clouds began to gather above the venue. Holiday nervously watched the concert, thinking of the $30,000 he'd invested and stood to lose with a rainout. But luck was on his side, as the Beatles played and left without so much as a drop of rain. As soon as the stands emptied, though, the heavens opened and poured forth, as Holiday noted, "one of the hardest rains I've ever seen."

City Park Stadium was later renamed Ted Gormley Stadium. After being ravaged by Hurricane Katrina in 2005, the field was in dire need of funds to restore it to playing condition. Fortunately, NFL star Reggie Bush donated $80,000 for renovations so high school games and other events could still be hosted at the venue. The playing field at Gormley Stadium is now known as Reggie Bush Field. The site of the Congress Inn would, in later years, be home to an assisted-living center that was eventually destroyed during Hurricane Katrina.

The '64 tour was beginning to wind down. Leaving the Crescent City, the Beatles found themselves "goin' to Kansas City" for the add-on concert they'd agreed to play for a sum seven times the amount they earned in New Orleans. In the bargain would be a clash of egos between John and Charles O. Finley, the flamboyant owner of the Kansas City Athletics.

PRIVATE COLLECTION

Mounted police officers had to be brought in to quell the crowd that ran onto the field. Sadly, no performance pictures could be found, only frames from a Super8 camera.

In addition to tickets and the generic program, quite a few collectibles survive from the show in New Orleans. Following the Beatles' stay, WNOE purchased all the bed linens from the Congress Inn, along with the microphones and cords that were used by the Beatles onstage. All of these items were cut up and sold with notarized certificates of authenticity. WNOE also distributed photographs of the Fab Four as well as a photo of Ringo surrounded by WNOE jocks. Copies of Mayor Schiro's proclamation were also distributed to anyone who visited City Hall in the weeks and months after the concert. Although unused tickets to the concert are rare, many have become available over the years. Apparently, several barriers were knocked over by exuberant fans as they entered City Park Stadium, and consequently, the tickets of those entering at that gate remained intact. As a matter of fact, more unused tickets than stubs have surfaced over the years.

KANSAS CITY

September 17, 1964
Municipal Stadium
8 p.m.

Charles O. Finley, the promoter who paid the Beatles $150,000 to alter their tour schedule, wears a Beatles wig and holds concert tickets with an American Flyers stewardess looking on.

IT WAS TO BE THE LARGEST FEE EVER PAID FOR A SINGLE PERFORMANCE in entertainment history up until that time—$4,838 a minute for a thirty-one-minute Beatles concert in Kansas City, Missouri. In today's dollars, that's more than $35,000 a minute. The KC show wasn't on the original itinerary and was never a consideration in the tour's planning stages. The fact is, it would never have happened had it not been for the colossal ego and unusually deep pockets of one man: forty-six-year-old Charles Oscar "Charlie" Finley, the flamboyant owner of the Kansas City Athletics baseball team.

While other promoters lined up early to present the group on their first tour of America, Charlie Finley stepped up to the plate a little late in the game. But after witnessing not only his daughter's excitement over the group but that of thousands of kids all over Kansas City, he wasn't about to let the Beatles tornado sweep past his hometown. He declared publicly that he would bring the band to town—at any cost.

Finley was a tycoon who had made his fortune selling insurance. In 1960 he purchased the Kansas City Athletics, a team he would move to Oakland, California, in 1968; after 1970, the team would be known simply as the A's. Finley not only developed a successful franchise (four-time World Series champions) but also introduced many innovative aspects to America's pastime. As if a check written for a staggering sum wasn't enough to secure the Beatles, he reportedly sweetened the deal with two boxes of green Athletics hats.

As the 1964 tour was being planned in early spring, Kansas City wasn't on anyone's radar screen. Norm Weiss of General Artists Corporation was fielding offers from cities as diverse as Troy, Michigan, Albuquerque, New Mexico, and even Buffalo, New York. After seeing the excitement build in late spring—and ticket sellouts at every stop—Finley knew he wanted a piece of the action. He decided he would meet Beatles manager Brian Epstein face to face and offer double the usual guarantee of $25,000 to add Kansas City to the schedule.

After being granted a meeting with Epstein in San Francisco, Finley flew to the city before the band's performance at the Cow Palace there. He

PRIVATE COLLECTION

On a scheduled "off day," the Beatles take questions from the Kansas City press. The press conference was held on the top floor of the Muehlebach Hotel.

PRIVATE COLLECTION

COURTESY OF JOSEPH A. TUNZI/JATPUBLISHING (2)

immediately handed the Beatles manager a check for $60,000. Epstein thanked Finley but refused it, saying that September 17 was a scheduled day off for the group. At that point in the tour, the Beatles were slated to play seven shows in six cities with no break. They deserved a day of rest, even late in the tour. But the persistent Finley wouldn't take no for an answer. He upped the ante, tempting Epstein with a $100,000 offer. Once again, Epstein declined.

Finley refused to let Epstein get the best of him. Three days later, while the group was in Los Angeles for the Hollywood Bowl show, he confronted Epstein once again. This time, however, Charlie O put even more money where his mouth was. He tore up the $100,000 check, threw it in an ashtray, and wrote out a check for the unprecedented sum of $150,000 for a single performance. Now Epstein took notice. Money like that would add substantially to the tour's profit. But he wasn't going to make the decision on his own. Asking Finley to wait a moment, he calmly took the check to the Beatles, who were absorbed

KANSAS CITY ATHLETICS

MUNICIPAL STADIUM
KANSAS CITY, MISSOURI 64141
HUMBOLDT 3-9911

CHARLES O. FINLEY
PRESIDENT

August 27, 1964

Mr. John Antonello, Director
City of Kansas City
Municipal Stadium
1310 Wyandotte Street
Kansas City 5, Missouri

Re: "Beatle" Novelties and Programs

Dear John:

Under separate cover I have forwarded to you my signed contract for rental of the Municipal Stadium on the night of September 17, 1964 – Beatle Night.

This contract rules me out completely on all concessions.

Since this is for charity, I do believe, John, that we are entitled to the concessions on all novelties and programs associated with the Beatles' visit to Kansas City.

I would appreciate tremendously your notifying, at your earliest convenience, as to the possibility of our keeping the concessions for charity of these articles.

Sincerely,

Charles O. Finley

COFinley/lr

Finley planned to donate the money from the sale of "Beatles" novelties and programs to charity (above). Kansas City (right) made certain that no beer would be sold at the stadium. The Muehlebach Hotel (upper right) sliced up sheets and pillowcases to further profit from their famous guests.

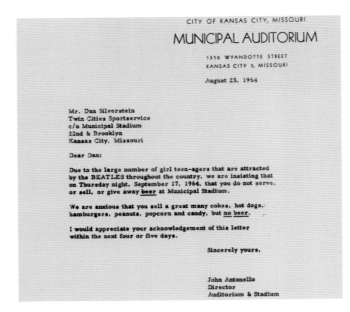

CITY OF KANSAS CITY, MISSOURI

MUNICIPAL AUDITORIUM

1310 WYANDOTTE STREET
KANSAS CITY 5, MISSOURI

August 25, 1964

Mr. Dan Silverstein
Twin Cities Sportservice
c/o Municipal Stadium
22nd & Brooklyn
Kansas City, Missouri

Dear Dan:

Due to the large number of girl teen-agers that are attracted by the BEATLES throughout the country, we are insisting that on Thursday night, September 17, 1964, that you do not serve, or sell, or give away <u>beer</u> at Municipal Stadium.

We are anxious that you sell a great many cokes, hot dogs, hamburgers, peanuts, popcorn and candy, but <u>no beer</u>.

I would appreciate your acknowledgement of this letter within the next four or five days.

Sincerely yours,

John Antonello
Director
Auditorium & Stadium

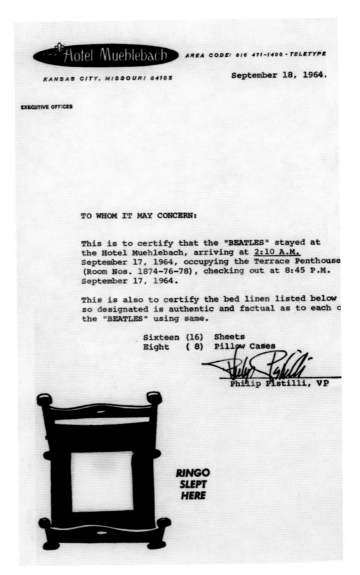

Hotel Muehlebach   AREA CODE: 816 471-1400 · TELETYPE

KANSAS CITY, MISSOURI 64105   September 18, 1964.

EXECUTIVE OFFICES

TO WHOM IT MAY CONCERN:

This is to certify that the "BEATLES" stayed at the Hotel Muehlebach, arriving at 2:10 A.M. September 17, 1964, occupying the Terrace Penthouse (Room Nos. 1874-76-78), checking out at 8:45 P.M. September 17, 1964.

This is also to certify the bed linen listed below so designated is authentic and factual as to each o the "BEATLES" using same.

Sixteen (16) Sheets
Eight (8) Pillow Cases

Philip Pistilli, VP

RINGO
SLEPT
HERE

---

in a card game, and informed them of the offer, explaining that they would be sacrificing a day off. Without missing a beat, John paused, looked up from his card game, and said, "We'll do whatever you want." The others nodded in agreement. The deal was done.

At that moment, entertainment history was made. No other musical performer had come remotely close to earning what the Beatles would earn in Kansas City on the night of September 17. At a time when Frank Sinatra was earning $10,000 a show, the Beatles would earn fifteen times that amount for one half-hour performance. With that guarantee, Finley assured himself a loss on the show. But for him, it wasn't about money.

In an August 1989 article in *Performance* magazine, Finley abridged the story a bit. He claimed that his only offer to Epstein was $100,000. The Beatles manager promptly rejected it, saying that he didn't want the group to lose a day off. If Finley wanted the Beatles in KC, it would take more money than that. Epstein told the promoter

KEWi 1440

BEATLE SPECIAL

Souvenir Ticket

September 17, 1964

CHARTER TRAIN AND BUS TRANSPORTATION $4.25

to wait and he'd discuss it with the group. He returned to tell Finley that the band would do the show, but it would cost him $150,000. Finley said he quickly wrote out a check before the price went any higher. Tour insiders have said that the negotiations were more intense and lengthy. However it came about, the fee was a record-breaker.

As the reality of a Beatles visit to Kansas City set in, Finley's staff concluded that in order to make his money back, their boss would need a large turnout at the 41,000-seat Kansas City Municipal Stadium. Hoping to recover from the guarantee, the Finley organization set ticket prices at $8.50, $6.50, and $4.50. The $8.50 price was the highest charged for a ticket on the entire tour (with the exception of those sold for the band's charity performance at New York City's Paramount Theatre). It's a wonder Epstein ever agreed to these prices, as he was intent on keeping the tickets affordable. When the demand for tickets began to stall, Finley authorized a $2 ticket, one of the lowest prices charged.

Perhaps the ultimate display of Finley's ego could be seen on the back side of all but the $2 tickets. Here was a picture of Charlie O himself, holding a picture of Ringo and sporting a Beatles wig. The caption below the photo read, "Yeah, Yeah!, Yeah! Today's Beatles fans are tomorrow's baseball fans," followed by the promoter's facsimile signature. On the front of the ticket, he made it clear who had brought the Beatles to KC: "Charles O. Finley," it read, "is pleased to present ... for the enjoyment of the Beatle fans in mid-America 'The Beatles' in person."

Bud Connell, the operations manager at KXOK in St. Louis, was good friends with George's sister Louise. Connell fondly recalls an early Beatles record that Louise gave to him to promote on the air well before the Sullivan shows. After listening, Connell gave her the bad news: "No way!" he told her. "The American teen wants single male vocalists, not groups." Connell would eat his words as his station in St. Louis teamed up with sister station WHB in Kansas City to charter a plane for 100 listeners to see a group—not a single male vocalist—in concert. Louise Harrison Caldwell would serve as a chaperone.

The Beatles' flight from New Orleans to Kansas City was rough as it worked its way through a storm system. The plane, bouncing around as it tried to weather the turbulence, was rattling its famous

Train ticket specials (above left) brought fans from the surrounding regions. The Muehlebach Hotel (top) where the Beatles occupied the Terrace Penthouse. Kansas City Municipal Stadium (above) met the wrecking ball in 1976.

passengers. Clarence "Frogman" Henry, one of the supporting acts, recalled, "That airplane was going down, down, down in that storm and I just knew we was gone." Fortunately, the plane arrived safely, though in a downpour, at 2 a.m. Only about 100 fans braved the rain to greet the group. On his notepad, *Kansas City Star* reporter C. W. Gusewelle captured the moment when the group descended the airsteps onto the tarmac. He wrote, "What the eye remembered was a sharp image of the faces of enthusiasm and indifference, of arrogance and imitated joy. And of course, the hair." Gusewelle then spent the next paragraph of his article on the most physically distinguishing feature of the Fab Four. "The hair of the Beatles is undoubtedly coiffed and sanitized beyond suspicion. But there is no escaping that it is the way you see hair worn by gandies and alkies and forgotten men, hanging lank and forlorn over the backs of their collars."

The group possibly opened the show with "Kansas City/ Hey-Hey-Hey-Hey," which would have been a slight variation to their standard set list and a tip of the hat to the City of Fountains.

The group was immediately ushered into waiting limousines and driven to the Muehlebach Hotel. Located at 12th Street and Baltimore Avenue, the hotel was built in 1915 by George Muehlebach, whose father, George Sr., owned Muehlebach Beer. Junior Muehlebach also built Muehlebach Field, which was later renamed Kansas City Municipal Stadium and was the venue for the Beatles concert. Among the hotel's most prominent guests was President Harry S. Truman, who used it as a quasi–White House, as it was near his hometown of Independence, Missouri. Before the Beatles arrived, hotel vice president and operations manager Earl Reynolds had the lobby cleared of all furnishings.

When the group reached the hotel, it took seven bellmen to transport the more than 200 pieces of luggage belonging to the entourage. As they entered their eighteenth-floor, $100-a-night suite, they noticed a table decked out with a Missouri country ham, apple cider, a mincemeat pie, and a watermelon—a gift from a local actress. Even so, they ordered a veritable feast from room service: buckwheat cakes, eggs, bacon, grilled cheese sandwiches, sliced tomatoes, toast, coffee, tea, milk, and orange juice. Frogman Henry, who was invited to partake in the lavish spread, commented that the Beatles had no idea how to eat a watermelon, as he observed them hitting and poking the fruit with a knife. Once again, a doctor was called in to treat Ringo for a sore throat.

Soon, a familiar face appeared. Charlie Finley, feeling that he "owned" the group, had marched up to rooms 1874, 1876, and 1878 to welcome the group he'd booked for $150,000. Entering their suite with Epstein, the promoter came face to face with John. Determined to get his money's worth (and give Kansas City fans a more memorable experience), Finley demanded of Epstein that the group extend their customary half-hour set by several more minutes. He felt it was his right to make such a request. After all, he'd paid $125,000 over their usual guarantee of $25,000. If necessary, he was willing to go higher.

Brian glanced at John, hoping he'd intercede. The Beatle stepped in and decided to toy with Finley a little, repeatedly telling him no even as the businessman upped his ante. It soon became a battle of wills between the baseball mogul and the Beatle. With each no from John, Finley would offer more money.

The more he offered, the more adamantly John would reject it. Finally, an exasperated Finley stormed out, calling the group "a bunch of boys."

The next evening, prior to leaving for the stadium, the Beatles held their usual press conference—this time on the top floor of the Muehlebach. One reporter asked, "Of all the questions you have been asked, what is the one question that you wish you had been asked at a press conference?" After a rare pause by the four Beatles, Paul simply said, "I guess we've been asked them all." The tour was clearly nearing its end.

Fans from all over the area were eager to attend this Midwest performance, and even a train derailment couldn't suppress their enthusiasm. The last car of a special "Beatles train" carrying 165 fans from Topeka, Kansas, jumped the tracks in route to Kansas City. Thankfully, there were no injuries, and buses were dispatched to transport the group to Municipal Stadium just in time for the show.

Kansas City Municipal Stadium was built as Muehlebach Field in 1923 and hosted the first Negro World Series that same year. In 1955, the stadium was razed and rebuilt as the home field for the newly christened Kansas City Athletics.

John infuriated Charlie Finley by refusing the flamboyant promoter's request to add songs to the set list, hoping to get his money's worth. "We never do more than eleven, Chuck," chided John.

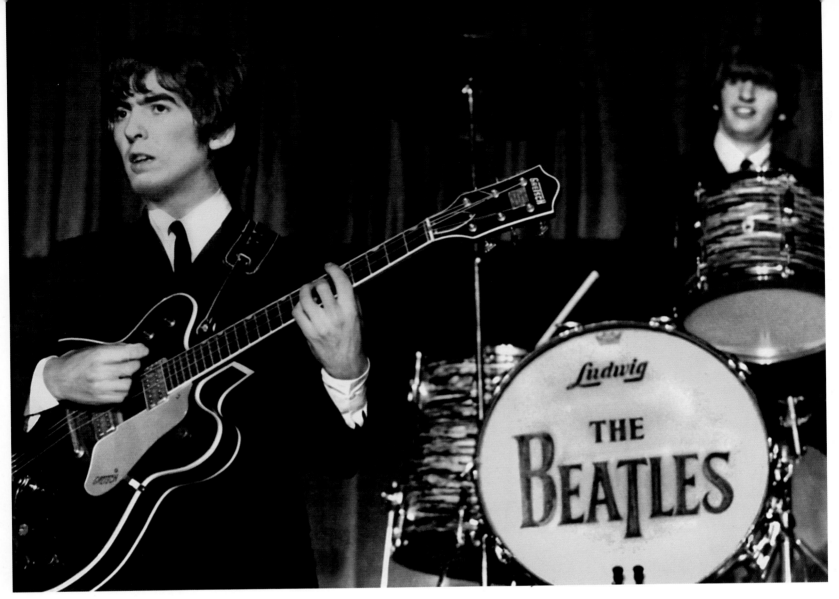

George and Ringo captured in a moment on the Kansas City stage.

As the Beatles arrived for the show, more than 40 percent of the Kansas City police force was on hand to keep order. Only a major flood and a recent tornado disaster had required more officers. In the dressing room as the group awaited their turn onstage, Finley made one final plea for an extended performance. Once again, John turned him down. "We never do more than eleven, Chuck," he said. "You shouldn't have paid all that money." Finley turned his back and left the dressing room in a huff.

In the end, the Beatles reportedly made one concession to the man who had paid so much to bring them to the city. Some fans recall they kicked off the show with a searing rendition of "Kansas City/Hey-Hey-Hey-Hey," which would have been the only time on the tour they played the medley. Their grinding guitars and screeching vocals pierced the warm Kansas City night, sending the audience of 20,280 into a frenzy. Finley had gotten his extra song, but had paid $125,000 more than the rest of the promoters on the 1964 tour.

Kansas City Times staff reporter Robert K. Sanford wrote that a "concerted scream rose in Municipal Stadium and hundreds of flashbulbs lit the park like harsh fireflies." One budding poet in the audience near the stage carried a sign that read, "You're the greatest Charlie O ... For you got us Dear Ringo ... I wish I may ... I wish I might ... get to talk to him tonight." As in New Orleans, the concert was threatened with cancellation as fans rushed the stage and general chaos ensued. Press officer Derek Taylor had to be brought out to quell the crowd and restore order so the show could go on. Once it ended, the boys were herded into limousines for the ride back to the airport. At 11:13 p.m. they departed for Dallas, their last official tour stop before their final performance, a charity benefit at the Paramount Theatre in New York City.

Finley had needed 28,000 fans in the stands to break even, so with just over 20,000 in attendance, he took a huge loss. Despite the fact that the concert wasn't a sellout, it was still one of the most highly attended shows on the tour. Finley boldly proclaimed the concert an overwhelming success despite the loss in gate receipts. "I don't consider it a loss at all," said the businessman. "The Beatles were brought here for the enjoyment of the children in this area, and watching them last night, they had complete enjoyment. I'm happy about that."

As a gesture of goodwill, Finley even donated $25,000 to Children's Mercy Hospital. In a final statement, he also thanked the concert crowd for being so well behaved.

In the 1990s, the Muehlebach Hotel was restored and became an extension of what is now the Kansas City Marriott Downtown. Municipal Stadium was demolished in 1976, and single-family homes now occupy the original site. Charlie Finley lived until 1996, with the Beatles' concert remaining one of his greatest personal accomplishments.

Just before the group left town, one fan sadly commented, "They are gone, gone. I'll never see them again." She was right. The Beatles never did make a return trip to Kansas City—which leads one to speculate just how much Charlie O would have paid the second time around.

Because KC was a late addition to the itinerary, there are few collectibles from this show. No poster or handbills were printed, although doing so may have attracted more fans. Only tickets and the generic North American program were used. All tickets but the $2 version have a picture of Finley on the back. Charlie O even had them printed in the colors of his beloved baseball team, using green, yellow, and white as a color scheme.

Perhaps the best-known and most commonly available collectibles from KC are the sheets and pillowcases the Beatles used while at the Muehlebach. Two enterprising businessmen from Chicago, Richy Victor and Larry Einhorn, contacted the hotel and offered $750 for all the group's bedding—sixteen sheets and eight pillowcases. The bedding was cut up into one-inch squares and mounted on official certificates of authenticity. What appeared to be a financial windfall for the two men actually resulted in very few sales, however. They weren't able to set up a distribution network in Kansas City, and as a result, none of the bedding squares sold in 1964. The men later placed them in storage, only to have a flood ravage the unit. The Paul and George certificates were completely destroyed and thrown out. The Ringo and John sheets were also damaged, but some survived and have sold to collectors over the years.

Ringo and his bandmates profited more than $4,800 a minute for their thirty-one minute performance, making entertainment history.

DALLAS

September 18, 1964
Memorial Auditorium
8:30 p.m.

Kathleen Lingo from the Dallas Civic Opera Association— an interesting choice—presented the boys with ill-fitting Stetson hats welcoming them to Texas.

©BOB JACKSON

AFTER A REWARDING NIGHT IN KANSAS CITY, Missouri, where the band earned an incredible $150,000 for one show, the Beatles' first North American tour began to wind down in the Southwest as the group said "howdy" to Dallas, Texas. Their September 18 visit to the city was the penultimate stop on an exhaustive tour that would span twenty-four cities in just thirty-three days. There would still be one more show to perform—a charity concert scheduled for New York's Paramount Theatre on September 20. But Dallas would be the end of the line for the packaged Beatles show that fans had flocked to see. The Bill Black Combo (which had performed for the entire tour without Black) would open for the last time. The Exciters would sing "Do Wah Diddy Diddy" and "Tell Him" just once more. Clarence "Frogman" Henry would go home to Louisiana, and Jackie DeShannon would shake her hips one final time, whipping the crowd into a frenzy (DeShannon did perform on the Paramount charity bill two nights later as well).

For the four lads from Liverpool, Dallas was probably the last place they wanted to see. Only ten months had passed since the shocking assassination of President John F. Kennedy. Given the fan frenzy that followed them throughout the tour, group members had a real fear that they might be shot as well. In the end, they soldiered on, giving the fans in Dallas one of their best performances and leaving the country hungry for a return in 1965.

Early on, Norm Weiss of General Artists Corporation (GAC) had suggested to Beatles manager Brian Epstein that the group finish the tour on September 19 at Houston's 30,000-seat Colt Stadium. The sponsoring station would be KNOZ, and they projected a potential gross of $100,000. The ever-conservative Epstein decided on a September 18 date at the smaller 10,000-seat Memorial Auditorium in Dallas, however.

Tickets went on sale on Monday, June 1, and were available for purchase only at the Preston Ticket Agency inside the Preston State Bank. Fans were seen lining up early Sunday night for a chance to buy one of the more than 10,000 tickets. By Tuesday afternoon, the concert was declared a sellout. They'd even sold out the tickets in an obstructed-view section behind Ringo's extra-tall drum riser. Such was the demand for tickets that fans were willing to settle for even a partial view of the band. The Preston Ticket Agency donated fifty obstructed-view seats to Dallas Services for Blind Children.

John, followed by the rest of the group (above), is mobbed by the fans at the Cabana. A fan is treated for her injuries (far left) after a plate-glass window broke in the front lobby of the Cabana Motor Hotel. Fans wave (left) as they look up towards the Beatles' room.

COURTESY MARK NABOSHEK (2)

Stephanie Pinter (far left with George above) holds her prized autograph set in her hand (shown at right). She and her friends were allowed into the inner sanctum of the groups' hotel suite.

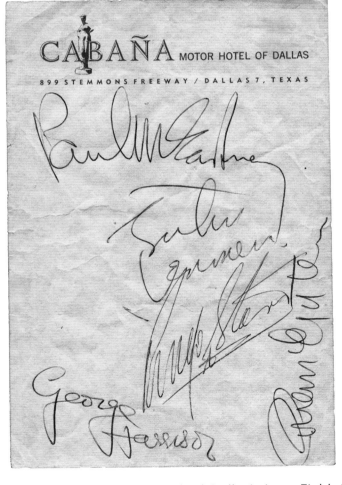

CABAÑA MOTOR HOTEL OF DALLAS

899 STEMMONS FREEWAY / DALLAS 7, TEXAS

The promoters for the Dallas appearance were none other than the Feld Brothers and their company, Super Attractions Inc. The D.C.-based promotion team of Irvin and Israel Feld (Baltimore and Dallas) and Franklin Fried's Triangle Productions (Chicago and Milwaukee) were the only promoters to sponsor two concerts on the same tour in different cities, something that wouldn't happen at all on the 1965 or 1966 tours. (The Felds did help co-promote the Las Vegas concert, but the Sahara's Stan Irwin did most of the legwork.)

Dallas Memorial Auditorium opened in 1957 and featured an enormous dome supported by only one column. Aside from the Beatles, it has hosted all manner of rock royalty, including Elvis Presley in 1976 and Led Zeppelin in 1977 (on the opening night of the band's final tour together). The venue still stands today but was merged in the 1970s with the larger Dallas Convention Center and renamed the Dallas Convention Center Arena.

The Felds gave both local teen stations, KLIF and KBOX, the opportunity to present the show, even though KLIF was far more popular, had higher ratings, and had found gold with its morning team, "Charlie and Harrigan." It was ultimately decided that no one station would sponsor the show and no station banners would be allowed to hang inside the auditorium. Instead, various deejays from across the area would take turns announcing the opening acts. KLIF's Dan McCurdy and Ron Chapman (Charlie and Harrigan), after winning a coin toss among the assembled deejays, would have the privilege of introducing the Beatles.

On the flight from Kansas City, a nervous John approached the designated press area. Journalist Larry Kane could sense his trepidation when the Beatle asked if he had been to Dallas. When Kane nodded in the affirmative, John asked, "A lot of guns, huh?" The Beatles had bought into the stereotype that Dallas was populated with gun-toting cowboys who exacted their own form of justice on the wild frontier. During their stay in Hollywood for the Bowl concert, the group had amused themselves by pulling Western-style guns from holsters as they lounged poolside.

There was a palpable heaviness in the air as the band's plane approached Dallas's Love Field, the same airport used by Air Force One during the Kennedy visit. On the ground, however, there was a much different feeling as approximately 2,000 fans pressed their noses against the chain-link fence lining the runway, awaiting the group's first visit to the great state of Texas. It was 12:40 a.m. on Friday, September 18. As the Beatles emerged from the plane, they were greeted by Kathleen Lingo, a representative of the Dallas Civic Opera Association (a somewhat strange choice!), who presented each Beatle with a white Stetson hat. Unfortunately, the hats were far too small and looked ridiculous perched atop their longish locks. They would later be replaced

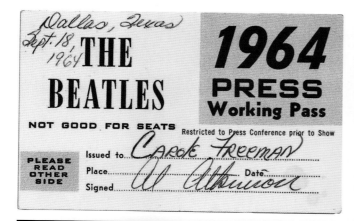

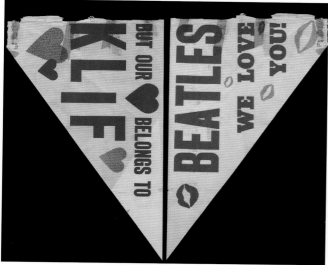

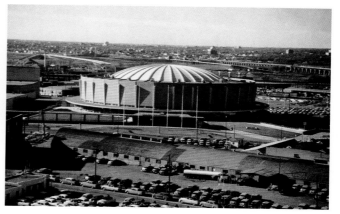

by black Stetsons given to the boys by the two co-presidents of the Dallas branch of the National Beatles Fan Club.

From the airport, the group's caravan traveled part of the route taken by President Kennedy's motorcade, including Dealey Plaza, which was directly across Stemmons Freeway from their accommodations at the Cabana Motor Hotel. By the time the band arrived, the fan count at the hotel had swelled to 1,800, as those who had watched the airport arrival rushed to the Cabana to join the 200 or so fans already assembled there.

The Cabana Motor Hotel, which was co-owned at the time by actress Doris Day, regularly entertained celebrities and politicians and was considered one of the city's swankiest inns. With its gaudy Grecian facade and lavish circular fountain, it was *the* place to be seen. The hotel also attracted its share of shadowy underworld types. Carlos Marcello, John Roselli, Jack Ruby, and Lee Harvey Oswald all had dealings there. It came as no surprise when, twenty years later, the hotel was turned into a minimum-security jail for Dallas County.

Derek Taylor later recalled the moment when they pulled onto the hotel property: "Our arrival ... was a shambles. Gum-chewing cops staked out the motel with riflemen 'round every lamppost." Police chief Jesse Curry enforced strict provisions to ensure the Beatles' safety in light of the recent assassination, assigning twenty-nine officers just to guard the Cabana. To avoid the crowds gathered in front of the hotel, the limos pulled around to the rear entrance. They soon discovered that the hotel was mobbed on

A press pass (upper left), and a KLIF pennant (far left) that was issued to fans at the concert. Doris Day co-owned the Cabana (above). Dallas Memorial Auditorium (left), remains virtually unchanged today. Carpet squares (below left), from the Cabana where the group had walked.

George and John (right) together with Paul (below) tote their white Stetson hats as they arrive safely inside the Cabana Hotel.

©BOB JACKSON (2)

all sides. Just to get inside, the Beatles had to run a gantlet of fans poised to tear them apart. They soon reached the safety of their ninth-floor suite (room 925), but George later wrote in his autobiography, *I Me Mine,* "Dallas was another madness … it was a terrible arrival there."

The Beatles would share the hotel that night with a group of American Legion conventioneers. As mostly teenagers congregated around the hotel and even swam in the giant circular fountain, one group of fans pressed their faces against the plate-glass window off the lobby until it suddenly gave way, sending four girls hurtling through. Ambulances were called and three girls were hospitalized with serious cuts and lacerations. Upon hearing of the distressing event, Larry Kane reported, the Beatles took it upon themselves to send flowers and call the hospital the next morning with get-well wishes for each of the girls.

In the safe haven of their well-appointed suite, the group found time to entertain the press as well as three fortunate fans: Stephanie Pinter and Yolanda Hernandez, co-presidents of Chapter 24 (the Dallas chapter) of the National Beatles Fan Club, and a third fan named Marie Leggett, arguably among the luckiest girls in Texas. But their meeting with the Beatles wouldn't have happened without months of careful planning and execution. Stephanie and Yolanda had begun preparing for the group's September visit as soon as the concert was announced—and they were determined to personally meet the Beatles. Stephanie's mother suggested that the girls shop for a unique "Texas-style" gift for the boys. She further suggested that Stephanie write a letter to Epstein, informing him that they had gifts to present to the Beatles when they arrived in the city. Incredibly, Stephanie received a personal reply from the manager with the news that he would try to arrange a meeting. Shopping at the world-famous Dallas

Neiman-Marcus, they bought four black Stetson cowboy hats as well as an oversized lighter, which they had engraved with a message to the boys.

As the day of the concert loomed, Stephanie and Yolanda spent hours enlisting deejays, newspaper reporters, police, and Memorial Auditorium officials to help them in their quest to meet the four musicians. Most importantly, they met with Michael Rosenstein, the Cabana's executive director, and Carole Hassell, its entertainment director, to ensure that they would have access to the hotel when the Beatles arrived. Working jointly with another local fan club, they even called a well-publicized press conference and implored those who attended the concert to "not lose control," saying that "the Beatles have threatened to cut the show to nine minutes if we don't behave."

Purposely leaving the black hats at home on the night of the group's arrival, the girls made the trip to Love Field. Seeing the size of the crowd already there, they decided to have Stephanie's mother drive

All smiles (top), the group faces their last press conference of the tour. Derek Taylor, with his assistant, Bess Coleman (above left), try to keep order. The Boys (above) seem delighted with a fan's letter.

All frowns in this Andy Hanson image as the Beatles await a barrage of questions from the press. Derek Taylor and Brian Epstein appear anxious as well.

them to the Cabana. After months of preliminary work, they were now in position on the ground at the hotel and armed with a letter from Brian Epstein.

Per Hassell's advice, they immediately headed to the back of the property, where the service entrance was located. There, they presented Epstein's letter to police officials and asked for Rosenstein. With Hassell at his side, Rosenstein came out to meet the girls, and soon they were seated in privileged territory—the hotel lobby—a few hours before the group's arrival. While plotting their next move in the hotel restaurant, they met a fellow fan club member, who informed them that she had booked an eighth-floor room with two other girls—one of them Marie Leggett. Their room was situated one floor directly below the Beatles' suite, so the three girls made their way up to it.

After the Beatles arrived at their suite in the early-morning hours, the girls excitedly tried to eavesdrop through air vents. They soon realized that this was their moment—the time to put all their planning into action. Stephanie and Yolanda decided to take the service elevator to the ninth floor and asked Marie to come along in case they were asked to show a room key. The other girls headed up the stairwell.

Cabana security guard Vernon Smart spotted trouble as girls began flooding onto the ninth floor "like crickets." As the elevator door opened onto the Beatles' floor, Stephanie, Yolanda, and Marie were met by two officers, who instructed them to ride back down. Suddenly they saw Hassell, who told security officials they were invited guests. Quickly thinking of their benefactor, they asked Hassell if Marie could come with them to the Beatles' suite. She consented.

The three girls, after some interrogation from road manager Neil Aspinall and press officer Derek Taylor, soon found themselves being escorted into room 925, the Beatles' suite, which was already teeming with reporters. All of their planning had paid off beautifully. For the next two hours, the girls had one-on-one conversations with each Beatle. Both Paul and John listened intently as Stephanie related how she'd made eye contact with JFK when his limo momentarily stopped next to her just minutes before the assassination. They talked with Ringo, whom they recalled as the most engaging, and conversed and shook hands with George.

Epstein wanted to know about the black Stetson hats the girls had purchased for the boys. Apparently the group hated the white hats they'd received at the airport and were beyond thrilled to hear that

Four pictures of the Fab Four answering questions. When asked about food in America, they responded that they could not find good English fish and chips.

black hats were forthcoming. They demanded them on the spot. Stephanie explained that they didn't have the hats with them, but would bring them to Memorial Auditorium. Of course, this was nothing more than a ploy on the girls' part to meet the group a *second* time.

As the meeting drew to a close around 3 a.m., Epstein asked Stephanie if she'd gotten the boys' autographs. When she admitted that she hadn't thought of it, Epstein reached for a hotel notepad and his pen and gave them to Stephanie so she could secure each Beatle's signature. Stephanie also asked Epstein to sign, as he'd been kind enough to arrange the meeting. He then suggested that a picture be taken of the girls with the group. Using Ringo's Polaroid camera, Taylor snapped two shots. In between the two photos, George asked Stephanie and Yolanda their ages. When they responded "Fifteen and sixteen," George jokingly said, "Brian, we have illegals in the room!" The girls were reminded to bring the hats to the venue and, before they left, were provided with

On stage at Dallas Memorial Auditorium. The group played one show in front of 10,500 fans.

passes for the press conference. It's unlikely that their feet touched the ground on their way out.

Having been up all night, the Beatles slept into the afternoon. When they awoke, they relaxed and made a few phone calls. Paul checked up on a ten-year-old girl who had been the victim of a recent hit-and-run accident and so couldn't attend the concert. They also checked on the fans who had been injured by the broken glass at the Cabana. Rumors quickly spread among the local press that the group would be shopping at Neiman-Marcus, but reporters and photographers arrived to find only Aspinall and Taylor shopping for gifts for the Beatles' wives and girlfriends as well as for Epstein, whose thirtieth birthday was the following day.

For the last time on the tour, the group was shuttled through a maddening crowd over to the venue. In the basement of Memorial Auditorium, they would give their final press conference of the tour. As they lounged in their dressing room, Stephanie and Yolanda arrived with the boys' black Stetson hats, which they immediately donned. The head of a second local fan club was also in attendance and presented them with engraved belt buckles and Western belts hand-tooled with their names.

Bert Shipp, a reporter for local ABC-TV affiliate WFAA, was able to get an exclusive one-on-one interview with the group by using the promise of autographs to bribe a police officer guarding the dressing room door. Shipp entered the empty room but soon found himself face to face with all four Beatles as they walked around a corner. He described them as polite, saying that they "took an imme-diate liking to my accent, which they thought was Texan but was really from New Mexico." He further recalled thinking, "Hey, the Beatles want a Texas accent? They're gonna get it." Noticing Paul's black Stetson, Shipp told the Beatle, "Bad guys wear black," to which Paul responded, "I'm going to be a good bad guy, how's that?" For the next ten minutes, Shipp had unfettered access to the group before the official press conference began. He asked them if they had seen the "presidential site." John responded exactly as if he had been on a multiple-city tour in a foreign country over a period of weeks: "It looked like a nice place when we drove to this place here, whatever this is."

Even though no radio station was allowed sole sponsorship of the concert, KLIF seemed to own the moment. The "Mighty 1190" supplied fans with pennants that read "Beatles we love you! But our heart belongs to KLIF" as well as Beatles sweatshirts custom-printed on the back with "KLIF Beatle Brigade."

Ringo Starr, with fans seated behind him, keeps the beat for John, Paul, and George, as they rock the Memorial Auditorium.

The station didn't sponsor the show, but they certainly went all out to have the fans believe they did. Banners were hung in the auditorium that read "Howdy Beatles ... Y'all come again." A bomb scare delayed the opening of the doors for thirty minutes, and police flushed out six fans who were hiding in bathrooms and beneath the bandstand. Once the all-clear had been given, the doors were flung open. Some 10,500 fans scrambled for their seats under the watch of 100 off-duty officers hired by Super Attractions, 200 officers lining the auditorium, and 200 more on standby.

Soon the press conference began. KLIF deejay Dan McCurdy (aka Charlie Brown) was amazed by the group's graciousness and how sensitive they were with their responses, despite being tired and out of sorts: "It just amazed me how they keep it up even at the very end of a long, long tour." Asked about the food they'd encountered in America, the Beatles were swift to agree that they could not find any decent fish and chips or tea. One girl asked if they were scared when they played live. John, alluding to the JFK tragedy, replied, "More so here perhaps." John had great fun mocking the reporters' accents, calling them "cuzzin." George was asked if he planned to make the black turtleneck his symbol, like Ringo's rings. In perhaps the most comical and sarcastic reply of the press conference, George, dressed in a coat and tie, commented, "Yeah, that's why I'm wearing one now!"

Dallas Morning News reporter Tony Zoppi was there as well. Having offended Derek Taylor with his review of the New Orleans show, he once again had the Beatles publicist ready to "have a go" at him, asking John why, if he held royalty in such high regard, he would say "Please spread the cream" instead of "God save the Queen." After the press conference, Taylor disparaged Zoppi—but after a few tense moments, both decided to go about their own business.

Meanwhile, when KLIF deejay Ron Chapman (aka Irving Harrigan) realized that the concert was about to begin, he slipped away from the press room, heading upstairs to find the stage manager. The other deejays were too busy looking for exclusive interviews to notice Chapman's absence. Upon finding the beleaguered stage manager, Chapman pulled the ultimate ruse and informed him that he was the emcee for the night and would be introducing the Beatles. "Thank God," the man replied. "Get up there and tell the kids to sit down and not throw things." As the deejays from KLIF, KBOX and Fort Worth's KFJZ came upstairs for their announcing duties, they were understandably upset to find Chapman in charge of designating who would do which introductions. It was decided that the only equitable way to determine who would introduce the Beatles would be a coin flip. Incredibly, it was Chapman who won the toss.

Ringo, sitting backstage with his feet propped up on another chair, confidently declared, "I could do another week." The other Beatles, longing for home, just stared at the drummer in disbelief, all deadpan.

After the opening acts had finished their sets, McCurdy and Chapman (as Charlie and Harrigan) walked onstage and slipped in a few illicit plugs for KLIF. Then, at 10:08 p.m., McCurdy bellowed, "And now ..." followed by Chapman's "... ladies and gentlemen ..." and then, in unison, "THE BEATLES!" Thunderous screams and flashbulb pops ensued, with the roof all but lifting off. For this performance, Ringo's drum riser was perched some fifteen to twenty feet above the auditorium floor. Because this was the final show of the regular tour, Paul thanked the supporting acts. Precisely thirty minutes later, following their usual set with its "Long Tall Sally" closer, the concert was over. After a month's worth of shows, they'd timed their act down to the minute.

By the time they left the stage at Memorial Auditorium that night, the group's fear of playing Dallas had dissipated. Ringo commented, "It was a wonderful crowd. You couldn't do much better than ending the tour on that note." Paul further added, "It was the best group we've played to on this tour. They were the screamin' kind, not the fightin' kind." Police chief Curry even had kind words for the fans of Dallas and the Beatles themselves: "I'm real proud of our young people," he said. "There was no flagrant misbehavior and they showed that they could enjoy the Beatles without tearing down the place." Finally, in a tip of his cap to the group that had captivated his city, Curry added that he "rather liked [The Beatles]. They impressed me as a bunch of fine boys." Curry's words were a stark contrast to the comments that Minneapolis's police chief would make about the group the following summer.

The next morning, Tony Zoppi wrote in his review that the Dallas concert "was Mardi Gras, V-E Day, the Texas-Oklahoma football game, and the Alamo all rolled into one—only louder." The sadness that had been so prevalent in Dallas for the previous ten months had been washed away—at least for the twenty-two hours and forty minutes when the Beatles had held court in the city. At the Cabana, operators

were fielding sixty calls an hour from kids wanting anything and everything the Beatles had touched. Director Michael Rosenstein refused, more focused on getting the hotel back in order.

Collectibles for the Dallas show are few and far between. The Feld Brothers printed only tickets and press passes and sold the generic program. Unused tickets for this show are extremely rare, and even stubs seldom turn up on the collectors' market. In November 1964, two months after the Dallas show, the Beatle Pom-Pom Company released official certificates, each bearing a piece of carpeting from the band's Cabana suite with the words "The Beatles Walked Here." Kids lined up for blocks to get one. Today, these certificates are the rarest of all Dallas memorabilia.

The boys play Dallas. Ringo's drum riser was built abnormally high— he towers over the rest of the band.

The Pigman Ranch
September 19, 1964

Brian Epstein and his boys. The manager shows off the antique telephone, a gift from the Beatles for his birthday. The group was en route to the Reed Pigman Ranch for a much needed rest day.

AFTER THE DALLAS CONCERT, the Beatles' plane lifted off from Love Field at 11:08 p.m. and headed to Missouri, where the boys would enjoy a well-deserved break at the secluded ranch of Reed Pigman, owner of American Flyers Airline. Dallas fans waved their good-byes for what would be the last time, as the Beatles would never play the city again. George, who hated flying, described the flight from Dallas to the Pigman Ranch: "We flew from Dallas to an intermediate airport where Pigman met us in a little plane with the one wing on top and with one or maybe two engines. It was so like Buddy Holly, that one; that was probably the closest we came to that sort of musicians' death. I don't mean it nearly crashed because it didn't, but the guy had a little map on his knee, with a light, as we were flying along and he was saying, 'Oh, I don't know where we are,' and it's pitch black and there are mountains all around and he's rubbing the windscreen trying to get the mist off. Finally he found where we were and we landed in a field with tin cans on fire to guide us."

After a short rest at the Pigman Ranch, where the boys rode horses, go carts and enjoyed the secluded atmosphere, the Beatles would fly from a remote airport near Alton, Missouri to the Big Apple where one final performance awaited them before returning home to the U.K.

Along with driving go-karts, and fishing, the Beatles rode horses through the expansive, secluded property wearing their now-fitted black Stetson hats that they received from the Dallas fan club. The entourage would fly out the next day to New York City where they would give one last performance in the States, a charity gig at the Paramount Theatre.

This image (opposite page) is one of the last "posed" photographs from the 1964 North American tour. Even while horsin' around on Pigman Ranch, the Beatles were never far from a photographer.

NEW YORK

**September 20, 1964
Paramount Theatre
8:30 p.m.**

AFTER A FEW HOURS' REST IN THE OZARKS as the guests of the Reed Pigman family, the Beatles boarded a plane that lifted off from a rural airport in Missouri, headed to the Big Apple. The charity performance at the Paramount Theatre would be the last show for the group, marking the end of their whirlwind first tour of North America. The Beatles would later fly back to England and enjoy a well-deserved eight-day rest before returning to EMI Studios to begin recording their second album of the year. They wouldn't play before a live audience again until Friday, October 9, when they kicked off their U.K. tour at the Gaumont Cinema in Bradford. The tour would constitute the group's only 1964 appearances in their home country and would wind up on New Year's Eve with a run of Christmas shows at the Odeon Cinema Hammersmith, London.

In England, the Beatles would play to much smaller audiences than they faced in North America, so the show at the cozy Paramount would be a great warm-up. The fortunate fans and patrons who occupied one of the 3,682 available seats at the Paramount were given perhaps the best live show yet.

In order to avoid the usual chaos at the airport, Captain Pres Cooper was instructed to land the Beatles' plane in a remote cargo area at Kennedy International at approximately 5 p.m. The landing site was two miles from the 400 fans assembled to greet the band. While this procedure was unusual for the 1964 tour, by 1966 it would be standard. The Beatles disembarked to relative calm, which was strange and eerie, as only six girls managed to get within 200 yards. Paul commented, "It's a change.... It's good.... I suppose." The entourage, which consisted of the Beatles, manager Brian Epstein, road managers Neil Aspinall and Mal Evans, and press officer Derek Taylor, was taken by helicopter to the Wall Street Heliport. Here they were met by Norman Weiss of General Artists Corporation, who had arranged limousine transport to the Paramount. The group was taken to Times Square and deposited at the theater entrance at about 6 p.m. The fans present were contained behind barricades erected by the police for crowd control.

The end of the road. The Riviera Idlewild was the last hotel of the 1964 North American Tour.

The Paramount Theatre, located on Broadway between 43rd and 44th Streets, was New York City's first great movie palace. Opened in 1926, it was styled after theaters in Chicago and was opulent even for the day. The lobby was modeled after that of Paris' famed Opera House, and the showroom welcomed the likes of Frank Sinatra, Glenn Miller, Benny Goodman, and Harry Belafonte. In 1956, the Paramount marquee featured a forty-foot-tall die-cut image of Elvis Presley for

the premiere of his first film, *Love Me Tender*. Both Alan Freed and WMCA's "Good Guys" show-cased some of the greatest-ever rock and pop stars at the Paramount, including Buddy Holly, Chuck Berry, the Everly Brothers, Sam Cooke, the Four Seasons, and Jan and Dean. Even a group called the "American Beetles" played there. The Paramount closed in early 1966 with a showing of the James Bond movie *Thunderball*. It was renovated for much-needed office space. The lobby was revived a few decades later by the World Wrestling Federation for a theme restaurant that eventually closed. In 2005, the Hard Rock Cafe chain transformed the old theater into one of its flagship properties, where, in the main dining area, patrons can still see the original stage used by the Beatles on the evening of September 20, 1964.

The performance scheduled for that night would benefit New York City's Retarded Infants Services as well as United Cerebral Palsy. Even though tickets were priced at $1.50 (the lowest on the tour) and $2.50, they were actually sold for charitable donations ranging from $5 to $100, with all proceeds going to the aforementioned organizations. The concert raised a large amount of money, as 380 seats were sold for $40 each ($15,200), 224 seats were sold for $100 each ($22,400), and the balance sold for between $5 to $25 a seat ($33,600).

Emceed by Ed Sullivan, Steve Lawrence, and Eydie Gormé, the star-studded bill also included Leslie Uggams ("House Built on Sand"), The Brothers Four ("Greenfields"), the Tokens ("The Lion Sleeps

The Fab Four pose backstage at the Paramount Theatre, shortly before their charity performance.

COURTESY OF UNITED CEREBRAL PALSY OF NEW YORK CITY

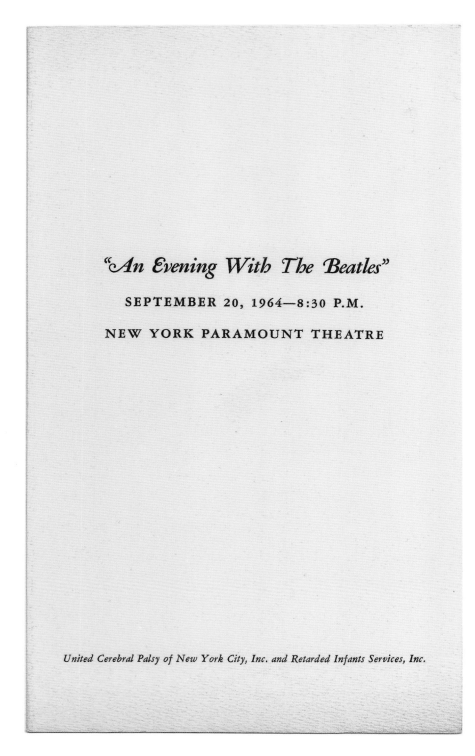

"An Evening With The Beatles"

SEPTEMBER 20, 1964—8:30 P.M.

NEW YORK PARAMOUNT THEATRE

United Cerebral Palsy of New York City, Inc. and Retarded Infants Services, Inc.

A special program was printed for the benefit concert that assisted United Cerebral Palsy and Retarded Infant Services of New York City.

Tonight"), Bobby Goldsboro ("See the Funny Little Clown"), the Shangri-Las ("Remember [Walkin' in the Sand]"), Nancy Ames (who would record "He Wore the Green Beret" in 1966), and Beatles tour standout Jackie DeShannon. Uggams was a huge Beatles fan and was in shock when she was led backstage by General Artists Corporation (GAC) tour manager Ira Sidelle to see all four of the boys sitting on the floor with none other than Bob Dylan. Paul told Uggams she reminded him of Shirley Bassey. The songstress was unfamiliar with Bassey, but when she later found out about the Welsh singer's popularity in the U.K., she took Paul's comment as a great compliment.

Outside, New York City's finest were trying to keep 4,000 fans, most without tickets, under control. One handmade sign expressed America's love for the group, saying, "Beatles Please Stay Here 4 Ever." It was a nice sentiment, for sure. But having logged thirty-three consecutive days in North America, the group was eager to get home.

Inside the Paramount, most of the seats were occupied by the elite of New York society, few of whom could comprehend Beatlemania or the effect the boys had on their fans. And as with the Royal Command Performance in London the previous year, the group would much rather have played for their die-hard followers than for well-heeled socialites. Tempers flared between the dignified older set and the young, screaming teenagers who were present, with the supporting acts urged to quickly finish their sets as a chant of "We want the Beatles" filled the elegant performance hall. Tour manager Bob Bonis took the boys to the wings of the theater for a glimpse of the anxious crowd. At 10 p.m., a full forty-five minutes before the group was scheduled to appear, Ed Sullivan introduced them for the last time in 1964 to an American crowd.

Uggams, who after her set watched the show with her mother from one of the front rows, became frightened as the crowd surged toward the stage. Still, she remembers the concert as a stupendous success. The interior of the Paramount was brightly lit from the constant pop of flashbulbs, and Taylor had to explain to journalist Gloria Steinem, there to interview John for *Cosmopolitan* magazine, that what she was seeing was not a lighting effect.

Those who attended the concert said that the Beatles' energy onstage and their earnest approach to their hits made for a magical evening despite a woefully inadequate sound system, perhaps the worst on the tour. Whether it was because the Beatles found comfort in the theater's small confines (which resembled the dance halls and cinemas they played in Britain) or because this concert was their last live performance in the States, they gave it their all. They finished their rousing set in twenty-five minutes and immediately left the theater, skipping a lavish champagne party that was planned in their honor in the downstairs lobby.

As in other cities, Manhattan hotels had turned the group away, fearing that their properties would be ripped apart. As a result, management decided to book the Riviera Idlewild Motel, near the airport, so they could make a quick getaway the next morning.

The fabulously new
Riviera
Idlewild Hotel

BELT PARKWAY at BAISLEY BLVD. · JAMAICA 34, N. Y.
Opposite J. F. Kennedy INTERNATIONAL AIRPORT

OF NEW YORK } SS.:
OF NEW YORK

U BARNEY, being duly sworn, deposes and says:

That he is the manager of Riviera Idlewild Hotel.

That said hotel is located at the Kennedy International Airport, Borough of Queens, City and State of New York, is owned and operated by Charnate, Inc., a New York corporation, and is known as the Riviera Idlewild Hotel.

3. That on September the 20th and 21st, 1964, the four members of the famous BEATLES were guests at the Riviera Idlewild Hotel. During said period THE BEATLES occupied rooms in said hotel and also used other facilities of the hotel including the service of food to them.

4. Charnate, Inc., the owner of the Riviera Idlewild Hotel, has sold to Ron Delsener the following enumerated items used by THE BEATLES on the occasion of their said visit to the hotel as guests thereof as aforesaid, namely:

8 face towels	8 bath towels	8 sheets	8 knives
8 forks	16 teaspoons	4 dinner plates	8 small plates
4 salad plates	4 cups	4 saucers	16 glasses
4 bathmats	3 serving trays	8 ash tmys	4 salt and pepper shakers
8 assorted used cakes of soap	12 assorted soda bottles	8 pillow cases	

5. This affidavit certifies the fact that each of the foregoing items, sold as aforesaid to Ron Delsener, was used by a member of THE BEATLES during their said visit at the Riviera Idlewild Hotel.

Sworn to before me this
day of October, 1964

The fabulously new
Riviera
Idlewild Hotel

BELT PARKWAY at BAISLEY BLVD. · JAMAICA 34, N. Y.
Opposite J. F. Kennedy INTERNATIONAL AIRPORT

OF NEW YORK } SS.:
OF NEW YORK

U BARNEY, being duly sworn, deposes and says:

That he is the manager of Riviera Idlewild Hotel.

That said hotel is located at the Kennedy International Airport, Borough of Queens, City and State of New York, is owned and operated by Charnate, Inc., a New York corporation, and is known as the Riviera Idlewild Hotel.

3. That on September the 20th and 21st, 1964, the four members of the famous BEATLES were guests at the Riviera Idlewild Hotel. During said period THE BEATLES occupied rooms in said hotel and also used other facilities of the hotel including the service of food to them.

4. Charnate, Inc., the owner of the Riviera Idlewild Hotel, has sold to Ron Delsener the following enumerated items used by THE BEATLES on the occasion of their said visit to the hotel as guests thereof as aforesaid, namely:

5. This affidavit certifies the fact that each of the foregoing items, sold as aforesaid to Ron Delsener, was used by a member of THE BEATLES during their said visit at the Riviera Idlewild Hotel.

Sworn to before me this
day of October, 1964

The fabulously new
Riviera
Idlewild Hotel

BELT PARKWAY at BAISLEY BLVD. · JAMAICA 34, N. Y.
Opposite J. F. Kennedy INTERNATIONAL AIRPORT

NEW YORK } SS.:
F NEW YORK

BARNEY, being duly sworn, deposes and says:

That he is the manager of Riviera Idlewild Hotel.

That said hotel is located at the Kennedy International Airport, Borough of Queens, City and State of New York, is owned and operated by Charnate, Inc., a New York corporation, and is known as the Riviera Idlewild Hotel.

3. That on September the 20th and 21st, 1964, the four members of the famous BEATLES were guests at the Riviera Idlewild Hotel. During said period THE BEATLES occupied rooms in said hotel and also used other facilities of the hotel including the service of food to you.

4. Charnate, Inc., the owner of the Riviera Idlewild Hotel, has sold to Ron Delsener the following enumerated items used by THE BEATLES on the occasion of their said visit to the hotel as guests thereof as aforesaid, namely:

5. This affidavit certifies the fact that each of the foregoing items, sold as aforesaid to Ron Delsener, was used by a member of THE BEATLES during their said visit at the Riviera Idlewild Hotel.

Sworn to before me this
day of October, 1964

The fabulously new
Riviera
Idlewild Hotel

BELT PARKWAY at BAISLEY BLVD. · JAMAICA 34, N. Y.
Opposite J. F. Kennedy INTERNATIONAL AIRPORT

NEW YORK } SS.:
OF NEW YORK

BARNEY, being duly sworn, deposes and says:

That he is the manager of Riviera Idlewild Hotel.

That said hotel is located at the Kennedy International Airport, Borough of Queens, City and State of New York, is owned and operated by Charnate, Inc., a New York corporation, and is known as the Riviera Idlewild Hotel.

3. That on September the 20th and 21st, 1964, the four members of the famous BEATLES were guests at the Riviera Idlewild Hotel. During said period THE BEATLES occupied rooms in said hotel and also used other facilities of the hotel including the service of food to them.

4. Charnate, Inc., the owner of the Riviera Idlewild Hotel, has sold to Ron Delsener the following enumerated items used by THE BEATLES on the occasion of their said visit to the hotel as guests thereof as aforesaid, namely:

8 face towels	8 bath towels	8 sheets	8 knives
8 forks	16 teaspoons	4 dinner plates	8 small plates
4 salad plates	4 cups	4 saucers	16 glasses
4 bathmats	3 serving trays	8 ash tmys	4 salt and pepper shakers
8 assorted used cakes of soap	12 assorted soda bottles	8 pillow cases	

5. This affidavit certifies the fact that each of the foregoing items, sold as aforesaid to Ron Delsener, was used by a member of THE BEATLES during their said visit at the Riviera Idlewild Hotel.

Sworn to before me this
day of October, 1964

Promoter Ron Delsener, who booked the group at Forest Hills, made a deal with the Riviera Idlewild Hotel. Along with bed sheets he bought up and sold silverware, plates, glasses and even "cakes of soap" the Beatles used during their stay.

As the seven limousines arrived at the Riviera, the entourage, especially the Fab Four, found it surprisingly quiet. No one seemed to notice as the group entered the lobby and adjourned to their rooms for their final night in America. Epstein, on the other hand, was furious when he learned that Taylor had taken a limousine to the Riviera that was meant for him. The Beatles' famous manager gave his publicist a thorough public thrashing. In disgust, Taylor resigned on the spot. While the two would later make up on the flight home, Taylor stuck by his decision to leave Epstein's employ. He would be replaced by Tony

The boys on stage. Well-heeled audience members—or their parents—donated more than $75,000 to charity for tickets to see the Fab Four.

Barrow for the 1965 and 1966 tours. In 1968, Taylor would again find work with the Beatles, returning after Epstein's death as the press officer for the newly formed Apple organization. He would work on several projects for the group until his untimely death from cancer at age sixty-five in 1997.

The Paramount show spawned a few collectibles. Because of the small size of the venue, unused tickets simply don't exist, and stubs are almost as rare. A special program titled "An Evening with the Beatles" was printed on white card stock, and a VIP ticket was issued to guests who sat in the boxes that lined the Paramount walls. Promotional material was also printed by United Cerebral Palsy and Retarded Infants Services of New York.

The group departed America aboard a commercial airliner bound for the United Kingdom. Considering the fan turnout at airports throughout the tour, it's surprising that only 150 fans came to say

good-bye. Before the plane took off, American Flyers Airline presented each Beatle with a black note-book that contained a detailed route map, flight itineraries, and a list of the tour cities and dates. All told, the Beatles had flown 22,441 miles since leaving London. In North America alone, they'd covered 13,645 miles in the air and logged forty-one hours and twenty-one minutes of flying time—a truly remarkable feat.

The tour was a huge success, and Epstein informed reporters at the airport that it had raked in over a million dollars—to be exact, $1,187,623.80 before expenses. The Internal Revenue Service exacted a 30 percent tax on the proceeds until attorney Walter Hofer and J. Blake Lowe, an attorney for the international accounting firm of Peat Marwick Mitchell & Co., successfully argued that NEMS Enterprises was not a permanent establishment in the United States. In 1968, NEMS and its successors were awarded the monies that had been withheld by the IRS in 1964: $297,815.09 plus 6 percent interest.

Norman Weiss had been correct in late March when he predicted that the Beatles' North American tour would be the most successful and profitable venture in entertainment history. Some critics were now falling in line with the dictates of Beatlemania, while others held fast to their belief that the bubble would soon burst. Having conquered American audiences, the Beatles would return to the United States in the summer of 1965 with renewed determination to win over any critics who remained while claiming any fans not yet converted.

Paramount Theatre officials escort a distressed fan (opposite page) out of the venue at the conclusion of the show. The group (above) answers a few last questions from the press before departing.

Hotels and Venues 1964

SAN FRANCISCO, CALIFORNIA | AUGUST 18–19: The Beatles stayed at the San Francisco Hilton (333 O'Farrell Street), which is still in operation. The concert was at the Cow Palace in nearby Daly City (2600 Geneva Avenue). The venue continues to hold events.

LAS VEGAS, NEVADA | AUGUST 20–21: The group played at the Las Vegas Convention Center on Paradise Road, one block south of Sahara Avenue. The building was demolished in 1990 to make way for larger convention facilities in the same location. The Fab Four occupied the Sahara Hotel and Casino (2535 Las Vegas Boulevard S.), which is currently closed and undergoing renovation.

SEATTLE, WASHINGTON | AUGUST 21–22: The Beatles checked into the Edgewater Inn (2411 Alaskan Way) and gave one concert at the Seattle Center Coliseum (305 Harrison Street). Both the hotel and the venue, now called Key Arena, are open today.

VANCOUVER, BRITISH COLUMBIA, CANADA | AUGUST 22: The first stop in Canada had the group playing at Empire Stadium on E. Hastings Street. The venue was demolished in 1993. The group had reservations at the Hotel Georgia but cancelled them, preferring to fly directly to Los Angeles after the concert.

LOS ANGELES, CALIFORNIA | AUGUST 23–26: The Beatles stayed in the private home of British actor Sir Reginald Owen in the Bel-Air section of Los Angeles (356 St. Pierre Road). Their reservations at the Ambassador Hotel were cancelled by hotel management. They played the historic Hollywood Bowl (2301 N. Highland Avenue). Both home and venue presently stand.

DENVER, COLORADO | AUGUST 26–27: The band played Red Rocks Amphitheatre, situated 10 miles west of Denver in Morrison, Colorado (17598 W. Alameda Parkway). The natural setting still hosts concerts today. After the show, the Beatles stayed at the historic Brown Palace Hotel (321 17th Street). The hotel is open and one can still order the same items from room service that the Beatles did: grilled cheese sandwiches and French fries.

CINCINNATI, OHIO | AUGUST 27: The Beatles' management cancelled the tour's reservations at the Vernon Manor Hotel (400 Oak Street) so the group could fly to New York after the concert. The Fabs played Cincinnati Gardens (2250 Seymour Avenue), which still hosts events today.

NEW YORK, NEW YORK | AUGUST 28–29: The Beatles played two shows at the Forest Hills Tennis Club in nearby Queens. The horseshoe-shaped stadium hosts an occasional concert and is currently trying to acquire landmark status from the New York Landmarks Preservation Committee. The boys spent two nights at the Delmonico Hotel (502 Park Avenue), which is still in operation.

ATLANTIC CITY, NEW JERSEY | AUGUST 29–SEPTEMBER 2: The group's stay at this seaside resort was their longest break on the 1964 tour. They stayed at the Lafayette Motor Inn (109 S. North Carolina Avenue), which has since been leveled; the site is now a parking lot. The Beatles played Convention Hall (2301 Boardwalk), which still hosts events.

PHILADELPHIA, PENNSYLVANIA | SEPTEMBER 2: The Fabs rocked Convention Hall (3400 Civic Center Drive, near Spruce), which was demolished in 2005. They flew to Indianapolis after the concert.

INDIANAPOLIS, INDIANA | SEPTEMBER 3–4: The entourage stayed at the Indianapolis Motor Speedway Motel (4400 W. 16th Street), which was demolished in 2009. The band played two shows at the Indiana State Fair, one in the Coliseum and another, in the evening, at the racetrack. Both venues are still operational and located on the fairgrounds (1202 E. 38th Street).

MILWAUKEE, WISCONSIN | SEPTEMBER 4–5: The stop in Wisconsin had the group playing the Milwaukee Auditorium (500 W. Kilbourne), which has since been reconfigured into a smaller venue and renamed the Milwaukee Theatre. The group stayed at the Coach House Inn (W. Wisconsin and 19th), which now serves as a dormitory for students attending Marquette University.

CHICAGO, ILLINOIS | SEPTEMBER 5: The Beatles played one show at the International Amphitheatre (4220 S. Halsted Street). It was demolished in 2009.

DETROIT, MICHIGAN | SEPTEMBER 6: Arriving after midnight, the boys were driven to the Whittier Hotel (415 Burns Drive), now a high-rise residential complex that is listed on the National Register of Historic Places. They played two shows at Olympia Stadium (5920 Grand River Avenue), an indoor venue that was demolished in 1987.

TORONTO, ONTARIO, CANADA | SEPTEMBER 7–8: The Beatles stayed at the Sheraton (now Omni) King Edward Hotel (37 King Street E). They played two shows at the historic Maple Leaf Gardens (60 Carlton Street). The venue has since been converted into a multipurpose building and named a National Historic Site of Canada.

MONTREAL, QUEBEC, CANADA | SEPTEMBER 8: The Beatles played two shows at the Forum (2313 St. Catherine Street), which met the wrecking ball in 1998. The entourage had planned to stay at the Queen Elizabeth Hotel, but threats forced them to cancel and fly on to Florida.

KEY WEST, FLORIDA | SEPTEMBER 9–11: The tour was diverted to Key West, rather than make the scheduled stop in Jacksonville, Florida, to avoid Hurricane Dora. The entire party stayed at the Key Wester Hotel (3675 S. Roosevelt). The property was torn down in 1999 and is now the location of the Hyatt Westward Pointe. The group had reservations for the Hotel George Washington (on the corner of Julia and Adams), but were denied rooms. The site is now occupied by the federal court system.

BOSTON, MASSACHUSETTS | SEPTEMBER 12: The group stayed at the Hotel Madison (76 Causeway Street). Ten years after the hotel's last guest left in 1976, it was demolished and replaced with the Tip O'Neill Federal Building. Boston Garden (150 Causeway Street), the venue where the Beatles played, was taken down in 1997.

BALTIMORE, MARYLAND | SEPTEMBER 13–14: The Fab Four rocked the Civic Center (201 W. Baltimore Street) for two shows and stayed nearby, at the downtown Holiday Inn (301 W. Lombard Street), which still serves customers today. The Civic Center was renovated and renamed the Baltimore Arena in the 1980s.

PITTSBURGH, PENNSYLVANIA | SEPTEMBER 14: The group's short visit here saw them play the Pittsburgh Civic Arena (66 Mario Lemieux Place; formerly another address), which was demolished over a period of nine months ending in 2012.

CLEVELAND, OHIO | SEPTEMBER 15: Arriving just after 12:30 a.m., the Beatles were taken to the Cleveland Sheraton at 24 Public Square, now a Marriott Renaissance property. The Fabs played one show at Public Hall (500 Lakeside Avenue), currently a multi-use entertainment and arts facility.

NEW ORLEANS, LOUISIANA | SEPTEMBER 16: Arriving after midnight, the entourage was horrified when they arrived at the Congress Inn, a one-level property surrounded by swamps. The property, situated on Chef Menteur Highway, was later transformed into an assisted-living center, then destroyed by Hurricane Katrina in 2005. The Beatles' venue, City Park Stadium (5400 Stadium Drive) is now called Tad Gormley Stadium and is still in operation.

KANSAS CITY, MISSOURI | SEPTEMBER 17: Once again arriving after midnight, the entourage was driven to the Muehlebach Hotel, now part of three wings of the downtown Kansas City Marriott Hotel (200 W. 12th Street). The Beatles' venue, Municipal Stadium (2123 Brooklyn Avenue), was demolished in 1976; the site is now occupied by a housing tract.

DALLAS, TEXAS | SEPTEMBER 18: The boys arrived in Dallas at 12:40 a.m. and were driven directly to the Cabana Motor Hotel (899 Stemmons Freeway), co-owned by actress Doris Day. The hotel was later transformed into an overflow minimum-security prison facility for Dallas County. It is sitting idle presently, although there are hopes of turning it into a residential complex. Dallas Memorial Auditorium (650 S. Griffin Street) is virtually unchanged and is now part of the larger Kay Bailey Hutchison Convention Center.

PIGMAN RANCH, ALTON, MISSOURI | SEPTEMBER 19–20: The Beatles spent two nights at this remote ranch, owned by American Flyers founder and president Reed Pigman Sr. The ranch was recently sold, and visitors can now stay on the property, which is near Walnut Ridge, Arkansas.

NEW YORK, NEW YORK | SEPTEMBER 20–21: The last stop on the tour was a charity gig at the Paramount Theatre, located at Broadway and 43rd Street. The theater closed in 1966 and was turned into retail and office space; currently a Hard Rock Cafe is located near the former entrance. The last hotel where the group stayed on its 1964 North American tour was the Riviera Idlewild Hotel (151-20 Baisley Boulevard) in Jamaica, New York, currently called the Garden Inn and Suites. The Beatles flew back to England on September 21.

Acknowledgments

Mike White, Mitch McGeary, and Kevin Curran for the inspiration to resurrect the idea, but in much different form than first envisioned. Mark Naboshek (Beatles book editor extraordinaire), Bruce Spizer (My Mentor!), Brad Zucroff and Bambi Nicklen at omnivorous media (need a book done? Have them do it—the best!), Sherri Schultz at Words with Grace (light edits), Amy Armstrong and Veronica Haas at Asia Pacific Offset, Bob Eubanks, Larry Kane, Mark Lewisohn, Aaron Bremner/Apple Corps, Tony Barrow, Randy Krone, Eric Cash, Steve McNutt (the Dallas gang), Larry Marion/Not Fade Away Gallery, Jeff Augsburger, Russ Lease, Steve Gunther, Erik Tarros, Gina Smith, Mark Benyas, Joe Tunzi/JAT Publishing, David Uebelhack, Gary Johnson/Rockaway Records, Pete Howard, Frank Caiazzo/Beatlesautographs.com, Thomas Vanghele/fab4collectibles.com, Paul Wane/Tracks UK, Graham Small, Jim Cushman, Melissa Ellis, Leisa Johnson, Gary Schroder, Luc Desilets, Lily Birkhimer/Ohio Historical Society, United Cerebral Palsy of New York City, Sara Schmidt, Vincent Vigil, Karen Marks, Fred Saxon, Clark Weber, Karen Mullarkey, Bob Burns, Dave Hull, Gary Park, Ivor Davis, Ed Diran, Stan Irwin, Lan Roberts, Pat O'Day, Gino Rossi, Zollie Volchok, Red Robinson, Julie Steddom, Don Martin, Jay Mack, Gary Allyn, Verne Byers, Cyril Brennan, Donnie Brennan, Tom Carney, Karl Mehlmann, Glenn Bell, Ted Scott, Dick Purtan, Dusty Rhodes, Alex Sinclair, Dino Santangelo, Ed Hamid Jr., Hy Lit, Jerry Baker, Art Schurgin, Bob Green, Jay Nelson, Dave Boxer, Michael DesRochers, George Morris, Kenneth Feld, Bruce Bradley, Arnie Ginsberg, Carl Hurd, Frank Luber, Linda Kirsch-Vinson, John Scott, Pat DiCesare, Chuck Brinkman, Bud Connely, Bert Shipp, Dan McCurdy, Ron Chapman, Leslie Uggams, Sid Bernstein, Jerry Bloom, Tony Taylor, Harry J. Miller, Indiana State Fair Commission, Charlie Murdock, Guy LiPierre, Dex Allen, John Rook, Joe Zingale, Art Schreiber, Jim Stagg, Bud Connell, Ray Otis, David Bedford, Sara Ferguson, Keith Sluchansky, Gotta Have It, Coi Gehrig/Denver Public Library, Lisa Jacob/Las Vegas Convention and Visitors Bureau, Gillian Gaar, Shelley Germeaux, Steve Marinucci, Nancy Stuenkel/*Chicago Sun-Times*, Erica Varela/*Los Angeles Times*, Julie Kanner/*Florida Times-Union*.

Design and Editorial

Created and produced by **omnivorous media**
2826 South Tioga Way, Las Vegas, NV 89117 | brad@omnivorous.com
Brad Zucroff/Creative Director and Designer
Bambi Nicklen/Photoshop Wizard and Production
•
Sherri Schultz/Copy Editor, Words with Grace
Seattle, WA | www.wordswithgrace.com

Colophon

Typefaces: **Whitney**—Designed by Tobias Frere-Jones for New York City's Whitney Museum in 2004
DIN 1451 Engshrift—Designed in Germany in 1931, used since as the standard for road signs and car plates
Franklin Gothic Extra Condensed—Designed in 1906 by Morris Fuller Benton, chief designer for American Type Founders

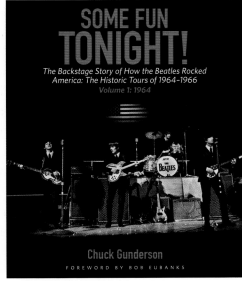
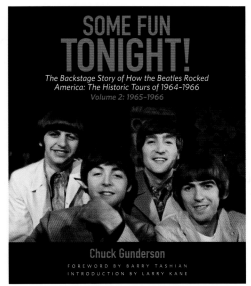
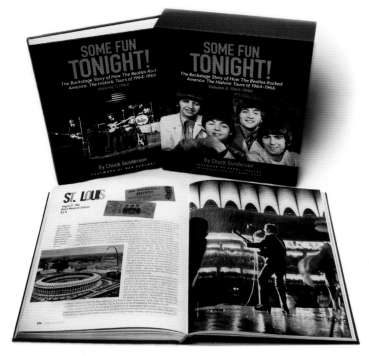